Voices of Innovation—Europe

Everyone talks about innovation, and we can all point to random examples of innovation inside of healthcare information technology, but few repeatable processes exist that make innovation more routine than happenstance.

How do you create and sustain a culture of innovation? What are the best practices you can refine and embed as part of your organization's DNA? What are the potential outcomes for robust healthcare transformation when we get this innovation mystery solved? Through timely essays from leading experts, the Voices of Innovation for Healthcare series consisting of three books showcased the widely adopted healthcare innovation model from HIMSS and how providers and payers could leverage it to increase their velocity of digital transformation. The most recent volume focused on how AI leverages the same framework and construct but zeroed in on artificial intelligence to include large language models, voice technology, and robotic process automation. Now the time has come for *Voices of Innovation—Europe*. While the Voices series has included European voices, the contributions have been limited. In important ways, the European market is vastly different from the US-based market. The payor- and government-based care make their approach to tech-enabled care different.

Using the HIMSS model for innovation as the structural framework, *Voices of Innovation—Europe* showcases the great innovations being implemented across their healthcare ecosystems. This structure will easily enable subsequent editions as advancements are made.

Voices of Innovation in Healthcare
Series Editor: Edward W. Marx

Everyone talks about innovation, and we can all point to random examples of innovation inside of healthcare information technology, but few repeatable processes exist that make innovation more routine than happenstance. How do you create and sustain a culture of innovation? What are the best practices you can refine and embed as part of your organization's DNA? What are the potential outcomes for robust healthcare transformation when we get this innovation mystery solved? Through timely essays from leading experts, the first edition showcased the widely adopted healthcare innovation model from HIMSS and how providers could leverage to increase their velocity of digital transformation. Regardless of its promise, innovation has been slow in healthcare.

Voices AI edition leverages the same framework and construct but zeroes in on artificial intelligence to include large language models, voice and robotic process automation.

Voices of Innovation—AI: Fulfilling the Promise of AI in Healthcare
Edited by Edward W. Marx, Sakshika Dhingra, Frank Papay and Piyush Mathur

Voices of Innovation—Europe: Fulfilling the Promise of Healthcare Technology
Edited by Sakshika Dhingra, Edward W. Marx, Aditi U. Joshi and Aline Noizet

Voices of Innovation—Europe

Fulfilling the Promise of Healthcare Technology

Edited by Sakshika Dhingra, Edward W. Marx,
Aditi U. Joshi, and Aline Noizet

Routledge
Taylor & Francis Group
A PRODUCTIVITY PRESS BOOK

Designed cover image: Brandon Marx, Senior Producer, Pyro Productions Studio

First published 2027
by Routledge
605 Third Avenue, New York, NY 10158

and by Routledge
4 Park Square, Milton Park, Abingdon, Oxon, OX14 4RN

Routledge is an imprint of the Taylor & Francis Group, an informa business

ISBN: 978-1-041-31668-8 (hbk)
ISBN: 978-1-041-31667-1 (pbk)
ISBN: 978-1-003-78017-5 (ebk)

DOI: 10.4324/9781003780175

Typeset in Garamond

For Product Safety Concerns and Information please contact our EU representative GPSR@taylorandfrancis.com. Taylor & Francis Verlag GmbH, Kaufingerstraße 24, 80331 München, Germany.

Contents

Foreword

I have known the books of Edward Marx for several years now, and from the very start, I was struck not only by their intellect but by their deep conviction that healthcare innovation must be a collaborative and human endeavor. When they invited me to write the foreword for this book on healthcare innovation in Europe, I didn't hesitate for a second. I said, "Count me in." Having followed their earlier work advancing thought leadership in digital transformation, writing this foreword feels much like joining a project destined to set the standard—a meeting of minds inspired by passion, purpose, and progress.

The other reason to me was the challenging moment in time we live in. Apart from financial aspects, we face doubling in demand in healthcare with decreasing trained staff and even geopolitical challenges on the horizon.

Whereas often it is assumed much of the innovation happens outside of Europe, during my travels for roughly 100 keynotes a year, I get to visit a lot of companies, institutions, startups, and the like, all proudly showing their innovation. In my opinion we do not lag in innovation, but we certainly do in terms of 'bragging' about the things we do.

That is where the book you are holding comes in for me as well.

This volume unites leading voices from across Europe—clinicians, policymakers, technologists, and entrepreneurs—each contributing a chapter that captures both the ingenuity and the humanity of healthcare transformation. The co-editors have built something extraordinary here: a mosaic of perspectives from across the continent that showcases the diversity and collaborative spirit that make European healthcare systems so distinct. By weaving together themes from the Nordics to the Mediterranean, the Baltics to the British Isles, and everywhere in between, they have created not only a book but a movement.

Innovation in healthcare has never been more urgent—or more possible. Across Europe, we encounter the same familiar truths: soaring workloads, aging populations, and the pressing need for sustainability and access. Yet in each of these challenges lies an opportunity. Innovation is not a luxury for some distant future; it is an imperative of the present. It is the means by which we honor our social contracts to provide equitable, efficient, and compassionate care to all. The contributors in this book understand this deeply. They do not write about innovation from an abstract academic distance—they live it, test it, and prove it in clinics, laboratories, policymaking chambers, and digital ecosystems across the continent.

Each chapter takes us inside a real use case, grounding ideas in context. We read about Portugal's experiments with telehealth equity, Estonia's pioneering digital health architecture, Germany's digital therapeutics legislation, the UK's advances in population analytics, and the Netherlands' success in empowered patient care models. Together these stories create a living atlas of European innovation—each example a testament to the creativity and resilience that unite rather than divide our healthcare systems. The message is clear: no single model fits all, but collective learning moves us all forward.

This book could not come at a more pivotal time. As the World Health Organization and European Commission both emphasize digital transformation as the path toward more sustainable and citizen-centered healthcare, leaders across Europe are asking how to translate vision into action. That is where this book shines. It offers practical frameworks and proven pathways for fostering innovation across governance, ethics, clinical impact, and technology adoption. It shows that innovation in healthcare is not about technology alone but about people—how we collaborate, design, listen, and learn.

As you turn these pages, I encourage you not only to absorb the strategies and success stories but to find inspiration for your own journey. Let this collection guide your thinking, challenge your assumptions, and fuel your commitment to building the healthcare systems our future demands. The transformation of healthcare is a collective responsibility, and each of us—whether clinician, policymaker, entrepreneur, or patient advocate—has a vital role to play.

I applaud Edward and every contributor for assembling this courageous and illuminating body of work. I have no doubt that readers will come away from this book energized, equipped, and ready to lead innovation where it matters most: in the service of better health, better access, and better outcomes for all Europeans.

Let this book be your invitation and your call to action. The future of healthcare innovation in Europe is being written right now. You hold one of its essential chapters in your hands. I hope to meet you in one of your journeys and mine, where we proudly share about the body of work also done on the European continent.

Lucien Engelen
CEO Transform.Health
Linkedin.com/in/lucienengelen

Introduction

When the Voices of Innovation series was launched in 2019, the goal was simple yet profound: to provide a platform for healthcare leaders to share the real, replicable practices that move innovation from theory into action. The belief then—which remains unchanged—that healthcare innovation is not only about technology but also about people, culture, and the courage to transform. Over time, what began as a single book became a movement of practitioners learning from one another, a living record of progress in an industry undergoing historic change.

Each volume of the Voices series expands that conversation. After the success of Voices of Innovation—Payer Edition and Voices of Innovation—AI Edition, readers began asking us to turn our lens toward Europe—a region that has long been a fertile ground for experimentation, collaboration, and system-level innovation in healthcare. That request led directly to the creation of this Europe Edition: a deep exploration of how European health systems, enterprises, and innovators are redefining the landscape of care.

The Europe Edition seeks to amplify the many voices that make European innovation unique. It brings together leading thinkers and practitioners from across the continent—clinicians, policy architects, digital pioneers, researchers, and health entrepreneurs—each contributing a chapter that captures a distinct dimension of innovation in context. The objective is not to present Europe as a monolith but as a rich mosaic of diverse ecosystems united by common values: equity, access, quality, and sustainability.

At its heart, this book explores the how of innovation. How do health systems balance public service and private enterprise? How do nations of different sizes, structures, and regulatory landscapes foster experimentation while maintaining public trust? How can innovation take root in societies that prioritize inclusion and safety without losing the agility required for transformation? Through each narrative, we seek to illuminate the processes, governance, partnerships, and persistence that make innovation thrive—across borders, disciplines, and generations.

This volume spans the European continent—north to south, east to west—through a collection of essays written by recognized leaders in health and digital transformation. Each contributor was invited not only to reflect on their theme but also to ground it in a tangible use case from a specific European country, creating a geographically and thematically balanced exploration of healthcare innovation. Taken together, these chapters form a kind of innovation atlas—a Europe-wide survey of what is possible when innovation is rooted in cultural understanding, policy vision, and community engagement.

The book is structured around core themes that mirror the universal stages of transformation:

- Foundations of Innovation—exploring strategy, leadership, funding, and governance;
- Technology and Digital Maturity—covering interoperability, data integration, telehealth, AI, and emerging digital infrastructure;

- Patient Empowerment and Experience—showing how human-centered design and co-creation shape sustainable impact;
- Collaboration and Ecosystems—demonstrating how cross-border partnerships and public–private alliances propel systemic change; and
- Future Horizons—reflecting on lessons learned and defining the path forward for a resilient, connected, European healthcare future.

Within these sections, readers will find both strategic insights and operational blueprints. Each story is framed within the same Voices of Innovation framework—emphasizing repeatable principles, measurable results, and practical relevance to leaders seeking guidance for their own transformation journeys.

The Voices approach rests on the conviction that successful innovation in healthcare follows a recognizable pattern—one that can be taught, modelled, and most importantly adapted. That framework emphasizes:

- Vision and Purpose—articulating a clear case for change anchored in patient and population needs.
- Partnership and Collaboration—breaking traditional silos through interdisciplinary and cross-sector cooperation.
- Iteration and Learning—viewing failure as feedback and progress as a collective endeavor.
- Sustainability and Ethics—ensuring innovations endure, scale, and align with public trust and societal values.

These concepts echo throughout the European Edition. What differentiates Europe on the global innovation stage is not the technology itself but the integration of human values into technological progress. Whether in the Netherlands' patient self-management programs, Germany's digital therapeutics law, or Estonia's national health data platform, European innovation demonstrates that modernization and equity can coexist—that digitization and compassion belong side by side.

This book does not aim to close the conversation on innovation—it aims to expand it. The essays that follow are snapshots of an evolving landscape: some describe successes already achieved; others outline work still in progress. All of them, however, share one unifying theme—the belief that shared knowledge accelerates shared progress.

We invite readers to approach this book as both a reference and a catalyst. Use it to benchmark ideas, learn from peers, and discover strategies that can be applied in your own organization or region. Let it remind you that the story of healthcare innovation is not written in isolation—it is a collective European narrative, shaped by collaboration, resilience, and vision.

Innovation in healthcare is no longer optional—it is essential. Through this edition of Voices of Innovation, we celebrate the ingenuity of Europe's healthcare leaders and reaffirm our shared commitment to better health for all.

Together, these voices form a chorus that transcends borders—a chorus calling us to imagine, build, and sustain the future of healthcare. The next chapters are their stories, and the next steps are ours.

Professor Shafi Ahmed *MD, PhD, FRCS, FRCS (Gen. Surg), PGDipEd, FFSTEd Consultant General, Laparoscopic and Colorectal Surgeon*

Acknowledgments

This edition of Voices of Innovation is dedicated to the clinicians who deliver care to millions—often at the expense of their own family lives. I salute your unwavering dedication and your steadfast commitment to placing the well-being of patients above all else. Your courage, compassion, and resilience continue to inspire the innovation this book seeks to amplify.

It is my hope that this volume brings fresh inspiration to healthcare professionals across Europe, encouraging new ways of thinking and working in support of the clinicians who serve at the very heart of our healthcare systems.

To my family and friends—thank you for being my backbone, my constant source of strength, and for always pushing me to reach for the stars and never settle for less. Your belief in me makes every page possible.

Sakshika Dhingra

I dedicate this book to my European family. I was born and raised in southern Germany in a city called Baden-Baden. My father Herbert Marx was born in Karlsruhe and my mother Ida Kollmansberger in Augsburg. Our family eventually settled in the United States. While we fully embraced our new country and citizenship, our hearts always longed for and appreciated our original homeland. This book is in appreciation for all my European relatives. My Oma and Opa. My aunts and uncles, cousins, and nephews and nieces. May this book have even a small part in advancing healthcare innovation throughout Europe.

Edward W. Marx

I dedicate this book to all of those working to make healthcare better, one patient at a time. To the innovators I've met across continents who are building solutions that actually work for the people using them. Europe's digital health landscape offers lessons the rest of the world needs to hear. Last, to my colleagues in medicine, practicing what remains the most challenging but most beautiful of professions.

Thanks to all my friends and family who have supported me throughout the many twists and turns of my life. You know who you are.

Aditi U. Joshi

I dedicate this book to all the innovators out there that are working on solutions to improve healthcare and patients' daily lives and believe in making healthcare more human, more personal, and more accessible. This book would not have been possible without the many individuals who believe that better health systems are built through collaboration, curiosity, and courage to innovate. May this book inspire others to keep innovating and push boundaries.

To my family and friends: thank you for your support over the years in this digital health journey.

Aline Noizet

Editors

Sakshika Dhingra is a transformative healthcare leader serving as clinical operations director at Humana, one of the leading health organizations in the United States. In her role, she drives operational excellence and innovation to improve outcomes for the Medicaid population—a US government-supported program that provides health coverage to low-income individuals and families. Over the course of her career, Sakshika has served across multiple payer organizations nationwide, consistently advancing initiatives that strengthen access, quality, and sustainability in healthcare. She is recognized for her strategic vision and for developing scalable frameworks that balance clinical effectiveness with operational efficiency. Residing in the United States, Sakshika is also a devoted mother and wife, finding her greatest joy in her family—her husband, Vivesh Sharma, and their inquisitive eight-year-old son, Aveer—who continue to inspire her commitment to innovation and care.

Edward W. Marx is CEO of Marx Advisory, a consultancy aimed at improving the marketplace experience for vendors and providers. A healthcare best-selling author of multiple books around innovation, transformation, and experience, all of his royalties are donated towards the eradication of cancer. His writings reflect his deep expertise gained while serving as CIO of the global Cleveland Clinic and NYC Health and Hospitals. He is an advisor for start-ups and multinational companies and sits on the boards of multiple health systems. He advises governments on digital transformation strategies. When not working, Ed competes internationally for TeamUSA Triathlon and is on pace to climb the Seven Summits. Ed is married to Dr. Simran Marx, and they share five children and more than five grandchildren.

Aditi U. Joshi is an emergency medicine physician, global health strategy consultant, and CEO of Ardexia, a digital health consultancy focused on clinician adoption and implementation. She has built 13+ digital health programs over a decade and advises on AI, RPM, and telehealth. She has worked with health systems, startups, and governments globally to ensure digital health technologies deliver measurable results and include the clinician perspective. Her experience spans implementations across three continents. She is the co-author of the bestselling book *Telehealth Success: How to Thrive in the New Age of Remote Care*, which outlines the Telehealth Success Framework used internationally to design and scale digital medicine programs. Dr. Joshi serves as an advisor to the American Medical Association's Digital Medicine Payment Advisory Group advising on reimbursement of digital medicine in the United States. She lives in Paris, France.

Aline Noizet is a connector by heart! A very active actor and recognized influencer in the health and innovation sector with a strong international network, she is on top of the latest digital health trends and technologies. With more than fourteen years working in the digital health and healthtech space, Aline has been supporting startups and corporations over the years through her own boutique consulting Digital Health Connector and has acquired strong international experience working with and for startups, investors, pharmaceuticals, payers, medtech, patient associations, regulators etc. Aline holds a Master of Arts (English literature and civilisation) from Lyon 3 University (France) and a Master of Business Administration from ESADE (Spain). Born in France, she has been living in Barcelona, Spain, for the past fifteen years, where she also founded Digital Health Innovators, a local community bringing together the actors of the digital health ecosystem.

Voices of Innovation Series

We published the original *Voices of Innovation—AI: Fulfilling the Promise of Information Technology in Healthcare* in the Spring of 2019. Little did we know that a few months later, COVID would completely disrupt life as we knew it. Innovation and digital transformation became everyday vernacular, and *Voices* went on to sell very well. Our publisher returned in late 2022 asking for a second edition. The publisher made a good point in that there were so many new stories of innovation born from the pandemic, it would help the industry to update the book. We updated almost half of the content with COVID-inspired innovations. *Voices*, 2nd ed., was published in July 2023.

With the success of the books, we heard requests from many other communities for voices that were increasingly specific to their healthcare vertical or focused on a particular topic.

We came out of the gate with *Voices of Innovation, Payer Edition*. Like their provider counterparts, payers also long to transform, and innovation is a catalyst to spark change of such magnitude. With Sachin Jain writing the foreword, we published *Voices Payer* in July 2024. An immediate bestseller, it was the first book ever written addressing the leverage of technology in the payer community.

We released *Voices AI* at a time when a great deal of buzz surrounded artificial intelligence, large language models, and robotic process automation. While many books had already been written on the topic, with more certain to follow, *Voices AI* distinguished itself by focusing on repeatable processes rather than examples that quickly lost relevance amid the rapid pace of AI innovation. While we applauded these other works, *Voices AI* was intended to serve as a practical handbook to support practitioners of that time—and those who would follow—in their AI-driven innovations.

With all these books in the Voices of Innovation series, our international friends started asking for their own editions specific to their countries. What works in the United States may not work so well in another country that likely happens to have a completely different kind of healthcare ecosystem. “Fair point,” we said. Since I have family roots in Germany, we began to think about creating a European specific edition. As this idea was socialized, more friends and colleagues raised their hands and said yes. No such collaborative efforts have been taken to share best practices across all the European continent previously. So what you are holding is pioneering work. Over twenty European countries are represented in *Voices of Innovation—Europe*. Each author shares a story of innovation where the principles that made each successful are transferable to other cultures and communities.

The beauty of *Voices* is that the books remain a set of global best practices where peers openly share their playbooks for transformation around a common structure for innovation that is easily adoptable for any sized organization. A leader can pick up a copy of *Voices* and instantly have access to a tried and tested framework for innovation with multiple case studies of how other payer organizations have succeeded, complete with results. This is the reason for the success of all the *Voices* books. Look for more *Voices* in the future.

Innovation Framework

HIMSS

AI Statement

Essay authors may have leveraged ChatGPT3 to source additional documented examples in healthcare to complement the others used in the article. We leveraged AI the same way we would search for examples using traditional methods such as Google or a public library for basic research.

Chapter 1

Blend Cultures

Include the organisation's larger community and ensure that institutional leaders are engaged and supportive of the proposed innovative strategies.

One of the first things you need to do to improve the odds of innovation success is ensure support and engagement from key organisational leaders. Innovation is hard to do in a vacuum. Often it takes a team, some of whom are directly involved and others who provide resources and political cover. As you embark on your innovation, take inventory of key decision makers, influencers, and culture. Identify both the individuals who will help you and those who might hurt you. The more organisational community and leadership engagement you develop, the higher the likelihood of overcoming the obstacles that will be on your path to innovation.

ENGLAND | INTEGRATING HOSPITALS, COMMUNITY, AND DIGITAL TEAMS—WHY CULTURE—NOT TECHNOLOGY—DETERMINES THE SUCCESS OF EUROPEAN HEALTHCARE INNOVATION | MLADEN MILOVANOVIC

Introduction: the Paradox of Digital Abundance

Healthcare innovation in Europe is frequently characterised by a paradox. Despite sustained investment in artificial intelligence, digital platforms, virtual wards, hospital-at-home (HaH) services, and remote monitoring, many initiatives fail to achieve durable impact at scale. This is not primarily due to technological limitations but to persistent organisational and professional fragmentation across European healthcare systems (NHS England, 2022; HIMSS Europe, 2023).

Digital transformation strategies across the European Union increasingly emphasise interoperability, data availability, and technological capability. However, technology alone does not determine system performance. Cultural alignment—defined here as shared norms of accountability,

DOI: 10.4324/9781003780175-1

trust, and decision-making across hospitals, community services, and digital teams—plays a decisive role in whether innovation is adopted, embedded, and sustained (Edmondson, 2018; Kotter, 2012).

This chapter examines cultural integration as a structural determinant of healthcare innovation in Europe. It demonstrates that while technology enables transformation, organisational culture determines whether transformation translates into system-level performance, workforce sustainability, and patient trust.

The Invisible Wall Inside European Healthcare Systems

European healthcare systems were largely designed around hospital-centred, specialty-driven, and episodic models of care. Contemporary healthcare delivery, however, is increasingly continuous, distributed, and population-oriented. Patients—particularly those with chronic conditions—move repeatedly between home, community services, outpatient settings, and hospitals, supported by digital technologies that generate real-time clinical data.

Despite this shift, organisational cultures remain segmented. Hospital clinicians are primarily trained to manage acute risk and inpatient complexity; community professionals focus on continuity, function, and social context; digital teams prioritise system reliability, scalability, and

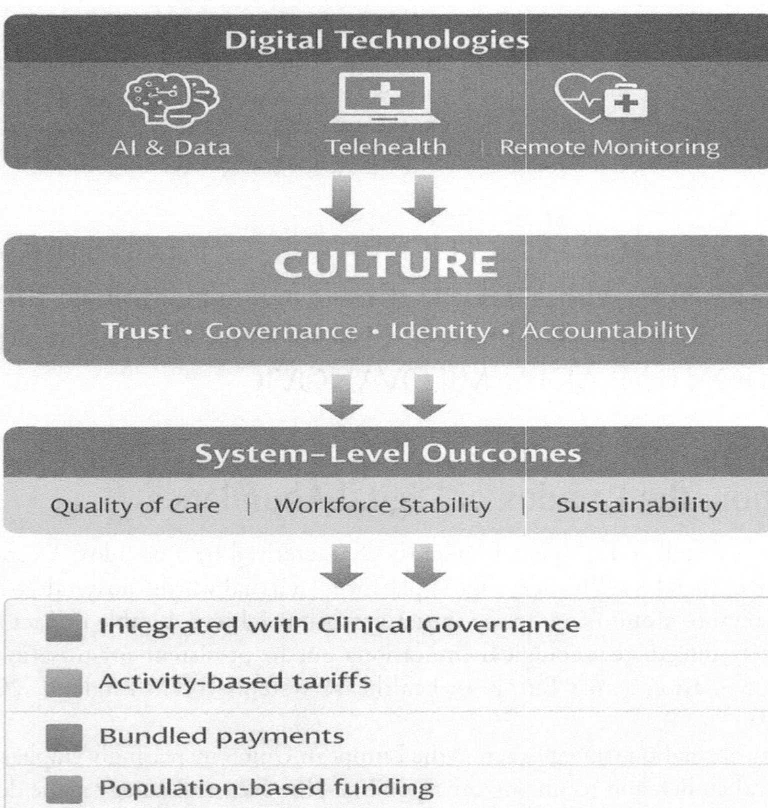

Figure 1.1 How culture drives Healthcare Innovation

data governance. Each perspective is legitimate within its domain. However, when these cultures operate in parallel rather than in coordination, care pathways fragment and innovation fail to scale (Porter, 2010; HIMSS Europe, 2023).

Technology tends to reinforce existing cultural patterns. In environments characterised by low trust or unclear accountability, digital tools are underutilised or resisted. Integration therefore represents a cultural and governance challenge rather than a purely technical one.

Culture mediates the relationship between technological capability and system-level outcomes. Identical digital technologies produce divergent results depending on whether professional identities, governance arrangements, and accountability mechanisms are aligned across hospitals, community services, and digital teams.

Cultural Integration as a Performance Mechanism

Cultural integration influences healthcare performance through identifiable and reproducible mechanisms. Comparative European experience suggests four mechanisms are particularly relevant:

1. Clinical trust, supported by shared governance and clearly defined accountability
2. Operational coherence, achieved through alignment of workflows across care settings
3. Workforce stabilisation, resulting from predictable work patterns and shared responsibility
4. Adaptive learning, enabled by joint review of outcomes and adverse events

These mechanisms help explain why comparable digital interventions lead to variable outcomes across regions and systems.

Table 1.1 Mechanisms through which cultural integration influences healthcare performance

Mechanism	*Description*	*Impact on care delivery*	*Supporting evidence*
Clinical trust	Shared governance and accountability	Earlier intervention; reduced defensive practice	Edmondson (2018)
Operational coherence	Aligned workflows across care settings	Reduced fragmentation; improved continuity	HIMSS Europe (2023)
Workforce stabilisation	Predictable workloads and shared responsibility	Reduced burnout; improved retention	Gray et al. (2015); NHS Confederation (2023)
Adaptive learning	Joint review of outcomes and events	Faster improvement cycles; improved safety	Edmondson (2018); NHS England (2022)

Source: Author synthesis based on Edmondson (2018), HIMSS Europe (2023), Gray et al. (2015), NHS England (2022), NHS Confederation (2023).

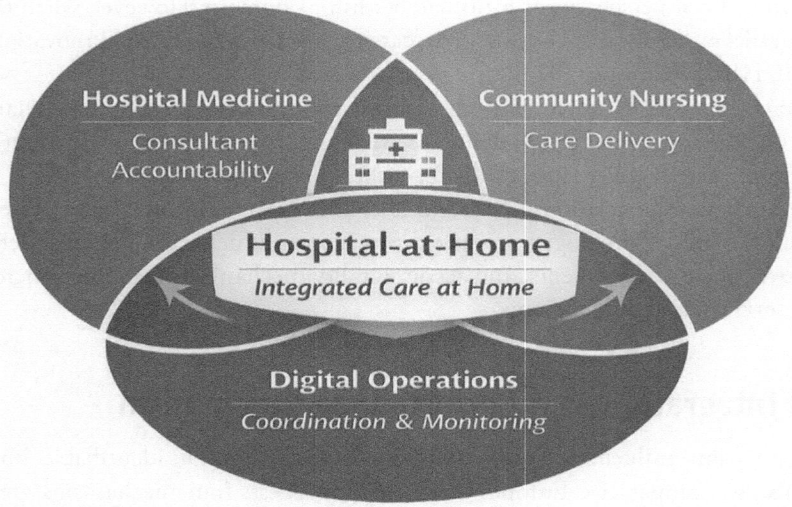

Figure 1.2 Hospital-at-Home as a Cultural Stress Test

Hospital-at-Home as a Cultural Stress Test

Hospital-at-home programmes provide a particularly informative case study for cultural integration. Evidence from Europe and North America indicates that HaH can deliver hospital-level care in patients' homes with outcomes comparable to, or better than, inpatient care (Levine et al., 2020; Federman et al., 2022).

HaH models challenge traditional organisational boundaries by relocating acute care delivery into the community. Successful programmes depend on high levels of trust between hospital consultants, community nurses, and digital operations teams. Research from Warwick Business School demonstrates that scalable HaH models consistently exhibit unified clinical governance, integrated digital infrastructure, and joint workforce arrangements (Milovanovic, 2022).

In these models, consultants retain ultimate clinical accountability, community teams deliver care as equal partners, and digital command centres support coordination rather than control.

Hospital-at-home integrates hospital medicine, community nursing, and digital operations within a single governance framework. Successful models preserve consultant-led clinical accountability while enabling digitally supported, community-based delivery.

NHS Virtual Wards: Cultural Integration at Scale

The NHS Virtual Wards programme represents one of the largest European efforts to operationalise integrated, digitally enabled care at scale. By 2023, more than 10,000 virtual ward beds were deployed across England (NHS England, 2022).

While early adopter integrated care systems (ICSs) reported reductions in length of stay and emergency readmissions, performance varied considerably. Systems that embedded virtual wards

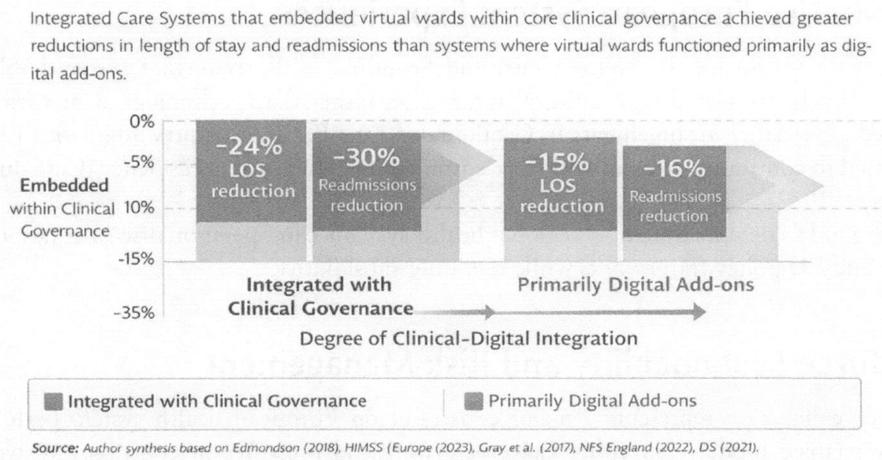

Figure 1.3 Degree of Clinical-Digital Integration & System-Level Outcomes

Table 1.2 Cultural integration models and system-level outcomes across selected European health systems

Health system	*Care model*	*Integration mechanism*	*Digital role*	*Reported outcomes*
Catalonia	System-integrated care	Joint governance	Shared infrastructure	30–40 % reduction in hospital utilisation
Basque Country	Integrated chronic pathways	Multidisciplinary leadership	Coordination-enabling	~20 % reduction in HF/COPD admissions
NHS ICSs	Virtual wards	Variable integration	Mixed	15–25 % LOS reduction (best performers)
Buurtzorg	Community nursing	Professional autonomy	Supportive	~40 % fewer care hours per patient
Scandinavia	Digital chronic care	Clinical–digital co-ownership	Embedded	15–30 % reduction in HF admissions

Source: Author synthesis based on García-Altés et al. (2019), Nuño-Solinís et al. (2016), NHS England (2022), Gray et al. (2015), Lindberg et al. (2022).

within existing clinical governance structures achieved more consistent results than those treating virtual wards as standalone digital initiatives (NHS Confederation, 2023).

Integrated care systems that embedded virtual wards within core clinical governance achieved greater reductions in length of stay and readmissions than systems where virtual wards functioned primarily as digital add-ons.

Comparative European System Experiences

Experiences from Spain, the Netherlands, and Scandinavia illustrate that system-level performance is closely associated with cultural integration rather than technological maturity alone. Integrated governance arrangements in Catalonia and the Basque Country align with EU objectives related to continuity of care, workforce sustainability, and system resilience (CatSalut, 2022; Osakidetza, 2022).

These models demonstrate how regional health systems can operationalise integration within national and EU policy frameworks while retaining subsidiarity.

Workforce Sustainability and Risk Management

Workforce exhaustion represents a major constraint on European health system performance. Digitally enabled models can either exacerbate workload pressures or contribute to workforce stabilisation, depending on cultural integration. Evidence suggests that integrated virtual wards and HaH programmes improve predictability, reduce night-time work, and enhance professional satisfaction (NHS Confederation, 2023).

Culturally integrated systems also demonstrate more effective risk management through shared clinical–digital governance.

Payment Models, Digital Maturity, and Patient Trust

Payment mechanisms influence organisational behaviour and cultural alignment. Activity-based funding tends to reinforce fragmentation, whereas bundled and population-based models support coordination and continuity.

Payment mechanisms shape organisational behaviour and culture. Population-oriented and bundled funding models support collaboration, cultural integration, and sustainable system performance.

The Future Trajectory of European Healthcare Systems

Looking ahead, the direction of European healthcare is likely to be shaped less by individual technologies than by the capacity of systems to operate as integrated, adaptive networks. Demographic ageing, rising multimorbidity, workforce constraints, and fiscal pressure will continue to challenge

Table 1.3 Governance and risk management approaches in fragmented and culturally integrated systems

Dimension	*Fragmented systems*	*Integrated systems*
Accountability	Dispersed	Shared
Digital oversight	Project-based	Joint clinical–digital
Risk response	Slow, blame-oriented	Rapid, learning-oriented
Data use	Retrospective	Real-time operational

Source: Author synthesis based on NHS England (2022), CatSalut (2022), Osakidetza (2022).

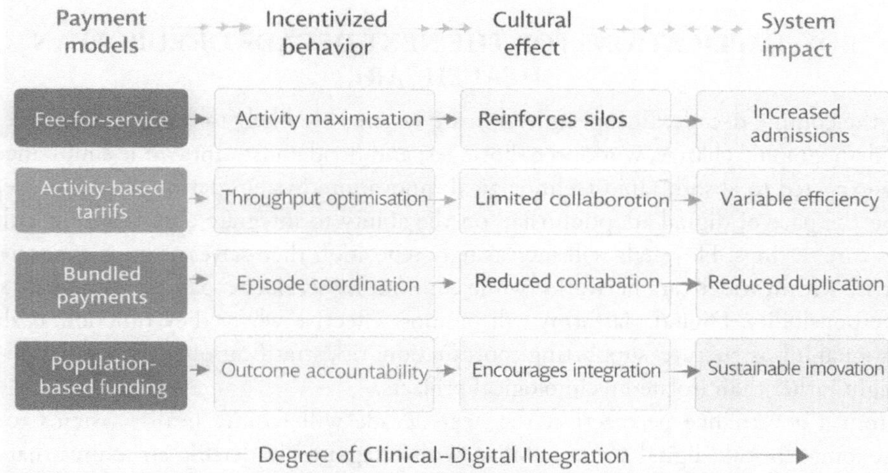

Figure 1.4 Payment Models & Their Influence

Table 1.4 Payment models and their influence on organisational culture and system performance

Payment model	*Incentivised behaviour*	*Cultural effect*	*System impact*
Fee-for-service	Activity maximisation	Reinforces silos	Increased admissions
Activity-based tariffs	Throughput optimisation	Limited collaboration	Variable efficiency
Bundled payments	Episode coordination	Encourages integration	Reduced duplication
Population-based funding	Outcome accountability	Supports shared identity	Sustainable innovation

Source: Author synthesis based on Porter (2010), CatSalut (2022), NHS England (2022).

hospital-centric models of care. In this context, future healthcare systems are expected to evolve towards distributed care architectures in which hospitals function as nodes of specialised expertise rather than default sites of care, community services assume expanded clinical responsibility, and digital platforms provide real-time coordination across settings. The success of this transition will depend on whether health systems can institutionalise cultural integration at scale—embedding shared governance, cross-sector accountability, and clinical–digital co-ownership as core system capabilities. Within the European Union, this trajectory aligns with broader policy objectives related to health system resilience, sustainability, and the European Health Union, where digitalisation is positioned as an enabler of continuity, prevention, and population-based care rather than an end in itself. Systems that achieve this cultural and organisational convergence are likely to be better equipped to absorb innovation, retain workforce, and deliver equitable, high-quality care under increasing complexity.

BOX: IMPLICATIONS FOR THE NEXT DECADE OF EUROPEAN HEALTHCARE

Over the coming decade, European healthcare systems are likely to face sustained pressure from demographic change, workforce shortages, and fiscal constraint, while simultaneously being expected to absorb rapid technological innovation. System performance will depend less on the pace of digital adoption than on the ability to integrate organisational cultures across care settings. Hospitals will increasingly reposition themselves as hubs of specialised expertise within wider care networks, while community services expand their clinical scope and responsibility. Digital platforms will be most effective where they function as shared operational infrastructure, supporting coordination, risk stratification, and population-level oversight rather than isolated technological projects.

From a governance perspective, the next decade will require health systems to normalise joint clinical–digital accountability, with integrated leadership structures that span hospitals, community providers, and digital teams. Workforce sustainability will remain a decisive constraint, making culturally integrated models—such as virtual wards and hospital-at-home—not only service innovations but strategic labour interventions. At policy level, alignment between payment models, regulatory frameworks, and integration objectives will be critical. Population-based and bundled funding mechanisms are more likely to support the cultural convergence required for continuity, prevention, and resilience. Within the context of the European Health Union, systems that succeed in institutionalising cultural integration are likely to be better positioned to deliver equitable, high-quality care while maintaining adaptability under increasing complexity.

Conclusion: Culture as Strategic Infrastructure

European healthcare innovation does not fail due to lack of technological solutions. It fails primarily because organisational cultures remain misaligned across care settings. Evidence from multiple European systems suggests that integrating hospitals, community services, and digital teams within shared governance frameworks improves performance, workforce sustainability, and patient trust.

Technology enables transformation. Cultural integration determines whether transformation endures.

References

Aguado, O. et al. (2020). Hospital at Home in chronic disease management: The Catalan experience. *European Journal of Internal Medicine, 13(4), 283–290.*

CatSalut (2022). *SISCAT Integrated Healthcare Model.* Government of Catalonia.

Edmondson, A. (2018). *The Fearless Organization.* Harvard Business Review Press.

Federman, A. et al. (2022). Hospital-at-Home for acutely ill adults. *Annals of Internal Medicine, 172(2), 77–85.*

García-Altés, A. et al. (2019). Hospital at Home in Catalonia. *International Journal of Integrated Care, 17(5), A279.*

Gray, B. H., Sarnak, D. O., & Burgers, J. S. (2015). *Home care by self-governing nursing teams: The Netherlands' Buurtzorg model.* New York, NY: The Commonwealth Fund.

HIMSS Europe (2023). *Digital Health Transformation Framework.*

Kotter, J. (2012). *Leading Change.* Harvard Business School Press.

Levine, D. et al. (2020). Hospital-level care at home. *New England Journal of Medicine, 382(3), 231–240.*
Lindberg, B. et al. (2022). Remote monitoring for heart failure. *European Heart Journal—Digital Health, 3(2), 203–213.*
Milovanovic, M. (2022). *Preparing for the Hospital of Future—Designing Hospital at Home Services.* Warwick Business School.
NHS Confederation (2023). *Delivering Virtual Wards.*
NHS England (2022). *Virtual Wards Delivery Guidance.*
Nuño-Solinís, R. et al. (2016). Integrated care in the Basque country. *Health Policy, 120(9), 1036–1045.*
Osakidetza (2022). *Strategy for Chronic and Integrated Care.* Basque Government.
Porter, M. (2010). What is value in healthcare? *New England Journal of Medicine, 363(26), 2477–2481.*

*****

FINLAND | ORGANIZATIONAL INNOVATION: BUILDING SUCCESSFUL TEAMS IN FINLAND'S COMPLEX HEALTH AND SOCIAL CARE LANDSCAPE | ANNIINA MUSTIKKAMAA AND ROBBIE HARLOW

Introduction

Innovation is hard, even more so in healthcare. Healthcare organizations around the world operate in highly complex, generally risk-averse environments where leadership aspires to innovate but may be impeded by patient safety laws, regulations, strict governance, and budget constraints. It makes sense too; healthcare is a costly, high-stakes industry in which the objectives are saving lives and preserving human wellbeing—aspirations that will always outweigh increased operational efficiencies or cost savings. Product innovation in healthcare should be slow, deliberate, and safe—not words Silicon Valley often associates with "innovation." With that in mind, healthcare organizations have an immense opportunity for organizational and process innovation that stands to increase the ultimate success of their product innovation. This essay examines how team-design and trust-building strategies helped a government digitization project in southern Finland, Lunna, to accelerate the successful uptake of new tools within a large health and social care setting.

An Introduction to Healthcare in Finland

Finland is a Nordic country of around 5.5 million people, where the administrative beating heart of health and social services is constituted by the Wellbeing Services Counties (WBCs), that is, the *hyvinvointialueet*. The WBCs, of which there are twenty-one spread across five regions, are responsible for clients' primary healthcare but also usually for services related to specialty healthcare, families and children, the elderly, mental health, substance-abuse, emergency situations, and more (Finns typically refer to patients as "clients," since healthcare recipients access both health and social services). WBCs are state funded, governed by locally elected officials, and they exist within one of the five larger regions, each of which coordinate cooperation and service provision.

Health and social care in Finland is predominantly publicly funded, coverage is universal, and life expectancy is high. Despite these strengths, Finland is sparsely populated, with only 19 people per square kilometer. Relatedly, Finns report the EU's second highest rate of unmet medical needs, largely due to high costs, long wait times and travel distance [1] [2]†. The rollout of digital services is a priority in Finland, as these services carry the promise of lower costs while decreasing wait times and eliminating the need for travel.

Project Overview

The Western Uusimaa Wellbeing Services County (LUVN) is the third largest WBC in the country, containing ten municipalities with over half a million inhabitants and employing almost ten thousand health and social care workers. The organization is divided into approximately sixteen service lines that together handle the core of health and social care service provision, not to mention numerous auxiliary support functions. LUVN initiated the Lunna digital services platform in response to citizens' growing desire for more advanced and cohesive digital services, and a core project objective was to reduce the number of different citizen-facing platforms from thirty-three to only five to ten by centralizing core services within Lunna. There were two key aspects to the Lunna project that drove the need for innovative team-design and trust-building strategies: the diversity of the service lines and emphasis on standardization across workflows and implementation methodology. The predominant thought was, if each service line deviates to their own way in solution design, implementation, training or governance, the project implementation will be slow, cumbersome, and inconsistent. The embodiment of this need to innovate materialized in the *Muutostiimi*, Finnish for "change team." The Muutostiimi, composed of internally recruited health and social care professionals, had the savvy and experience to effectively communicate with service lines all the way from frontline staff to service line leaders, building trust at every step of the project. Furthermore, the Muutostiimi was dedicated to their service line, handling a wide variety of project functions alongside their service line. This gave each service line a single, dedicated project liaison which reduced fragmentation and streamlined communications between the project team and frontline managers.

Hiring and Structuring the Right Team

As with many Wellbeing Services Counties (WBCs) in Finland, LUVN received EU funding designated for digital transformation initiatives like Lunna; however, facing the complex structure of the service lines and desire for consistency across the implementation, LUVN added its own funding to staff up and hire the Muutostiimi. The team was responsible for a myriad of project activities, including project management, workflow design and decision support, professional education, line manager support, go-live assistance, and post-implementation follow-up and benefits analysis. The intent was for these eleven individuals to serve as consistent, visible points of contact—"faces of change"—who could accompany service lines throughout the entire transformation process. Unlike traditional project models, where service design, training, reporting, and go-live support are handled by separate functional teams, each service line in the Lunna project typically worked with one to two dedicated change support staff across all phases. This structure enabled deeper contextual understanding of each service line's operational realities and personnel, while also allowing the project to maintain coherence and coordination across service lines through close collaboration within the change management team and centralized project oversight.

The composition of the Muutostiimi was key in ensuring quality and speed of implementation. Team members were drawn primarily from nursing, physical therapy, and social care backgrounds, allowing them to communicate fluently and efficiently with service line managers and to credibly interpret real needs and specific constraints. This shared professional language and experience helped generate high trust levels between the Muutostiimi members and their counterparts.

An innovative approach to team-building within the Muutostiimi was also pivotal to the team's success. The team spent their first two weeks of onboarding in the classroom where they learned about the Lunna project, the project's stakeholders, the different service lines they would be working with, standard working methods, and change management principles. Furthermore, the team was given plenty of exposure to leadership and understood the overall executive strategy for Lunna. This intensive training and contact with the project brass nurtured a sense of comradery within the team early on and generated a sense of duty to the project's goals. This effort represented significantly more training and preparation than is the norm for digitization projects in Finland and allowed the team to feel comfortable asking each other for support as well as sharing and collaborating to solve challenges they would later encounter within their respective service lines.

Although the Muutostiimi were largely effective in their primary function as change managers, the Lunna project, like any other, had its challenges. One noteworthy obstacle the team faced concerned service line workflow deviation. Initially, team members struggled to fully understand how individual service lines would use Lunna, as workflows had been designed independent of the Muutostiimi group. This made it difficult for the team to interpret design decisions and translate them into practical training. Eventually, the Muutostiimi team members recognized the issue and assumed greater responsibility for workflow design, which increased workload but significantly improved their understanding of service line requirements and inter-service line commonalities. If the project had not assigned a team member per service line, the Muutostiimi's bandwidth to do this work would have been severely hampered. This small tweak to ensure staff had bandwidth to identify and pivot to solve unforeseen project issues may not scream innovation to some, but it is a subtle organizational innovation that paid dividends for LUVN. Additionally, as the Muutostiimi developed these workflows across service lines, the initial effort put into team-building made workflow standardization easier as team members felt comfortable communicating more frequently and honestly about challenges and deviations—another minute but invaluable organizational innovation.

Conclusion

Innovation in any setting is tough, especially in healthcare. That said, hiring a motivated, right-sized team that already has the skill to effectively communicate and build meaningful relationships with stakeholders is a cornerstone to success. Sometimes those people come from IT, but sometimes not. Sourcing implementation teams that are willing to learn and are excited for new challenges may cost more upfront, but it may lead to better outcomes and save money and headaches down the road. Product innovation will always carry inherent risks but the most sinister of those risks is failed adoption. A brilliant product is never going to work, no matter how great it is, if the users fail to use it and use it well. This is where organizational and structural innovation comes in handy. Healthcare organizations can heighten their chances of successful product innovation by thinking deeply about how to build the right teams to implement those products. When implementation teams like the Muustiimi walk in lockstep with operations, the risk of a failed implementation lowers significantly. LUVN was successful in implementing Lunna because they took an innovative approach to building their implementation team, a team that was built to speak the language of their end users and dedicate time to educating and listening to their end users. They were staffed adequately from the beginning, received robust training, and were built up as a team instead of just thrown together haphazardly and left to their own devices. With five go-lives already under the belt, many service lines are inspired to invent and introduce new digital services through Lunna, and the Muutostiimi team members continue to play a vital part in the future of LUVN and its citizens.

*****

GERMANY | SURMOUNTING THE ORGANIZATIONAL IMMUNE SYSTEM: A TALE FROM THE TRENCHES, OR THE HANGOVER AFTER THE PARTY: WHY "INNOVATION THEATER" DIES IN THE TRANSFER GAP (AND HOW TO ACTUALLY WIN) | JASMIN SARIC

Introduction: The Table Soccer Fallacy

We have all been there. The "Innovation Lab" launch party. The air is filled with excitement, the scent of freshly brewed cappuccino, and the faint chemical smell of a thousand sticky notes. There are table soccer tables. There are whiteboards covered in phrases like "Disrupt or Die" and "Fail Fast." The CIO gives a speech about how we are going to act like a startup. We are going to be agile. We are going to break things.

And then, six months later, we realize we didn't break the market; we just broke the procurement process.

I have spent over fifteen years operating at the often-painful intersection of investors, corporate giants, and scrappy startups. I hold a PhD in computational linguistics, which means I have studied how to crunch large piles of textual data. But I also spent sixteen-plus years at a major pharmaceutical company where I co-founded a digital lab, and later I served as CEO of a digital oncology startup. I have lived on all sides of the table.

Here is the uncomfortable truth I have learned: Most corporate innovations fail not because of a lack of ideas but because of a lack of *architecture and culture*. We are great at generating sparks in the lab, but we are terrible at carrying that fire back to the corporate "mother ship" without it getting extinguished by the cold winds of annual budgets, compliance, IT security, and "business as usual."

This essay is not about how to brainstorm better. It is about the unsexy, gritty, essential work of innovation transfer. It is about how we move from "innovation theater"—where we pretend to be startups—to "venture clienting" and strategic integration, where we actually generate value.

The Diagnosis: Why "Playing Startup" Doesn't Work

In my presentation "Corporate Innovation: Dare to Win," I often show a slide contrasting the "Corporate Tanker" with the "Innovation Speedboat." The narrative is seductive: The Corporation is slow, bureaucratic, and risk averse. The Lab (or Startup) is fast, agile, and risky. The logic follows that if we just build Speedboats and tether them to the Tanker, the Speedboat will pull the Tanker toward the future.

In reality, the Tanker usually just runs over the Speedboat without even noticing it.

When we were building the digital lab, the challenge wasn't hiring data scientists or finding cool use cases. We could do that. The challenge was the "organizational immune system." When you try to graft a Silicon Valley culture onto a 100-year-old German pharmaceutical company, the antibodies come out in force. You aren't fighting a competitor; you are fighting the internal reality that a "Pivot" looks suspiciously like a "Planning Error" to a traditional controller.

The antibodies didn't always look like blockers; sometimes they looked like "strategic realignment." The entire team would spend six months building a product that solved a massive pain point, proving the value with hard data and happy users. You felt bulletproof. But then you'd run into the invisible wall of corporate narrative. You weren't killed because you failed; you were killed because the company decided to change it or your "North Star" over the weekend.

I remember presenting a project that had just hit 100% of its targets, only for a VP to lean back, nod slowly, and say:

"This tool solves a real problem, yes, but it solves a problem we have strategically decided to stop caring about. It simply doesn't map to the new roadmap, so we're putting it on hold."

We call this "Innovation Theater." It manifests in specific symptoms:

1. **MVP Purgatory:** We built endless minimal viable products (MVPs) that prove the user wants it, and the technology works, but never scale because nobody budgeted for the integration.
2. **The "Not Invented Here" Syndrome:** The core business looks at the lab's output with suspicion. "That looks cute," they say, "but it won't work in *real* operations."
3. **Metrics Mismatch:** The lab is measured on "learnings" or "activities" (hackathons hosted, pitches presented, etc.), while the core business is measured on P&L.

As I argued in *Dare to Win*, "Hope is not a strategy." To win, we need to stop treating innovation as a magical creative act and start treating it as a structured business process with a clear ambition to change how business operates.

The Strategic Pivot: Architecture Over Ideation

To bridge the chasm between a digital lab and the corporate core, you don't just need a new idea; you need transfer architecture that defines a new target state or structure. I learned the hard way during this process—and had to realize even more deeply later on—that this transformation piece is the real challenge. Not every company has to go through it; in some cases, for good reasons, you have a running oil tanker that delivers. For those organizations, innovation can be managed at arm's length externally.

However, if you choose to bridge the gap, you must recognize that while innovation requires three distinct phases, most organizations stop after the second, leaving the most critical work undone:

1. **Ideation & Incubation**: Discovering the solution.
2. **Validation**: Proving the concept through an MVP.
3. **Transfer & Scaling**: Fully integrating the solution into the core business—this is what startups call the growth phase.

The 1:5 Ratio: The Hidden Cost of Cultural Transformation

Phase 3 is where the "bodies are buried." The most common mistake in corporate innovation is underestimating the "Scaling Gap." It is crucial to understand that the ratio of investment between discovery (Phases 1+2) and scaling (Phase 3) is roughly 1:5 (this is my humble guess). This means that for every effort (e.g. "Euro") spent on the "cool" tech and the MVP, you need five times the effort (e.g. "Euro") to handle the organizational friction of integration.

This 1:5 ratio represents the massive cultural shift required to transition from a traditional organization of engineers—often optimized for "zero-error" and rigid planning—to an agile, digital-first organization. This transformation is the real challenge because it requires:

- **Organizational Absorption Rate**: The percentage of validated pilots that successfully migrate from the lab to a permanent budget line in the core business. It is crucial to have the support of the board.
- **Time-to-Internal-Scale**: The duration between a successful pilot and full operational rollout across the target business unit should be measured and regularly reported to the board.
- **Talent Fluidity**: The number of "core" employees who have cycled through the lab and returned to the business with agile competencies, effectively acting as "internal champions" for innovation.

This investment transforms the organization from a rigid engineering culture—optimized for zero-error and long cycles—into an agile, digital-ready ecosystem and needs clear ambition and support by the board.

A Tale from the Trenches: The Digital Lab Experience

When we established the transfer processes at our digital lab, we realized we couldn't simply "throw code over the wall" to IT. We had to front-load the transfer. Before a single line of code was written for a minimum viable product, we sat down with the eventual business "owner" developed the idea, the pitch deck, got approval from all different stakeholders (including the board), involved IT from the beginning, and so on.

At our digital lab, our primary focus was always the business ambition: identifying where we could create the most significant impact for patients and the company. However, we realized that high-level ambition must be underpinned by operational reality. To ensure this, we allocated our best people—not just to code but to act as strategic partners—helping the business units work out their pitch decks and define the true value proposition.

Once the ambition was clear, we asked the difficult, forward-looking questions about the budgets and resources that would become necessary once the "hype" of the pilot faded. We asked: "If this works and scales, do you have the long-term budget to own it? Who will manage the support tickets in three years?"

This "accountability-first" approach moved us from a "technology push" to a "demand-pull" model—solving the high-stakes problems that actually kept our leaders awake at night or at least helping them to better understand what the target state of digital transformation could be.

The Pathway Forward: Venture Clienting & Ecosystems

If building internally is too slow or the cultural price of the 1:5 ratio is too high, the modern pathway is venture clienting. During my time as a startup CEO, I saw the corporate side's flaws: months of meetings and vendor risk assessments designed for multinationals, not 20-person teams.

Corporates don't always need to build (intrapreneurship) or buy (CVC). Often, they just need to be the best possible customer. In the venture client model, the corporation offers a paid pilot to validate a solution. This aligns incentives perfectly:

- **The Startup** gains essential revenue and a marquee logo for their deck.
- **The Corporate** gets immediate access to cutting-edge tech without the risk of an acquisition or the sluggishness of internal R&D.

However, even this requires "transfer architecture." You need fast-track procurement, a "sandbox" environment for safe data access, and a simplified legal framework to succeed.

Conclusion: Dare to Execute

The value of innovation (VOI) is not measured by the number of ideas generated but by how many survive the transfer into the real world. We must move past the "romance of the garage" and focus on the "mechanics of the bridge." We need fewer evangelists and more architects.

My advice for the next generation of leaders, earned from the scars of both winning and losing:

- **Don't build what you can't land**: Without a receiver in the core business, you are just building toys.
- **Respect the Tanker**: You can't steer the corporate tanker by shouting at it; you must understand its "engine room"—procurement, legal, and IT—better than the captain does.
- **Dare to Win**: It is easy to play it safe with hackathons. It takes courage to kill a "zombie project" or force a hard conversation about budget.
- **Mind the Strategy**: Clearly understand if your are executing on a strategy as PR for shareholders, or on a strategy creating value for shareholders

Innovation is messy and frustrating. But when you finally bridge that gap—seeing a tool you nurtured actually saving lives or optimizing a global chain—it is the best job in the world.

Let's get back to work.

*****

UK | NHS BLENDED CLINICAL AND DATA CULTURES TO SCALE AI IMAGING | EDWARD W. MARX, SAKSHIKA DHINGRA, ALINE NOIZET AND ADITI U. JOSHI

Technology is hardly ever a starting point of innovation in healthcare. In the majority of cases, it starts with pressure. In the United Kingdom, that strain was too great to disregard as the demand of diagnostic imaging kept on increasing, whereas the number of radiologists continued to decrease. At the end of the 2010s national hospitals serving the National Health Service (NHS) were experiencing weeks or even months-long backlogs in reporting.[1] Clinicians got frustrated, patients were spending more time to get answers, and leaderships were experiencing increased scrutiny. The problem was clear. The solution was not. Artificial intelligence already showed potential in imaging research settings, especially in the field of chest X-rays, CT scans and stroke detection. However, taking those initial successes and putting them into habitual clinical practice in a complicated, publicly funded health system was a much more difficult task. Pilot shortage was not required in the NHS.[2] It required one that scaled in real clinical processes and in the actual environments. A single algorithm or vendor could not be the successor in eventual AI imaging success in the NHS. It has appeared as a conscious mixture of cultures, clinical, technical, operational and regulatory ones, each of which introduced another side to a common acute issue.

A System Under Strain

Radiology is the core of modern medicine. Almost all patient pathways will engage imaging somewhere, either in the diagnosis process, in the planning of treatment or in the monitoring of the patient. In the UK, the volume of imaging activities rose more than 30% in ten years, and the radiology workforce was much slower, which created a bottleneck in EDs, cancer pathways and elective care. Clinicians had an inkling that technology would be beneficial; however, there was a lot of doubt. Most radiologists had witnessed earlier IT implementations that had not decreased workload but rather increased workload.[3] The initial discussions on AI brought up the question of accuracy, bias, liability and the fear, which might or might not be articulated, that automation can take over professional judgment. Meanwhile, data scientists and technology vendors also tended to have problems with familiarizing themselves with clinical realities. Algorithms that were trained on selected datasets were not consistently effective in the variability of imaging in the real world.[4] Technical excellence would not be enough to achieve success. It would require trust.

Bringing the Right People to the Same Table

Among the first lessons acquired in NHS AI imaging initiatives was the fact that innovation could not be assigned to one department. The involvement of radiologists, IT teams, clinical safety officers, hospital executives and external partners had to be involved at the beginning. Instead of defining AI as a radiology initiative, a number of NHS trusts presented it as an organizational issue that has been system-wide.[1] Clinical leaders were also requested to provide not assessing performance metrics only but to assist in defining what useful actually meant in practice. The data scientists had been invited to reading rooms in order to see what was going on. Projects that had imperfect early results were also provided with visibility and protection by executive sponsors.[4] This mixture of cultures contributed to raising such hard questions at an early stage. Where would the results of AI be found in the workflow? What would be done with the discrepancies in human and algorithm? Who was responsible for making the decisions? Through collective efforts in solving these problems, the teams escaped the retrofitting trap of governance once it was deployed.

From Pilot to Practice

Another breakthrough was the AI tools that are capable of assisting timing-sensitive diagnoses, especially stroke and chest imaging. In stroke care, where the ability to swiftly detect large vessel occlusions in CT scans is of importance, AI algorithms able to do so quickly provided a distinct value proposition: the quicker the identification of the blockage, the quicker the intervention. Some NHS trusts launched AI systems which alerted stroke teams within minutes of the image being taken of suspected cases.[5] Notably, radiologists were not replaced by the AI. Rather it served as an early warning system which ensured that the urgent cases were given priority even in the peak working hours. Radiologists did not lose influence on the decision-making process, and their role changed in nuance.[6] Instead of being the gatekeepers of all images, they turned into authenticators and integrators of the clinic: they relied on AI outputs as a supplementary information source in their competencies. This re-packaging assisted in decreasing resistance and enhancing the information that technology was there to assist but not replace professional judgment.

Leadership and Cultural Permission

This level of innovation needed to be visible in terms of leadership support. Signaling that experimentation was not only a possibility but also a requirement, the NHS executives played a key role. They recognized that the first deployments would not be flawless and learning was an element of improvement. Such national institutions as NHS England and NHSX also contributed to this culture by developing comprehensive assessment frameworks and the procurement routes to AI technologies.[2,5] These organizations offered top-down assistance rather than leaving individual hospitals to deal with the regulatory uncertainty on their own but offered common advice on clinical safety, data governance and performance monitoring. This support was combined with bottom-up clinical involvement.[4] The two of them brought about a background in which innovation could not be an isolated success story but could start developing throughout the system.

Measurable Outcomes

The outcomes of such attempts were becoming harder and harder to disregard. The use of AI-assisted imaging at NHS locations showed a drop in reporting turnaround time, especially in emergencies. In stroke paths, there were qualitative gains, as well as time saving in tens of minutes, which is eternity when brain tissue is in question. There were better confidence reports of making prioritization decisions by clinicians during the high-volume periods. The junior radiologists also received extra support, and the senior clinicians also enjoyed the fact that the system allowed bringing up small things that would have been postponed.[6] Most importantly, AI imaging decreased cognitive load, perhaps. Technology enabled clinicians to work on complex interpretation and interaction with patients, the side of the care that is most linked to human skill, by managing repetitive triage processes.

Lessons in Blending Cultures

The experience of the NHS using AI imaging highlights one of the most basic realities regarding healthcare innovation: it is not about the tools but rather about the alignment. One ingredient alone was the technology itself. Another important thing was how the various professional cultures were ready to interact with each other in a way that is honest and respectful. Radiologists got to know how to express their requirements so that they could be converted into technical requirements by data scientists. Engineers came to appreciate the art and flexibility in clinical judgment.[5] Leaders got to know that innovation needed patience and visibility, and there must not be short-term pressure on performance. These cultures merged together, and thus, the NHS turned AI into a hypothetical possibility into a viable ability.[3] It was a process that could not be done in a straight line or simply enough, but it was reproducible, exactly what healthcare systems require in terms of innovation courses.

Conclusion

The UK has yet to embrace AI imaging. There are still new applications, such as cancer detection and musculoskeletal imaging. However, the legacy that might outlast the longest of such first attempts might not be the algorithms themselves but the shared muscle memory which they developed. By deciding on people versus technology, NHS failed to resolve its imaging issues. It only managed to do so by not dividing them. By so doing, it had shown that sustainable innovation in healthcare begins when different cultures cease to work around each other and begin to work together.

References

1. Cushnan, D. et al. (2021). Towards nationally curated data archives for clinical radiology image analysis at scale: Learnings from national data collection in response to a pandemic. *Digital Health.* 7:205520762110486. https://doi.org/10.1177/20552076211048654
2. Doherty, G., Hughes, C., McConnell, J., Bond, R., McLaughlin, L., McFadden, S. (2025). Integrating AI into medical imaging curricula: Insights from UK HEIs. *Radiography.* 31(3):102957. https://doi.org/10.1016/j.radi.2025.102957
3. Hassan, M., Borycki, E.M., Kushniruk, A.W. (2024). Artificial intelligence governance framework for healthcare. *Healthcare Management Forum.* 38(2). https://doi.org/10.1177/08404704241291226
4. Morley, J., Murphy, L., Mishra, A., Joshi, I., Karpathakis, K. (2022). Governing data and artificial intelligence for health care: Developing an international understanding. *JMIR Formative Research.* 6(1):e31623. https://doi.org/10.2196/31623
5. Alami, H. et al. (2025, November 9). Artificial intelligence governance in health systems: A systematic review of frameworks and an integrative model proposal (preprint). https://doi.org/10.2196/preprints.87448
6. Freeman, S. et al. (2025, April 9). Developing an AI governance framework for safe and responsible AI in healthcare organisations: A protocol for a multimethod study (preprint). *JMIR Research Protocols.* https://doi.org/10.2196/75702

*****

GERMANY AND SWITZERLAND | DRIVING HEALTHCARE INNOVATION ACROSS GERMANY AND SWITZERLAND: THE PT EHEALTH GMBH EXPERIENCE WITH KHZG FTB, EAM EVALUATION, AND KIS STANDARD | TATJANA PARMAKOVIC WITH FELIX PENNER

The Human Frequency of Innovation

In the era of precision-focused orthopedic care, where every millimeter can be a patient's biggest advantage in mobility, the surrounding digital systems often resemble an untreated fracture: crucial but neglected, undermining the flow of progress.

Healthcare technology has been, for decades, regarded as a secondary actor, shadowed behind the clinical assets it ostensibly serves. Yet the journey from a clinical lens into a health IT perspective has revealed a transformative truth that reshapes priorities: innovation is not a commodity to be purchased or following a trend—it is a culture that requires deliberate cultivation across every tier of an organization.

At pt ehealth, our experience has demonstrated that the mastery of code, while essential, is not the defining factor of successful digital transformation. Instead, innovation stems from the art of managing blended cultures. It is about forging harmony between the precision-driven world of surgeons; the structured, logic-oriented approach of IT professionals; and the meticulous oversight of finance managers. When these distinct organizational "languages" find a common purpose and align with a unified vision, innovation transcends rhetoric to become a life-changing reality for patients.

Setting the Context: A Tale of Two Systems and a Third Way

European healthcare currently acts as a dynamic experimental ground for diverse innovation models. Navigating this landscape demands not only technical savvy but also cultural adaptability—a need to become a chameleon who can read and respond to differing regulatory and financial climates.

The German Mandate: The Hospital Future Act

Germany's Hospital Future Act (KHZG) stands as a bold federal mandate, designed to accelerate digital modernization through fiscal incentives. Hospitals are under tremendous pressure to complete Fast Track Bundles (FTB) 2 to 6, a comprehensive roadmap covering everything from patient portals and medication safety to cybersecurity hardening. This is more than digitizing paperwork—it is a strategic leap into building an integrated digital healthcare ecosystem.

The Swiss Monetary Impasse: Fiscal Discipline in Innovation

Switzerland faces a contrasting challenge. Its decentralized system fosters efficiency but often at the cost of innovation momentum. Though desires for sophisticated enterprise architecture management (EAM) systems exist, capital remains tied up in outdated infrastructures. The dilemma stifles agility and hampers large-scale digital transformation.

To make matters worse, the procurement of clinical information systems (CIS) follows a certain paradigm. Historically, Swiss hospitals invest significant time and resources in tenders that over-customize systems to fit idiosyncratic workflows, resulting in skyrocketing costs and feature creep. This leads to complex, costly, and cumbersome solutions that stagnate rather than accelerate innovation.

The Third Way: Bridging Cultures and Systems

pt ehealth proposes a third way: a pragmatic, adaptive approach that combines institutional mandates and financial realities with inclusive stakeholder engagement. We function as cultural translators, weaving together Germany's top-down regulatory momentum with Switzerland's cautious, budget-conservative innovation style. Through this synthesized model, we help institutions modernize sustainably and strategically.

Define Your Innovation: The Strategic Cultural Synchronizer

Innovation cannot reside solely in technical "how to" guides or static policies. It thrives best when it permeates the culture at all levels of an organization—where technology and human factors coalesce.

The Top-Down, Bottom-Up Approach in Germany

Our German projects do not settle for mere compliance with KHZG's FTB 2–6 mandates. Instead, we map statutory requirements directly to tangible clinical challenges. For example, we involve surgeons deeply, ensuring their perspectives shape tool development so that digital innovations assist rather than obstruct clinical workflows.

Contract Potential Analysis in Switzerland

Our forensic financial innovation methodology scans existing contracts for "dead capital"—fees spent on underutilized or obsolete IT services. Upon revealing substantial savings, we bring together finance and IT teams who rarely collaborate, supporting dialogue that transforms relationships and reallocates savings toward strategic EAM initiatives. The cost reduction of up to 18% on license fees and hardware spending demonstrates that innovation can be self-funded when financial waste ("muda") is identified and eliminated.

From IT Projects to Investment Decisions

To move innovation beyond aspiration, healthcare organizations must evaluate digital initiatives with the same rigor applied in the financial industry. At the project level, we apply DCF models, NPV calculations, Monte Carlo simulations, and confidence interval analysis to assess uncertainty, risk exposure, and value creation.

This approach reframes digital transformation from a cost discussion into a risk-adjusted investment decision. It provides executive leadership with transparent, comparable metrics to prioritize initiatives across clinical, IT, and operational domains. At the same time, it establishes a common financial language that extends beyond internal governance—serving as a foundational data basis for external investment decisions by banks, institutional investors, and alternative financing partners. Innovation that cannot demonstrate economic plausibility under uncertainty risks losing credibility, regardless of its technological promise.

Operationalizing Innovation at Scale

At the organizational and operational level, sustainable innovation requires objective measurement of efficiency—not intuition. By combining technology enablement with industry-standard process management methods, healthcare organizations can quantify performance improvements.

Applying principles such as Little's law enables leadership to correlate work-in-progress, throughput, and cycle time across clinical and administrative processes. When embedded into governance and operational dashboards, these metrics transform digital systems from passive enablers into active instruments for continuous performance optimization. This analytical discipline is essential for scaling innovation beyond pilot projects into day-to-day operations and financial decision making.

Standard-First Deployment: Disrupting the Swiss CIS Model

Challenging the entrenched paradigm of hyper-customized clinical information systems, we spearheaded an initiative requiring hospitals to adopt standardized cloud-based CIS solutions—a radical cultural realignment. This approach shifts the burden from endless system tailoring onto the organization adapting clinical workflows to best practice standards embedded in the software. It is a cultural and operational pivot from "bending software to fit us" to embracing evolution in clinical processes for sustained digital success.

Preparing Healthcare Institutions for Quantum Readiness

While quantum computing remains emergent, its implications for healthcare institutions are immediate—particularly in the domains of cybersecurity, data integrity, and long-term architectural decisions. Quantum readiness should not be interpreted as premature technology adoption but as institutional preparedness.

From a governance standpoint, organizations must begin assessing post-quantum cryptographic resilience, especially where sensitive patient data, long retention periods, and cross-border data exchange are involved. Decisions made today regarding encryption standards, identity management, and data lifecycles will determine whether future transitions can be executed smoothly or under crisis conditions.

Equally important is architectural foresight. Enterprise architectures should be evaluated for algorithm agility, modularity, and the ability to swap cryptographic components without systemic disruption. This readiness mindset mirrors earlier transitions in healthcare IT, where institutions that prepared early avoided costly, reactive overhauls.

Quantum readiness, therefore, is less about computing power and more about organizational maturity—the ability to anticipate disruptive shifts and embed resilience into governance, architecture, and strategic planning long before disruption becomes operational reality.

Case Study: The Reality of Cross-Border Transformation

Part I: Germany—Orthopedic Hospital & KHZG Implementation

Our collaboration with a leading orthopedic hospital epitomizes the scale and depth of digital transformation under KHZG's Fast Track Bundles:

- **FTB 2 & 3:**
  Empowering patients became a focal point. We enabled patients to upload X-rays digitally before consultations, significantly reducing delays and streamlining care coordination. Nursing documentation was integrated into a single interoperable digital file accessible in real-time, bridging communication gaps.
- **FTB 4 & 5:**
  Leveraging AI, we developed risk modeling tools tailored for surgeons' decision-making processes and embedded automated medication safety checks to prevent harmful prescribing or administration errors. These advances not only improved safety but enhanced the confidence of clinical teams in digital tools.
- **FTB 6:**
  Cybersecurity presented a formidable cultural barrier. Surgeons initially perceived it as a competing priority that compromised speed and efficiency. With this in mind, our IT security officers organized forums for physicians in which cyber risks were translated into clinical terms—to show how security measures are not obstacles but safeguards that enable the rapid and secure introduction of AI-powered innovations. This cultural bridge-building was crucial to creating acceptance and establishing cybersecurity as an enabler, not a hindrance.

Part II: Switzerland—Unlocking EAM through Financial Realignment

A Swiss healthcare provider sought to implement an EAM solution but lacked the budget to justify the investment. Through a meticulous audit, we exposed "dead" costs in hardware and license deployments. By promoting dialogue between finance and IT—departments that traditionally avoided working together—we created a shared understanding.

The resulting 18% annual cost reduction was repurposed to fund the EAM evaluation process. This negotiation and reconciliation between cultures not only unlocked funds but sparked a self-funding innovation mechanism, setting a precedent for financial transparency and partnership that extends beyond IT procurement.

Part III: The Standard-First Cloud-KIS: The New Frontier in Swiss Healthcare

Confronting the "complexity trap" associated with Swiss CIS implementations, our latest project took a pioneering path:

1. **Phase 1—Standard Installation:** We installed a cloud-based CIS in its standard, unmodified form, resisting the temptation to immediately customize.

2. **Phase 2—Gap Analysis:** A comprehensive clinical workflow review identified deviations where the standard system did not meet clinical realities. This objective audit prevented unnecessary feature creep while illuminating true crucial needs.
3. **Phase 3—Must-Have Configuration:** We implemented tweaks only for essential functions, ruthlessly rejecting "nice-to-have" modifications that would complicate maintenance or delay delivery.

The project's upcoming "Big Bang" launch, involving a wholesale switch from the legacy CIS to the new cloud system overnight, presents significant cultural and operational risks. Success hinges on the entire hospital staff's willingness to discard entrenched habits and embrace a more streamlined, efficient future. This transformation is more than technical—it is an evolution in mindset.

Lessons & Barriers: Crossing the "Valley of Resistance"

Digital transformation is rarely a straightforward journey; it is a "team of teams" endeavor requiring constant vigilance against internal resistance.

- **Legacy Mindset:**
  Veteran physicians often resist digital documentation, perceiving it as bureaucratic or time-consuming. Identifying "culture champions," early adopters savvy with technology, proved invaluable. These champions serve as peer influencers demonstrating how new systems can save time and reduce frustration, shifting perception from resistance to advocacy.
- **Governance Reality:**
  Managing change in healthcare environments resistance is the norm—a critical lesson across all transformation initiatives is the acknowledgment that approximately 85% of individuals are inherently resistant to change. This is not a healthcare-specific phenomenon but a fundamental human trait. Consequently, innovation cannot rely on voluntary adoption alone. It must be governed.

Effective change therefore requires clear top-down sponsorship, explicit prioritization, and visible accountability at executive level. When leadership treats digital transformation as optional or negotiable, resistance fills the vacuum. Conversely, when change is framed as a strategic imperative—supported by governance structures that align incentives, responsibilities, and decision rights—adoption accelerates despite initial skepticism. Cultural change, in this sense, becomes a leadership discipline rather than a grassroots hope.

- **The Complexity Trap:**
  Our initial Swiss EAM plans failed because they were overly complex. We learned the value of "stress simplicity": if a concept cannot be explained clearly and simply, it risks rejection. Simplifying solutions and communications support broader acceptance.
- **Funding Fog:**
  Bureaucratic hurdles can obscure clinical priorities. We found that consistent, in-person communication is essential to keep teams focused on the shared patient-centered goals and prevent delays or scope creep.

The Human Element: Innovation With Empathy

At pt ehealth, we firmly believe "one is too small a number for innovation." Progress is fueled through collective effort, shared purpose, and mutual respect. Appreciating small victories—whether a smooth parameter configuration or a milestone in KHZG compliance—is critical. Such recognition builds momentum and morale.

Innovation challenges assumptions and egos, particularly for physicians who may feel distanced from IT initiatives. By involving frontline healthcare professionals directly in the design and rollout of solutions such as the "standard-first" CIS, we promote ownership rather than imposition. This participatory approach ensures that new solutions feel like genuine tools co-created by their users rather than alien mandates.

Empathy for the stress and uncertainty that accompany change forms the bedrock of our cultural approach, enabling resilience and adaptability.

A Blueprint for the Future: Scaling Across Borders and Systems

Our cross-border experience unveils a replicable model for healthcare leaders worldwide seeking digital transformation:

- **Carry out a Cultural Inventory:** Map out allies and skeptics early. Engage culture champions who can influence peers and identify resistance pockets that require tailored strategies.
- **Audit Existing Resources:** Quantify existing "dead capital" to avoid unnecessary expenditure and reallocate savings for innovation funding.
- **Bridge the IT-Clinical Divide:** Ground technological roadmaps in real clinical needs, ensuring solutions are practical and clinician-friendly.
- **Standardize and Simplify:** Reject over-engineered solutions. Embrace standardized, cloud-based platforms for cost-effectiveness, maintainability, and timely delivery.
- **Maintain Transparent Communication:** Prioritize openness and frequent dialogue among all stakeholders to maintain alignment and adapt swiftly to evolving demands.

This blueprint imagines a future unconstrained by national borders or legacy systems—a healthcare ecosystem propelled by rich data flows, security, and seamless patient-centered care.

Closing Remarks: Harmonizing the Future of Healthcare Innovation

pt ehealth's journey exemplifies the power of managing blended cultures, demonstrating that sustainable innovation emerges not from piecemeal technology acquisition but from the synthesis of human insight and technical prowess. As Europe gears up for challenges ahead—especially in cybersecurity, advanced data analytics, and harmonizing best practices across nations—the imperative to dismantle the "uncured fractures" within healthcare's digital fabric grows ever more pressing.

Together, by transcending language differences, cultural divides, and organizational silos, we pave the way for a thriving healthcare culture—responsive, resilient, and relentlessly progressive.

Innovation, at its core, is human. It's about understanding, connection, and courage to change. And it is through managing blended cultures that we unlock its fullest potential for the benefit of every patient's life.

*****

GERMANY | ADDING WHEELS TO A STATIONARY SYSTEM—HOW GERMANY'S MOBILE DENTAL INNOVATION REACHED A GENERATION LEFT BEHIND | TOBIAS LIPPEK

Note: Patient and provider names have been changed to protect privacy.

The Phone Call That Changed Everything

Dr. Weber's* phone rang at 7:47 AM on a Tuesday morning in March 2024. On the other end was the director of a nursing home. Her voice cracked as she described an 87-year-old resident who hadn't seen a dentist in four years. His infected tooth had turned into sepsis. He was in the hospital, fighting for his life.

"We called every dentist within 50 kilometers," she said. "No one comes to us anymore."

Dr. Weber was the last dentist in that district willing to make house calls. He was sixty-four years old. And he was exhausted.

This is not a story about one patient. This is a story about 5.7 million Germans like him—immobile, invisible, and underserved by a healthcare system built for a world that no longer exists. This is a story about what happened when we stopped waiting for patients to come to us and started going to them.

This is the story of how we had to reimagine German dentistry.

Setting the Context: The Culture We Inherited

For decades, German dentistry operated on a deeply embedded cultural principle: the independent practitioner model. Every dentist was an entrepreneur. You graduated, secured substantial financing (today's practice acquisition costs average €300,000–€770,000), bought a practice, and spent the next forty years bearing every clinical, financial, and administrative risk alone.

This culture built extraordinary quality. German dentistry became renowned worldwide for precision, clinical autonomy, and excellence. But it also built extraordinary rigidity.

By 2024, the model showed profound structural cracks:

The Demographic Shift: The average age of German dentists reached 53.4 years. In Eastern Germany, over 50% were older than 55. The Baby Boomer generation was retiring en masse, and far fewer young dentists wanted to follow the traditional path.

The Capital Barrier: Young dentists increasingly rejected the model of taking on hundreds of thousands of euros in debt for practice ownership, especially as they sought work-life balance and different career paths.

The Immobility Wave: Meanwhile, 5.7 million Germans became care dependent. They couldn't come to the dentist. And the dentists, bound to their stationary practices by economic necessity and professional culture, couldn't—or wouldn't—come to them.

The result was what we call the "Care Effect": Within six months of entering a nursing home, residents' oral health collapses. Infections soar. Aspiration pneumonia rates spike. In Germany, poor oral hygiene increases pneumonia mortality by up to 57%.

The eighty-seven-year-old patient was not an exception. He was becoming the rule.

We had inherited a culture of excellence that was inadvertently creating exclusion. And we faced a choice: defend the status quo, or complement it with something new.

Defining the Innovation: Building the Collective

In early 2024, I co-founded 32bit Mobile Medizin with Dr. Sebastian Geiger, bringing together two perspectives that healthcare transformation requires: systematic infrastructure thinking and frontline clinical experience.

I had spent years coordinating innovative projects in Berlin's public services—youth welfare, public health, child protection. I'd seen how well-intentioned individuals burn out trying to fix structural problems. I'd watched brilliant social workers, nurses, and doctors sacrifice themselves at the altar of broken systems while administrators called them heroes.

Sebastian brought clinical reality—facing the challenges of integrating mobility into dentists' workflows, both on hardware and software levels.

We surveyed the landscape of mobile dentistry in Germany and found a paradox: individual dentists were attempting mobile care, but there was no collective infrastructure, no shared equipment, no standardized training. Every mobile dentist was reinventing the wheel.

We realized: You cannot solve a cultural problem with individual heroism.

The traditional culture—the independent practitioner—needed to meet a new culture: the Collective. Not as a replacement but as a complement. The stationary model would remain vital for standard care. We would build the missing infrastructure for those the stationary model couldn't reach. From that synthesis, we could create something stronger than either could achieve alone.

The Case Study: The Mobile Medical Hub-and-Spoke

Our model is simple in concept, complex in execution:

The Hub: A central infrastructure node handling sterilization, administration, logistics, and regulatory compliance. Our first hub will open in Herxheim, Rhineland-Palatinate, in Q3 2026, with Berlin following.

The Spokes: A fleet of certified mobile medical units—not converted buses but purpose-built, medical device-certified dental clinics on wheels—that deploy to rural areas and care facilities across Germany.

But the innovation wasn't the vehicle. It was the professional identity we created: the Care Pioneer.

The Care Pioneer Model

We told young dentists: "Don't take on crushing debt. Don't become an administrator managing staff and insurance billing. Just be a doctor."

We offered them:

- Employed positions with 4-day workweeks
- Fair, transparent compensation
- Zero entrepreneurial risk while maintaining clinical autonomy
- And something even more valuable: the chance to specialize in geriatric and special-needs dentistry as a respected expertise, not a fallback

In return, they join a collective mission to reach the unreached.

The Tariff: Culture Through Compensation

Traditional dental practices use opaque salary negotiations and individual incentives. We created something different: the collective tariff—a transparent compensation model where every role, from dentist to dental assistant to driver, receives fair base pay. But the real innovation lies in what we choose to reward beyond the baseline.

We built a point system that makes values tangible. Dentists earn points for specialized training in geriatric dentistry, dementia care, and—critically—sign language for deaf patients. Dental assistants earn points for expertise that stationary practices often overlook. Drivers earn points for commercial licenses and willingness to work in underserved "dental deserts."

But we also reward commitment to the mission itself: working more than 50% of your time in mobile units earns points. Taking on the challenges of non-ideal clinical conditions earns points. These aren't abstract values on a mission statement. They're concrete factors in your compensation.

By embedding these values into the economic structure, we made the invisible visible. Compassion became quantified. Flexibility became a skill. The willingness to serve became a professional credential.

This wasn't charity. This was cultural engineering through economic design. We weren't asking people to sacrifice for the mission. We were aligning economic incentives so that serving the mission became the rational economic choice.

The Human: When an Apple Changes Everything

The 87-year-old patient who nearly died from sepsis was our warning signal. Another patient—let's call her Mrs. Klein*—became our proof of concept.

Mrs. Klein, 82, lives in a care facility near the border. She has advanced dementia. For three years, she refused to eat solid food. The staff attributed it to cognitive decline.

When our mobile unit arrived for routine screening, our dentist didn't force her into an unfamiliar chair or try to transport her to an external clinic—both would have triggered fear and resistance in a dementia patient. Instead, he sat by her bedside. Using our portable handheld X-ray, he identified a severe abscess under her dental bridge in 30 seconds.

Because we were mobile, we didn't need to schedule hospital transport. We treated her right there, in her familiar room, with her favorite nurse holding her hand.

Two days later, the nursing director called us.

"She ate an apple today," she said.

That moment—an elderly woman with dementia eating an apple—is why we navigate bureaucracy. That is the metric that transcends all others. That is the human truth beneath every innovation framework.

Mrs. Klein's daughter sent us a video. Her mother was singing—a song from her childhood. She was smiling for the first time in two years.

"You gave me my mother back," the daughter wrote.

Vision: The Fourth Pillar

We don't envision mobile care as a niche service. We envision it as the Fourth Pillar of the German healthcare system, standing alongside hospitals, specialist practices, and Public Health Services.

By 2030, our vision:

- Every nursing home in Germany receives quarterly dental visits—as standard of care
- Mobile units operate nationwide, integrated with the Public Health Service for systematic screening
- Care pioneers are trained and employed in a profession young dentists choose because of its mission, not despite it
- A collective tariff model becomes the standard for mobile healthcare workers across Europe

The Cultural Shift

Mobile dental care is no longer seen as "secondary" but as specialized expertise in geriatric care, special needs dentistry, and complex patient management under non-ideal conditions.

The independent practitioner model remains vital for standard dental care. We complement it, not replace it. Together, the stationary and mobile models form a complete system that serves all patients, regardless of mobility.

Repeatability: A Model for Others

For organizations considering similar innovations, our journey offers three transferable lessons:

1. **Economic Alignment is Cultural Alignment** You cannot ask people to sacrifice financially for mission work. Design compensation structures that make the right thing the economically rational thing.
2. **Technology Should Be Invisible** Don't force users to "adopt" technology. Embed it so seamlessly that they forget it's there.
3. **Complement, Don't Confront** We positioned ourselves as the missing piece. This turned potential opponents into collaborators.

Any healthcare organization facing access gaps for mobility-impaired populations can adapt this model: senior care (medical, not just dental), rural healthcare, disability services, or post-acute care.

The principles remain the same: collective infrastructure, transparent incentives, technology that serves humanity, and respect for existing professional cultures.

Wrapping Up: The Architecture of Hope

In architecture, there's a principle: load-bearing walls cannot be removed without replacing their function. For seventy years, the independent practitioner model was the load-bearing wall of German dentistry. We didn't remove it. We added a new structural element.

We are proving that excellence and equity can coexist, that innovation doesn't require choosing between quality and access, that a profession can transform itself before crisis forces change.

The HIMSS Innovation Pathway "Blend Cultures" asks us to include the broader community and ensure institutional leaders are engaged and supportive. We've created a synthesis—one that honors the clinical excellence of traditional practice while addressing the moral imperative of universal access.

Dr. Weber, the exhausted 64-year-old who took that call in March 2024, visited our hub in Berlin last month. He's considering joining the Collective. He thought his career was ending. Now he sees it beginning again—not alone but together.

The patient who nearly died from sepsis? He's still in the nursing home, receiving quarterly preventive care. He's eating well. No infections.

Mrs. Klein still has dementia. We didn't cure that. But she's eating apples. She's singing. She's present.

Because in the end, patients don't care about our business model or our innovation frameworks. They care that when they needed help, someone came.

And that is the only innovation that truly matters.

*****

RUSSIA | NATIONAL MEDICAL RESEARCH CENTER FOR HEMATOLOGY | EDWARD W. MARX

The Alchemy of Progress: Blending Cultures at Russia's National Medical Research Center for Hematology

Introduction

In the demanding and precise world of modern medicine, progress is rarely the product of isolated genius. Instead, it emerges from the sophisticated integration of diverse perspectives, disciplines, and cultural frameworks. The National Medical Research Center for Hematology (NMRCH) in Russia stands as a premier example of this principle in action (NMRCH, 2023). Far more than a mere hospital or research institute, NMRCH functions as a dynamic nexus where a multifaceted approach to cultural blending—spanning professional, regional, and international spheres—fuels groundbreaking advancements in hematological research and clinical practice. By intentionally weaving together the distinct threads of scientific rigor, clinical pragmatism, regional diversity, and global collaboration, the Center has crafted a unique ecosystem that accelerates innovation from the laboratory bench to the patient's bedside, solidifying its role as a leader in the global fight against blood diseases.

National Medical Research Center for Hematology Outcomes

Before we dive deep into how NMRCH successfully blends cultures, let's look at the results of this intentional approach. Much of NMRCH success is dependent on blending cultures. Russia itself is an eclectic mix of researchers, scientists, and clinicians from all over the world. The results speak for themselves.

Major clinical advancements:

- Pioneering Blood Transfusion Techniques. As the world's first institute of blood transfusion (established in 1926), it has historically led innovations in transfusion medicine, including improved storage methods and safety protocols for blood products (Ivanov et al., 2022).
- Advanced Cellular Therapies. Research includes developments in bone marrow transplantation and CAR-T cell therapies for hematologic malignancies, enhancing treatment protocols for leukemia and lymphoma (Zhang, 2022).
- Genomic and Molecular Diagnostics. Implementation of next-generation sequencing and molecular profiling to guide personalized treatment strategies for blood disorders (Petrova, 2021).
- Focus on AI-driven precision medicine, automated diagnostics, and next-generation cell therapies.
- Expansion of telemedicine platforms for remote patient monitoring in hematology.

Major research achievements

- Pioneering Transplantation Techniques. Conducted Asia's first successful syngeneic bone marrow transplant (1964), establishing foundational protocols for hematopoietic stem cell transplantation that improved survival rates for leukemia and aplastic anemia patients.
- Breakthroughs in Gene and Cell Therapy. Advanced CAR-T cell therapies for relapsed/refractory blood cancers, achieving high remission rates in clinical trial. Pioneered gene therapy solutions for genetic blood disorders like thalassemia and hemophilia, with experimental treatments showing potential for functional cures (Zhang, 2022).
- Precision Medicine and Diagnostics. Leveraged multi-omics technologies to identify novel biomarkers and therapeutic targets, enabling personalized treatment strategies for hematologic malignancies. Integrated AI-assisted diagnostic tools for rapid and accurate classification of blood cancers (Petrova, 2021).
- National Treatment Guidelines and Protocols. Developed evidence-based clinical guidelines and standardized protocols for blood diseases, adopted nationwide to ensure consistent care quality. Established large-scale biobanks and disease registries to support translational research and epidemiologic studies (Volkov, 2023).

Major public health advancements.

- Reduced Mortality and Improved Survival. Contributions to HSCT and targeted therapies have significantly increased 5-year survival rates for leukemia and lymphoma patients in regions served by these centers. Enhanced blood transfusion safety through improved screening and storage techniques, reducing transfusion-transmitted infections.

- Accessibility and Equity in Care. Expanded access to advanced therapies via national healthcare partnerships and reduced-cost treatment programs. Telemedicine and remote consultation initiatives have improved care access for rural and underserved populations.
- Global Collaboration and Knowledge Sharing. Led multinational clinical trials and research consortia (e.g., with NIH, European hematology networks), accelerating the adoption of innovations worldwide (Zhang, 2022). Training programs for hematologists from developing countries, building capacity for blood disease management globally.
- Policy and Health System Strengthening. Influenced national health policies by providing data-driven insights for resource allocation. Addressed public health crises through agile research responses.

National Medical Research Center for Hematology Human Capital Strategy

To better understand the need to blend cultures to maximize outcomes, there are some key facts and strategies to better understand the environment. NMRCH's success stems from treating research and human resources as interdependent pillars. By fostering a culture where scientific ambition and staff growth mutually reinforce each other, the center achieves both cutting-edge innovation and operational excellence.

- Hierarchical Expertise and Specialized Roles. The center employs over 1,400 staff, including 10 professors and 35 doctors of sciences, 160 candidates of sciences (PhD-level). Roles are divided across clinical teams, research scientists, technical and support staff (lab technicians, data analysts).
- Integration of Research and Clinical Practice. Staff engage in translational research, bridging laboratory discoveries to patient care. For example, clinicians contribute to clinical trials, and researchers access real-world patient data to refine studies. This dual role ensures that innovations are directly applied to improve treatment outcomes.
- Talent Development and Training. Junior researchers and clinicians train under senior experts, fostering mentorship and skill transfer. Continuing education: Regular workshops, seminars, and collaborations with global institutions (e.g., European hematology networks) keep staff updated on advancements. Leadership in national guidelines: Senior experts lead the development of standardized treatment protocols adopted across Russia. Mentorship programs: Junior researchers and clinicians are paired with senior experts (e.g., professors or doctors of sciences) to cultivate specialized skills in areas like genomics, stem cell transplantation, or immunotherapy. Career pathways: Clear trajectories allow staff to advance in research, clinical leadership, or both, reducing turnover and retaining institutional knowledge.
- Collaborative Ecosystems. Interdisciplinary teams: Hematologists work alongside immunologists, geneticists, bioinformaticians, and AI specialists to tackle complex problems (e.g., multi-omics research). National and international networks: Staff participate in consortia (e.g., with the WHO, European hematology societies) to share knowledge and resources.
- Collaborative and Interdisciplinary Culture. Internal networks: Teams from different departments (e.g., immunology, bioinformatics, and clinical hematology) jointly design studies, ensuring diverse expertise feeds into research goals. External partnerships: Collaborations

with global institutions (e.g., WHO, European hematology networks) bring external insights and shared resources.

- Operational Efficiency and Resource Allocation. High-volume clinical practice: With ~5,000 patients treated annually and 300+ bone marrow transplants per year, staff gain extensive hands-on experience. Focus on high-impact research: Resources are prioritized for projects with immediate clinical applications.

This human-resource model enables NMRCH to maintain its status as Russia's leading hematology institution, driving innovations in treatment while improving national healthcare standards.

National Medical Research Center for Hematology Three Step Process for Blending Cultures

The Fusion of Clinic and Laboratory

The most fundamental cultural blend within the NMRCH is the intentional erosion of barriers between its research and clinical arms. In many medical institutions, a cultural chasm can exist between researchers, who are driven by the slow, meticulous process of scientific discovery, and clinicians, who operate in the fast-paced, immediate-decision environment of patient care. NMRCH actively dismantles this divide through structural and philosophical integration.

This is achieved through dual-role positions where senior physicians are also principal investigators, ensuring that research questions are directly informed by the challenges and anomalies observed in daily patient care. Conversely, laboratory scientists regularly participate in clinical rounds and tumor boards, gaining a firsthand understanding of the human impact of their work. This creates a powerful feedback loop: a clinician's frustration with the limitations of a current leukemia therapy can directly seed a researcher's new investigation into drug resistance, while a breakthrough in cellular immunology in the lab can be rapidly translated into a pilot clinical trial for lymphoma patients within the same institution.

This professional blending fosters a shared language and a unified mission. The culture is not one of "researchers versus doctors," but of collaborative teams working on different facets of the same problem. This synergy is evident in the Center's pioneering work in areas like haploidentical bone marrow transplantation and the development of CAR-T cell therapies for refractory cancers, where success is entirely dependent on the seamless cooperation of immunologists, geneticists, intensive care specialists, and nursing staff.

Integrating Regional and National Diversity: A Tapestry of Talent

As Russia's leading hematology institution, NMRCH leverages the vast human capital of the nation itself, blending regional perspectives and expertise into a centralized hub of excellence. Russia's immense geographical and demographic diversity presents a challenge but also a unique opportunity. The Center addresses this by actively recruiting talent from across the country's extensive network of medical academies and research universities, from Moscow and St. Petersburg to newer science hubs in Tomsk, Novosibirsk, and Kazan.

This deliberate regional integration serves multiple purposes. First, it brings together diverse scientific traditions and problem-solving approaches, enriching the Center's intellectual pool. A geneticist from Siberia might approach data analysis differently than a colleague trained in Moscow, leading to more robust and innovative research methodologies. Second, it allows NMRCH to better understand and address the specific hematological needs of Russia's diverse population. Epidemiological patterns for blood disorders can vary across regions due to genetic, environmental, or socioeconomic factors. By having a staff that reflects the nation's diversity, the Center can tailor its research and public health initiatives to be more effective and equitable.

This internal blending is supported by national policy alignment. The Center's experts play a key role in developing standardized national treatment guidelines, ensuring that advancements pioneered in Moscow are effectively disseminated and implemented across eleven time zones. This process itself is an act of cultural blending, as protocols must be adapted to the logistical and resource realities of different regional healthcare systems, creating a dynamic, nationwide conversation about best practices.

Embracing International Influence: The Global Scientific Commons

No leading research institution can afford to operate in isolation, and NMRCH exemplifies the profound benefits of blending national expertise with international collaboration. The Center actively participates in the global scientific commons, engaging in a continuous exchange of knowledge, talent, and technology. This international blending occurs on several levels.

Strategically, NMRCH is an active partner in multinational clinical trials and research consortia, working alongside organizations like the European Hematology Association (EHA) and the American Society of Hematology (ASH). These partnerships provide access to larger patient cohorts for studies, validate findings across diverse genetic backgrounds, and allow Russian researchers to contribute to setting global standards of care. Furthermore, the Center fosters a flow of people through exchange programs, where its young scientists and clinicians train at leading institutions in Europe, Asia, and North America, and vice versa. These returning scholars bring back not only technical skills but also new cultural attitudes toward innovation, collaboration, and scientific communication.

The integration of international talent, particularly from other post-Soviet states and beyond, further enriches the Center's culture. This creates a multilingual, multinational environment where the best ideas can emerge from any corner. The adoption of English as a common language for international publications and conferences ensures NMRCH's research is accessible to the world, while its domestic work remains grounded in Russian. This outward-looking posture ensures that the Center remains at the cutting edge, able to rapidly incorporate global breakthroughs in genomics, AI-driven diagnostics, or novel therapeutics into its own practice.

Conclusion: A Model of Synergistic Innovation

The National Medical Research Center for Hematology in Russia demonstrates that the path to medical excellence in the 21st century is not through cultural isolation but through intentional and strategic integration. By masterfully blending the distinct professional cultures of research and clinical practice, it ensures that its science is relevant and its treatments are cutting-edge. By harnessing the regional diversity of Russia itself, it builds a stronger, more representative national institution capable of addressing the health needs of all its citizens. And by enthusiastically engaging with the international scientific community, it remains a dynamic and competitive player on the world stage, both contributing to and benefiting from global knowledge.

This multifaceted cultural alchemy is the true engine of NMRCH's success. It transforms potential tensions between the lab and the clinic, the center and the regions, and the national and the international into a powerful synergistic force. The result is an institution that is more than the sum of its parts—a place where cultural diversity is not merely managed but leveraged as the fundamental fuel for discovery, ultimately leading to longer, healthier lives for patients with hematological diseases in Russia and around the world.

References

1. NMRCH (National Medical Research Center for Hematology). (2023). *Annual Report 2022.* Moscow: National Medical Research Center for Hematology.
2. Ivanov, A., Petrov, D., & Smirnova, T. (2022). History of hematology in Russia. *Journal of Medical History,* 66(4), 512–528.
3. Petrova, E. (2021). Interdisciplinary teams in translational medicine. *Blood Advances,* 5(18), 3561–3568.
4. Volkov, S. (2023). Russia's national health strategies. *The Lancet Haematology,* 10(3), e175–e180.
5. Zhang, L. (2022). Global partnerships in CAR-T therapy. *Nature Medicine,* 28(9), 1804–1810.

Chapter 2

Use People in IT

Do not create an over-reliance on people or on technology; use both resources in concert.

Often we rely too heavily on technology as we embark on innovation. Sometimes innovation starts at the other extreme with people but little incorporation of automation or tools. The best innovations tend to be the result of a strong balance at the intersection of people and technology. Always take an inventory of people and technology to ensure balance. It is the ability to take the best of people and technology, then meld them together, that ignites innovation.

PORTUGAL | PEOPLE-CENTERED DIGITAL HEALTH INNOVATION IN PORTUGAL AND THE AZORES | SAKSHIKA DHINGRA

Introduction

Healthcare systems worldwide face an enduring paradox: while digital technologies promise efficiency, access, and quality, their success ultimately depends not on algorithms or platforms but on people. Nowhere is this paradox more evident than in geographically diverse regions, where population dispersion, workforce shortages, and aging demographics intensify pressures on healthcare delivery. Portugal—and particularly its autonomous region of the Azores—offers a compelling illustration of how healthcare innovation can succeed when technology is implemented through human-centered IT practices and sustained by collaboration and active listening.

Over the past decade, Portugal has pursued one of Europe's most ambitious digital health strategies, embedding telemedicine, national health platforms, and interoperable data systems within its public National Health Service (Serviço Nacional de Saúde, SNS). These initiatives did not succeed merely because of technological sophistication but because policymakers, clinicians, IT professionals, and patients were actively involved in design, adaptation, and continuous improvement (ISO 9241-210, 2019). The Portuguese case demonstrates that innovation in healthcare is not a technical challenge alone but a socio-technical one—requiring trust, collaboration, and human capability.

DOI: 10.4324/9781003780175-2

Background

Portugal operates a tax-funded, universal healthcare system that serves over 10 million citizens, complemented by private and social sectors. Despite relatively strong health outcomes, the system has faced persistent challenges, including regional inequities, long waiting times, and limited access to specialized care in rural and island regions (OECD, 2023).

The Azores, an archipelago of nine islands in the Atlantic Ocean, exemplifies these challenges. Geographic isolation, small populations, and weather-dependent transportation make centralized healthcare delivery inefficient and often impractical. Historically, patients requiring specialist care were transported to mainland Portugal at significant financial and social cost (Direção-Geral da Saúde [DGS], 2019).

In response, Portugal embraced digital health transformation as a strategic priority. National strategies such as the National Health Plan 2021–2030 and the Digital Transition Action Plan positioned information systems, telehealth, and data integration as enablers of equity and resilience (Ministério da Saúde, 2021). Crucially, these strategies emphasize capacity-building, stakeholder engagement, and co-creation, reflecting an understanding that technology alone cannot reform healthcare systems.

Defining the Innovation

The innovation examined in this essay is people-centered digital healthcare delivery, operationalized through two interlinked principles:

1. **Using People in IT**:
   This principle recognizes healthcare IT not as an autonomous system but as a tool that amplifies human expertise. It involves investing in digital skills, redefining professional roles, and integrating clinical judgment with technological decision support.
2. **Collaborating and Listening**:
   This refers to structured and informal mechanisms through which healthcare systems engage clinicians, patients, policymakers, researchers, and technologists in dialogue. It emphasizes feedback loops, participatory design, and shared ownership of innovation.

Together, these principles align with socio-technical theories of healthcare innovation, which argue that outcomes depend on the interaction between technology, organizational culture, and human agency (Greenhalgh et al., 2017).

Case Study: SNS 24 and Telemedicine in the Azores

SNS 24: A National Digital Gateway

The SNS 24 platform is Portugal's flagship digital health service, offering telephone and online access to health advice, triage, appointment scheduling, e-prescriptions, and COVID-19 management. Initially launched as a health advice line, SNS 24 evolved into a comprehensive digital gateway during the COVID-19 pandemic, handling millions of interactions annually (Serviços Partilhados do Ministério da Saúde [SPMS], 2022).

While technologically robust, the system's effectiveness relies heavily on trained nurses and healthcare professionals who conduct clinical triage supported by standardized algorithms. Rather than replacing human decision-making, the platform structures it—allowing professionals to make consistent, evidence-based judgments while maintaining empathy and contextual sensitivity.

Evaluations by SPMS and the OECD show that SNS 24 reduced unnecessary emergency department visits and improved patient navigation across care levels (OECD, 2023). These outcomes underscore the principle of *using people in IT*: the platform succeeds because skilled professionals are embedded at its core.

Telemedicina dos Açores

The Telemedicina dos Açores program represents a regionally adapted innovation responding to geographic constraints. Implemented through collaboration between the Azorean Regional Health Service (Serviço Regional de Saúde dos Açores) and national digital health authorities, the program connects local primary care units with mainland specialists in fields such as cardiology, dermatology, neurology, and ophthalmology.

Local clinicians collect patient data using digital diagnostic tools (e.g., digital ECGs, imaging systems) and transmit them securely for specialist interpretation. Importantly, the process is collaborative rather than transactional: local clinicians remain active participants, discussing cases and integrating specialist feedback into patient care.

Studies indicate that the program significantly reduced patient transfers to the mainland, lowered costs, and improved continuity of care (DGS, 2019; WHO, 2021). These benefits emerged not from technology alone but from interprofessional trust and communication, cultivated over time.

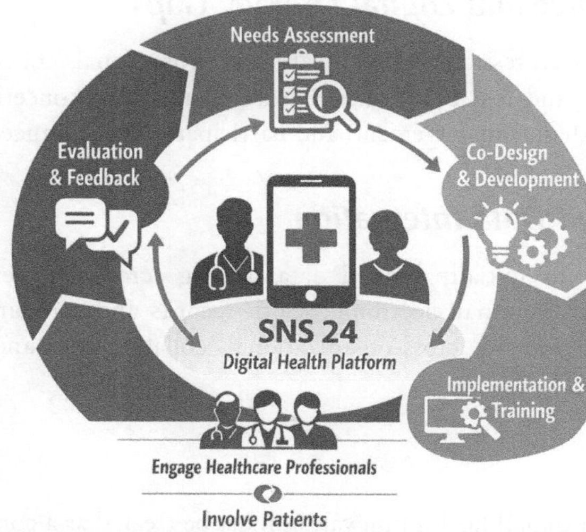

Figure 2.1 Human-centered design cycle applied to the SNS 24 digital health platform.

Note. The figure illustrates the iterative human-centered design process underlying the SNS 24 platform, emphasizing continuous feedback from healthcare professionals and patients. Adapted from ISO 9241-210 (2019), World Health Organization (2020), and Serviços Partilhados do Ministério da Saúde (2022).

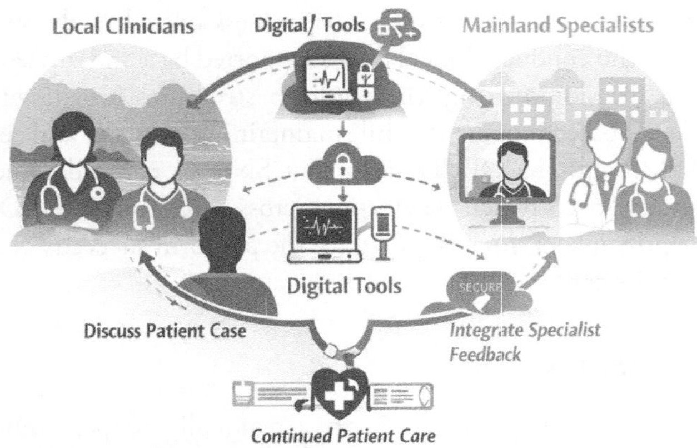

Figure 2.2 Human-centered telemedicine care model in the Azores.

Note. Figure 2.2 depicts the human-centered telemedicine model used in the Azores, where digital tools support collaboration between local clinicians and mainland specialists while preserving continuity of patient care. Based on Direção-Geral da Saúde (2019) and World Health Organization (2021).

Barriers and Lessons Learned

Despite its successes, Portugal's digital health journey has encountered notable barriers.

Workforce Resistance and Digital Literacy Gaps

Early implementations faced resistance from healthcare professionals concerned about increased workload, data security, and loss of autonomy. Addressing these concerns required sustained investment in training, change management, and participatory governance (SPMS, 2020).

Interoperability and Data Integration

Fragmented legacy systems initially limited data sharing across care levels. Progress toward interoperability—through national electronic health records and standardized data models—highlighted the importance of cross-organizational collaboration and consensus-building (European Commission, 2022).

Lessons Learned

The central lesson is that digital health innovation must be treated as a continuous learning process, not a one-time deployment. Mechanisms for feedback, iteration, and adaptation proved as important as technical specifications.

The Human Aspect of Innovation

At the heart of Portugal's digital health transformation lies a redefinition of professional and patient roles.

Healthcare professionals transitioned from being passive users of IT systems to co-designers and interpreters of digital tools. Nurses in SNS 24 exemplify this shift, combining clinical expertise with algorithmic support to guide patients effectively.

Patients, too, assumed more active roles. Platforms such as the SNS 24 mobile app and MySNS portal enable individuals to access health records, prescriptions, and test results, fostering engagement and health literacy (Ministério da Saúde, 2021).

In the Azores, the human aspect is particularly salient. Telemedicine strengthened relationships between local clinicians and mainland specialists, reinforcing professional confidence and reducing isolation. This illustrates how digital tools can enhance, rather than erode, human connection when designed intentionally.

Vision for the Future and Repeatability

Portugal's experience offers a replicable model for other regions facing similar constraints. Key elements include:

- National coordination with regional flexibility
- Investment in human capacity alongside technology
- Structured collaboration across sectors
- Continuous listening to users

Looking ahead, Portugal aims to expand AI-supported clinical decision tools, predictive analytics, and personalized medicine, while maintaining ethical oversight and human accountability (OECD, 2023).

For other health systems, the core transferable insight is clear: digital health innovation scales sustainably only when people are empowered, heard, and trusted.

Conclusion: Reaffirming the Framework

Portugal and the Azores demonstrate that healthcare innovation succeeds when framed through "using people in IT" and "collaborating and listening." Digital platforms like SNS 24 and telemedicine networks did not transform care because they were technologically advanced but because they were socially embedded.

By aligning technology with human expertise and fostering collaboration across institutional and geographic boundaries, Portugal has created a resilient, inclusive digital health ecosystem. This case reinforces a broader truth for healthcare innovation worldwide: technology is the enabler, but people are the innovators.

References

Direção-Geral da Saúde (DGS). (2019). *Telemedicina em Portugal: Avaliação e Perspetivas*. Lisbon.

European Commission. (2022). *Digital Health and Care in Europe*. Brussels.

Greenhalgh, T., Wherton, J., Papoutsi, C. et al. (2017). Beyond adoption: A new framework for theorizing and evaluating nonadoption, abandonment, and challenges to the scale-up of health technologies. *Journal of Medical Internet Research*, *19*(11), e367. https://doi.org/10.2196/jmir.8775

ISO 9241–210. (2019). *Human-Centred Design for Interactive Systems*.

Ministério da Saúde. (2021). *Plano Nacional de Saúde 2021–2030*. Lisbon.
OECD. (2023). *OECD Reviews of Health Systems: Portugal 2023*. Paris: OECD Publishing.
Serviços Partilhados do Ministério da Saúde (SPMS). (2020). *Estratégia Nacional para a Transformação Digital da Saúde*. Lisbon.
Serviços Partilhados do Ministério da Saúde (SPMS). (2022). *Relatório de Atividade do SNS 24*. Lisbon.
World Health Organization. (2020). *Human-Centred Design for Digital Health*.
World Health Organization (WHO). (2021). *Digital Health in Small Island Health Systems*. Copenhagen: WHO Europe.

*****

ROMANIA | BALANCING TECH AND TRAINING IN ROMANIAN TELEMEDICINE | ADITI U. JOSHI

In 2001, while much of the world was still adjusting to the early era of the commercial internet, the Romanian Space Agency (ROSA) launched a visionary project: the Demonstrative Pilot of Telemedicine. The goal was to create a future where geography would no longer dictate the quality of healthcare. This pioneering effort focused on diagnostic, clinical, and educational applications, serving as a landmark in the country's health history. Yet, for nearly two decades, that vision remained largely dormant. The initial effort lacked a ready workforce, standardized education, and a supporting legal framework.

It took the global catalyst of 2020 to prove a global innovation phenomenon: you can legislate technology into existence overnight, and you can fund infrastructure with millions of Euros, but you cannot "download" the human competence required to use it effectively. As Romania began its rapid digital transformation, it became clear that the real bottleneck was not the speed of the internet or the cost of the hardware but the readiness of clinicians and patients to operate in a virtual clinical space. There was a need to move from a pilot mentality to a national strategy that balances technical infrastructure with human empowerment.

A Landscape of Necessity

Romania's healthcare system has long struggled with a stark demographic and geographic lottery (Ćwiklicki et al., 2020). A significant portion of the population resides in rural or mountainous areas, creating medical deserts as we see in other countries (Ćwiklicki et al., 2020). Chronic shortages of medical personnel in these regions have historically meant that a patient's health outcomes were inextricably linked to their zip code. The traditional model of care required patients to travel long distances to urban hubs, a journey that was often a barrier to care in itself, leading to delayed diagnoses and worsened chronic conditions.

The arrival of the COVID-19 pandemic turned these chronic challenges into an acute crisis, but it also acted as a propellant. Between 2018 and 2022, the Romanian government moved with unprecedented speed to provide a foundation for digital health. This began with Government Emergency Ordinance 8/2018, which amended a former Health Reform Law to address personnel shortages through digital means. This was solidified by Government Decision 252/2020 and later by Government Decision 1133/2022, which approved comprehensive implementation norms for scheduling, data privacy, and payment mechanisms.

The financial barriers were dismantled by a €400 million allocation from the National Recovery and Resilience Plan, with €100 million specifically targeted at telemedicine support and up to €300 million for hospital digitalization. The legal barriers had also been overcome meaning Romania had built the tools required for digital innovation and adoption. The only thing left was creating a way for clinicians to follow.

The Competency Framework

In this context, the innovation is not the telemedicine platform but the systemic integration of a competency-based educational framework into the national health workforce.

This strategy seeks to harmonize the infrastructure with the people by adopting internationally recognized guidelines (Focsa et al., 2025), such as the

- World Health Organization (WHO) Digital Health Competency Framework (DHCF)
- International Society for Telemedicine & eHealth (ISfTeH) standards
- European Health Telematics Association (EHTEL) recommendations

Romania defined telemedicine strictly as a medical act performed exclusively by licensed medical professionals. This is opposed to the broader definition of telehealth which includes administrative, operational, and preventive activities. Even in this case, telemedicine involves diagnosis, treatment, and therapy, requiring the development of standardized training modules (Focsa et al., 2025). These modules ensure that a remote consultation meets the same rigorous clinical standards as an in-person visit, focusing on technical proficiency, ethical considerations, and the unique challenges of remote patient management.

The Overarching Ecosystem of Romanian Digital Health

To understand the progress in Romania, one must look at the three interdependent pillars that now form the digital health ecosystem: the academic, the clinical, and the industrial. This "team of teams" approach ensures that innovation is not happening in a vacuum but is supported by a robust network of experts.

The Academic Pillar: Training the Next Generation

At the heart of this transformation are the medical centers. Institutions in Timisoara, Cluj-Napoca, Iasi, and Bucharest have shifted their curricula to include medical informatics and digital health tools as core disciplines. A standout initiative is the Erasmus+ TEAM project, launched in November 2023 (Focsa & Rotaru, 2025). This project, involving the University of Medicine and Pharmacy Victor Babes, is a cross-European collaboration that develops micro-credentials in telemedicine. These are accredited learning pathways designed to bridge the gap between technical IT skills and clinical practice (Focsa & Rotaru, 2025). Furthermore, the Center for Innovation and e-Health at the University of Medicine and Pharmacy Carol Davila recently hosted specialized courses focusing on both the theoretical legal frameworks and the practical skills required for virtual care.

The Clinical Pillar: Evidence-Based Implementation

The clinical results of this human-tech synergy are becoming visible through targeted pilot programs and cross-sectional studies. For example, research into telerehabilitation for Parkinson's disease has shown significant improvements in walking performance and patient engagement. Similarly, the RoboTeleRehab system, a home-based robotic cardiac telerehabilitation system, demonstrates how technology can assist in post-acute care. In these models, the technology is sophisticated, but the success is dependent on the role of the human therapist who interprets biometric data and adjusts treatment in real-time. In diabetes care, researchers have developed validated tools to assess patient adherence to telemedicine, ensuring that the platforms are optimized based on real patient needs rather than just technical specifications.

The Industrial Pillar: Co-Designing with the Frontline

The ROHEALTH cluster, established in 2015, serves as the industrial nexus, bringing together research, industry, and clinical entities. Through initiatives like the TELMed project, which supports thirty-five small and medium-sized enterprises (SMEs) in the health sector, personnel are being trained to assimilate new technologies related to Industry 4.0. This ensures that when platforms like eTELEDOC (emergency telemedicine) are rolled out, the practitioners have already been involved in the design and testing phases. This prevents an over-reliance on technology for its own sake; instead, the technology is built to fit the human workflow, ensuring that engineers and clinicians speak the same language.

Barriers and Lessons Learned: The Literacy Paradox

One of the most profound lessons learned in the Romanian journey is the "literacy paradox" (Luca et al., 2021). One can build a multi-million-euro digital infrastructure, but if the end-user lacks digital literacy, the progress stalls. While the government was making massive investments, only 40% of Romanians were using the internet to search for health information, significantly below the EU average of 55%. More strikingly, 33.2% of the population demonstrated "problematic" health literacy, and 7.5% had "inadequate" levels. This means nearly 40% of the population faces significant challenges in processing and acting upon health information.

Meaningful advancement requires an Educational strategy. For telemedicine to be equitable, the clinician must be more than a doctor; they must also be a "digital navigator." As a navigator, they must be trained to help the patient with basic digital literacy. This is particularly true for the elderly or those with less access to technology.

Access must not be mistaken for adoption. Digital tools do not solve health disparities; they often highlight them unless the strategy for people is as robust as the strategy for the tools.

The Human Aspect of Telemedicine

As more technology is integrated into care, the human aspect becomes *more* important, not less (Saigí-Rubió et al., 2022). Website manner, or digital empathy, is its own clinical skill (Galpin et al., 2021). This refers to the ability to project empathy, build virtual rapport, and conduct an effective clinical assessment through a screen or over chat. This skill is as important as bedside manner is in in-person practice; it allows for successful patient-physician relationships and builds trust in both the system and medical care.

Many clinicians, particularly family doctors, have expressed concerns about diagnostic uncertainty or the fear that they might miss a physical cue that only an in-person visit could reveal

(Saigí-Rubió et al., 2022). During the pandemic, over a quarter of general practitioners reported that while teleconsultations were manageable, they were often more time-intensive and fraught with technical difficulties. This is a human barrier that technology cannot solve alone. The solution lies in training clinicians to use the digital interface, learning digital empathy skills and virtual physical exams. By learning advanced remote communication skills and utilizing high-fidelity IoT monitoring, the clinician can actually gain *more* comprehensive data (such as continuous biometric tracking) than they would in a brief, ten-minute in-person visit. The human touch is not lost; it is simply redefined for a digital age.

A Roadmap for the Future

The Romanian experience provides a clear roadmap for other health systems transitioning to digital practices. To achieve a balance between personnel and platforms, a four-part strategy is required:

1. **Synchronize Policy and Pedagogy:** Never pass a law regarding digital health without simultaneously funding a national training program. Legislation provides the "what," but education provides the "how." Clinician adoption often fails due to the lack of effective training.
2. **Incentivize Micro-Credentials:** Recognize that clinicians are time-poor. Provide bite-sized, accredited training, like the Erasmus+ TEAM pathways, that build digital confidence incrementally.
3. **Bridge the Gap with Digital Navigators:** Invest in programs that train nurses, administrative staff, and community health workers to assist patients with the technology, ensuring that no one is left behind.
4. **Embrace Interdisciplinary Teams:** Progress is a collaborative sport. Ensure engineers, clinicians, and data scientists are in constant dialogue. Use virtual communities and clusters like ROHEALTH to promote telemedicine usage and improve patient satisfaction.
5. **Address the Literacy Gap Directly:** Integrate health and digital literacy training into public health campaigns. The 66.5% of highly educated individuals who use the internet for health must be the starting point, but the 17% of those with low education must be the ultimate goal.

The Alchemy of Progress

Progress is not a sprint; it is a marathon of collaboration. By intentionally melding the €400 million in digital infrastructure with the standardized education of the TEAM project, the PALMED initiatives, and university reforms, Romania is making true on its goal of innovation started decades ago.

Technology alone is an insufficient catalyst for this type of change. The alchemy of progress happens when we stop treating technology as a separate entity and start treating it as an extension of human care. Romania's story is a testament to the fact that the most important hardware in healthcare will always be the humanity behind the technology. Technology should empower the best tools that science can provide. By focusing on the intersection of educational competencies, regulatory policies, and technological infrastructure, we can ensure that modern care is not just digital but deeply human.

References

1. Ćwiklicki, M., Schiavone, F., Klich, J., & Pilch, K. (2020, March 4). Antecedents of use of e-Health services in Central Eastern Europe: A qualitative comparative analysis. *BMC Health Services Research, 20*(1), 171. https://doi.org/10.1186/s12913-020-5034-9. PMID: 32131820; PMCID: PMC7057573.
2. Focsa, M., & Rotaru, V. (2025, May 15). Developing a telemedicine curriculum with micro-credentialing: Insights from the erasmus plus TEAM project. *Studies in Health Technology and Informatics, 327*, 1029–1033. https://doi.org/10.3233/SHTI250539. PMID: 40380645.
3. Focsa, M. A., Rotaru, V., Andronic, O., Marginean, M., & Florescu, S. (2025). Bridging gaps in telemedicine education in romania to support future health care: Scoping review. *JMIR Medical Education, 11*, e66458. https://doi.org/10.2196/66458
4. Galpin, K., Sikka, N., King, S. L., Horvath, K. A., Shipman, S. A., & AAMC Telehealth Advisory Committee. (2021, July). Expert consensus: Telehealth skills for health care professionals. *Telemedicine and e-Health, 27*(7), 820–824. https://doi.org/10.1089/tmj.2020.0420. Epub 2020 Nov 25. PMID: 33236964.
5. Luca, M. M., Mustea, L., Taran, A., Stefea, P., & Vatavu, S. (2021, July 20). Challenges on radical health redesign to reconfigure the level of e-Health adoption in EU countries. *Frontiers in Public Health, 9*, 728287. https://doi.org/10.3389/fpubh.2021.728287. PMID: 34354976; PMCID: PMC8329364.
6. Saigí-Rubió, F., Borges do Nascimento, I. J., Robles, N., Ivanovska, K., Katz, C., Azzopardi-Muscat, N., & Novillo Ortiz, D. (2022, October 27). The current status of telemedicine technology use across the World Health Organization European region: An overview of systematic reviews. *Journal of Medical Internet Research, 24*(10), e40877. https://doi.org/10.2196/40877. PMID: 36301602; PMCID: PMC9650581.

*****

EUROPE | WHAT EMERGENCIES REVEAL ABOUT HUMAN CAPACITY IN HIGHLY OPTIMIZED HEALTHCARE SYSTEMS | MERGIME GERGURI

Context

In an emergency C-section, something changes. Protocols exist, checklists exist, and technology is readily available. And yet, in the moment when seconds matter, none of these elements truly leads.

Time compresses. Roles become secondary. Communication narrows to what is essential. Decisions are made without deliberation in the usual sense, and movements are precise, coordinated, and often faster than conscious reasoning could allow. No one pauses to optimize or debate options, and still, actions are remarkably accurate.

What becomes visible in these moments is not chaos but a different mode of functioning. Clinicians respond with a clarity and creativity that often exceed what is accessible during routine operations. Solutions emerge that were not rehearsed, attention sharpens, presence deepens, and the team operates as a coherent unit, even though no additional tools have been introduced and no new skills have been taught.

Importantly, these capacities do not appear because people suddenly become more intelligent or more experienced. They appear because the usual way of operating no longer suffices.

Outside of emergencies, modern healthcare systems function under very different conditions. Processes are standardized, roles are clearly defined, and technology supports efficiency, safety, and scalability. Decision-making is distributed across protocols, dashboards, and increasingly, intelligent systems. This structure has enabled extraordinary progress. Outcomes have improved, errors have decreased, and complexity has become manageable at a scale that would otherwise be impossible.

In this normal operating mode, professionals perform reliably, often at a very high level. They follow procedures, interpret data, and execute tasks with consistency. The system is designed to minimize variability, reduce uncertainty, and prevent deviation. Under these conditions, automation and digital tools are not only helpful. They are essential.

And yet, the contrast with emergency situations raises a quiet but important question.

If the abilities observed in emergencies were learned skills, they would need to be trained explicitly. If they were the result of new information, they would require additional data. But neither is the case.

What emergencies reveal is not something newly acquired. It is something temporarily uncovered.

As a physician who has worked across acute care, public health, and industry, I have seen this pattern repeat itself across settings. The same individuals who operate competently within highly optimized systems demonstrate a markedly different quality of attention and action when routine structures no longer carry the situation.

This is not an argument against technology or artificial intelligence. On the contrary, it acknowledges their role in advancing healthcare beyond what would otherwise be possible. But it does suggest that technological progress primarily supports and amplifies the mode of functioning that is already dominant.

Technology reduces tasks, increases speed, and stabilizes processes. What it does not automatically do is shift how humans function internally.

The question is not whether innovation is progressing. It is.

The more relevant question may be whether progress at the level of systems is accompanied by a corresponding development in the way humans engage with them.

Emergencies offer a brief glimpse of what becomes possible when habitual modes of operation fall away. Not because a crisis is desirable but because it exposes capacities that remain largely unused under normal conditions. Understanding this distinction becomes increasingly relevant as healthcare systems continue to integrate more powerful digital and AI-enabled technologies, technologies designed to optimize routine operations but which inevitably interact with how humans are already functioning within those systems.

Define the Innovation

The innovation described here does not introduce a new technology, platform, or clinical protocol. It begins with a different understanding of how human functioning operates within highly optimized systems.

Most healthcare innovation efforts implicitly assume that performance improves when systems reduce cognitive load, standardize decision pathways, and automate repeatable tasks. Within this logic, digital tools and AI are designed to take over what is predictable, allowing humans to focus on what is complex, relational, or uncertain. This assumption is not wrong. But it is incomplete.

Observations from emergency settings suggest that human functioning is not simply a matter of having more time, better tools, or fewer tasks. What changes in emergencies is not workload but mode. People do not merely do less. They function differently.

The system does not change. The human does.

Under routine conditions, healthcare professionals primarily operate in a stabilized mode of execution. Attention is distributed, decisions are mediated by structures, and actions follow established pathways. This mode is efficient, reliable, and essential for large-scale systems. In emergencies, however, this mode temporarily collapses.

What emerges is a form of functioning characterized by direct attention, rapid integration of information, and action that is neither purely reactive nor procedurally driven. The same individuals, with the same training and the same tools, access a different quality of presence and decision-making.

In highly optimized healthcare environments, digital systems increasingly mediate attention, decision-making, and responsibility. Dashboards, alerts, documentation requirements, and AI-supported recommendations shape not only what clinicians do but how they engage cognitively and emotionally with their work.

Within this context, "use people with IT" requires more than balancing task allocation between humans and machines. It requires conscious design choices that determine whether technology narrows human functioning to procedural execution or supports access to higher-order integration, situational awareness, and embodied decision-making.

The question is therefore not how much technology is used but how it structures human attention. Systems that continuously fragment focus may increase efficiency while simultaneously reducing the likelihood that clinicians can access the same integrated modes of functioning observed in emergency situations.

The innovation, therefore, lies in designing systems where technology stabilizes what should be stabilized, while organizational structures intentionally preserve space for modes of attention, decision-making, and coordination that are otherwise only accessed under extreme conditions.

Case Study—Emergency C-Section

The shift becomes particularly visible in acute obstetric emergencies.

During an emergency C-section, the clinical environment changes within seconds. A situation that is usually governed by clearly defined roles, standardized communication patterns, and established procedural sequences suddenly exceeds what routine structures can fully contain. Time pressure becomes absolute, uncertainty is real, and responsibility is immediate.

In such moments, teams do not abandon protocols. Surgical checklists, anesthetic safety steps, and clinical guidelines remain present. However, they no longer function as the primary drivers of action. Instead, they recede into the background.

What takes precedence is a different quality of coordination. Communication becomes minimal and precise. Information is exchanged without elaboration. Decisions are made without extended comparison of options. Actions follow one another seamlessly, often without explicit verbal instruction. Each team member appears to anticipate what is needed next.

From the outside, this can look like intuition or instinct. From within the situation, it feels neither emotional nor impulsive. It is focused, clear, and remarkably efficient.

Importantly, nothing new has been added. The same clinicians are present, the same training applies, and the same technology is available. What has changed is not competence but access.

Under these conditions, clinicians often perform actions they would not normally attempt under routine circumstances. They adapt techniques in real time, integrate information rapidly across disciplines, and respond to subtle changes without conscious deliberation. Solutions emerge that were not rehearsed and would be difficult to plan in advance.

Once the emergency resolves and the patient is stabilized, the system returns to its default operating mode. Roles are re-established, documentation resumes, and decisions are again mediated through protocols and digital systems. The heightened clarity and coherence that characterized the emergency gradually dissipated.

What remains is a contrast. The same individuals, working within the same system, demonstrate two markedly different modes of functioning. One is stable, procedural, and optimized for continuity. The other is integrated, decisive, and adaptive under conditions where standard pathways no longer suffice.

This contrast is not limited to obstetrics. Similar patterns can be observed in trauma care, intensive care units, and other acute settings. The emergency C-section illustrates it particularly clearly because it compresses time, responsibility, and consequence into a narrow window where habitual modes of operation are temporarily suspended.

The relevance of this observation lies not in the emergency itself but in what it reveals about human functioning within complex systems.

Barriers & Lessons Learned

The primary barrier to translating insights from emergency situations into routine healthcare settings is not a lack of awareness, competence, or intention. It is structural.

Modern healthcare systems are deliberately designed to prevent conditions in which uncertainty, immediacy, and improvisation dominate. Standardization, protocols, and digital systems exist to reduce risk, ensure consistency, and protect patients at scale. From a system perspective, emergencies represent failure states that must be minimized.

As a result, the modes of human functioning that emerge in emergencies are implicitly treated as exceptions rather than signals. They are tolerated under necessity but discouraged under normal conditions. Once stability is restored, systems quickly revert to configurations that prioritize predictability, documentation, and procedural adherence.

This creates a structural asymmetry. Healthcare systems actively reinforce one mode of functioning while offering little space for others. Over time, this shapes how professionals habitually engage with their work. Attention becomes fragmented across tasks and interfaces, decision-making is increasingly mediated by tools, and responsibility is distributed across layers of process and oversight.

This is not inherently problematic. It is what allows complex systems to function safely and at scale. The difficulty arises when this becomes the only supported mode of operation.

A common assumption in digital transformation is that automation and AI will free humans from routine tasks, allowing them to become more relational, reflective, or creative. In practice, however, reducing task load does not automatically change how people function internally. Time saved is often reallocated to additional complexity rather than deeper engagement.

The lesson from emergency settings suggests that access to different human capacities is not primarily a function of time or workload but of structural conditions.

Human Aspect

From the perspective of those working within the system, the difference between these modes of functioning is often difficult to articulate. Outside of emergencies, most professionals do not experience themselves as overwhelmed or disengaged. They are capable, committed, and effective.

What changes over time is not performance but texture. Attention becomes increasingly distributed, inner dialogue rarely pauses, and bodily signals are often noticed late, if at all. This does not feel like dysfunction. It feels like participation in a well-functioning system.

Because functionality remains intact, the cost remains largely invisible.

In emergencies, many clinicians later describe a different quality of experience. Despite extreme pressure, there is often a sense of clarity, immediacy, and inner alignment. Fatigue may be present, but fragmentation is not.

This contrast suggests that certain human capacities are not lost but simply remain underused when systems do not call for them. Digital tools and AI do not impose a mode of functioning. They amplify what is already dominant.

From a human perspective, the question is therefore not whether technology should be adopted but whether systems intentionally support access to a broader range of human functioning.

Vision for the Future

The vision implied by these observations is not one of replacing existing structures, nor of introducing new layers of intervention. It is a shift in perspective.

Rather than asking how technology can further optimize performance, the question becomes how systems can be designed to preserve access to multiple modes of human functioning. Routine execution and adaptive presence are not competing states. They are complementary.

For healthcare leaders, this perspective invites a different set of innovation questions. Instead of asking only how digital systems can further optimize workflows, it becomes relevant to examine how interfaces, communication structures, and escalation pathways influence human presence and decision quality.

Small design choices, such as how many handovers fragment responsibility, how alerts interrupt attention, or how much contextual synthesis is delegated to humans versus systems, can significantly shape which modes of human functioning are accessible in routine operations. These choices are rarely framed as human-capacity decisions, yet they directly influence clinical performance under both stable and unstable conditions.

Technology continues to do what it does best: stabilize, support, and scale. Organizational design ensures that human capacities are not narrowed in the process.

The future of healthcare innovation may depend less on what new technologies are introduced, and more on which human capacities remain accessible within them.

Returning to "Use People With IT"

Within the HIMSS Innovation Pathway, "use people with IT" is often interpreted as a question of balance between human work and technological automation. The observations described in this essay suggest a more nuanced perspective.

Technology does not merely redistribute tasks. It shapes the mode in which humans function within healthcare systems. Highly optimized digital environments stabilize routine execution, but they may also unintentionally narrow access to human capacities that become visible in emergency situations.

Using people with IT therefore requires more than efficiency gains or advanced tools. It requires intentional system design that preserves human presence, integration, and situational awareness alongside technological optimization.

Emergencies reveal that these capacities already exist. Innovation lies not in creating them but in ensuring that healthcare systems do not render them inaccessible during normal operations.

*****

SWEDEN | HOLDING THE LINE: HOW KAROLINSKA UNIVERSITY HOSPITAL BALANCED HUMAN JUDGMENT AND AI IN CLINICAL DIAGNOSTICS | SAKSHIKA DHINGRA, EDWARD W. MARX, ADITI U. JOSHI AND ALINE NOIZET

Swedish healthcare trusts in money. It is the interface between clinicians and patients, institutions and the populace, and the professionals who must make difficult decisions in a pressurized situation. At the time that artificial intelligence started to enter clinical diagnostics, especially in radiology and pathology, that trust was a source and a danger at the same time. It was not about whether AI could enhance diagnostic performance but whether it could be presented in a way that would not strip the human judgment that the center of care is based on. A practical example of the success of innovation when people and technology are created in a well-thought-out way is the experience of Karolinska University Hospital in Stockholm. Karolinska did not focus on automation itself but instead made AI a strategic assistant to clinicians but never a substitute. There is an even bigger lesson within this disciplined approach: sustainable innovation appears when technology is people centered and not when people are being asked to adjust to technology.

A Diagnostic Pressure Point at a National Referral Hospital

Karolinska University Hospital is a national referral center with complex care as well as one of the largest academic medical centers in Europe. Similar to most of the high-income medical systems, it was under an increasing diagnostic pressure due to the aging population, the rise in screening programs, and the increase in the expectations of precise medicine. This was especially true of radiology and pathology departments. When screening breast cancer was implemented as a single procedure, radiologists went through thousands of mammograms each year. It was monotonous physically and time-consuming. Fatigue was also identified as a clinical risk factor not because of incompetence but because of volume. Leaders were not just worried about throughput but the sustainability of the workforce in the long term and clinician well-being. Initial discussions around AI anticipated fears. Would algorithms deskill clinicians? Overreliance: would diagnostic instincts be undermined? So, who might be held responsible when human judgment and machine results were at variance? These queries defined a conservative value-conscious way ahead.

Designing AI *With* Clinicians, Not *Instead* of Them

Right at the start, the Karolinska leadership set one clear rule: AI would be implemented in areas where it would reinforce clinical judgment. This was the guiding principle in the selection of technology and the implementation strategy approach. Instead of having complete automated diagnostic systems, the hospital was interested in decision-support tools. They served to identify areas of concern, to indicate anomalies, or to prioritize cases but never made a final diagnosis. The responsibility was strictly human. Radiologists and pathologists provided continuous and early input throughout the implementation process. They were involved in the process of setting industry-acceptable thresholds of performance, checking false-positive thresholds, and determining how AI results were displayed visually in already existing workflows. Notably, clinicians still had the power of veto. The tools that seemed to add cognitive load or disrupt the clinical flow were stopped, redesigned, or discarded. This was a strong cultural message: technology will be a welcome member of clinical practice and not a requisite.

Training People Alongside the Machines

Karolinska acknowledged the fact that the implementation of AI is a human change process more than a technical change process. Each implementation was accompanied by structured training. Clinicians not only received education on the use of AI tools but on their operation, such as sensitivity, specificity, and algorithmic bias. According to the demystification of the technology, AI was approachable instead of threatening. Clinicians were taught when to believe alerts and when to doubt them as well as how to interpret the confidence levels. With time, the perception of AI has become less black box and more of a junior colleague, which is beneficial, erroneous, and context specific. Such openness gave rise to informed trust. Making decisions became evidence based and not ideology based.

Case Study: AI as a Second Reader in Breast Cancer Screening

Breast cancer screening was one of the most effective uses at Karolinska. Mammograms used to traditionally be read twice by two radiologists. With the pressure of the workforce rising, leaders started to consider AI a complementary reader instead of a replacement. Research carried out in Swedish screening services showed that AI-assisted double reading did not affect the cancer detection rate and reduced radiologists' load (Amann et al., 2020). In other designs, AI reliably replaced a single human reader, freeing up the time of a specialist but maintaining the quality of the diagnosis. To clinicians, the benefit was not represented in terms of productivity. Rather, executives emphasized reduced clinician fatigue, greater focus on complex cases, and improved continuity of screening programs. This framing mattered. AI was also framed as a defender of professional standards and not a threat to them.

Pathology: Redirecting Human Attention Where It Matters Most

The same principles were applied in the field of AI in pathology. Digital pathology tools were also added to screen slides in advance identifying areas of interest to further analysis. Review of normal tissue was more efficiently done, and other pathologists would focus their expertise on frequent or complex observations. Again, AI did not diagnose. It curated attention. Pathologists expressed that there was better workflow and less visual strain and maintained complete interpretive authority (Boonstra et al., 2020). This minor translocation of energy demonstrated the strength of coordinating individuals and technology: machines processed size and human beings meaning.

Governance as a Human Safeguard

Balance was important with the help of governance. AI applications were incorporated into the existing clinical accountability frameworks and were not used alongside them. There were clear guidelines on how these discrepancies between the AI output and the judgments of clinicians were to be dealt with. The disagreement initiated review in the vast majority of cases and not override. Audits of usage patterns were done to identify overreliance or underutilization. These feedback controls made sure that AI was an assistive technology and not a decision-maker (Porter & Lee, 2015). The conversation also involved the patients. It was highlighted as well that AI helped clinicians and did not replace them. This openness was in harmony with the rest of the Swedish culture of openness, and it was able to maintain trust among people.

Leadership That Resisted Extremes

Karolinska's leadership was silent but firm. They opposed pressure by vendors to go all automated and distrusted those who considered digital tools harmful in the first place. They were the mediators instead. Rollouts were staged. There was a cumulative construction of evidence. The process of training not only targeted the physicians but also the nurses, technicians, and junior clinicians. The concept of innovation was developed as a collective duty and not part of the technological elite. This forbearance was rewarded. Artificial intelligence tools that survived this critical examination had a higher chance to survive, develop, and grow.

Lessons in Using People With IT

The experience of Karolinska University Hospital illustrates several practical lessons for healthcare organizations seeking to integrate artificial intelligence into clinical environments.

First, AI adoption must begin with a clearly defined human role. At Karolinska, AI tools were designed explicitly as decision-support systems rather than autonomous diagnostic engines. This principle preserved clinician authority and ensured that technology reinforced professional expertise rather than replacing it.

Second, clinician involvement in system design is essential. Radiologists and pathologists were included early in the implementation process, shaping performance thresholds, user interfaces, and workflow integration. This participatory approach increased trust in the technology and ensured that AI tools complemented existing clinical practices.

Third, education and transparency reduce resistance to innovation. By training clinicians to understand algorithmic limitations, confidence levels, and potential biases, Karolinska transformed AI from a mysterious "black box" into a comprehensible clinical tool.

Finally, governance structures must protect human accountability. Clear policies ensured that disagreements between AI output and clinician judgment triggered review rather than automatic override. This safeguarded professional responsibility while allowing technology to assist clinical decision-making.

Together, these lessons highlight an important principle: successful digital transformation occurs not when technology replaces human expertise, but when it amplifies the strengths of the people using it.

Conclusion: A Sustainable Path Forward

Karolinska University Hospital demonstrates that the integration of artificial intelligence into healthcare does not require choosing between technological advancement and human judgment. Instead, sustainable innovation emerges when both evolve together.

By positioning AI as a supportive partner rather than a substitute for clinicians, Karolinska maintained trust among healthcare professionals and patients alike. Decision-support tools enhanced efficiency and diagnostic accuracy while preserving the interpretive authority and ethical responsibility of medical professionals.

This balanced approach offers an important model for healthcare systems worldwide. As AI technologies become increasingly sophisticated, the temptation to automate decision-making will continue to grow. Yet the Karolinska experience suggests that long-term success depends less on the sophistication of algorithms and more on the careful alignment of technology with human expertise, governance, and professional culture.

Ultimately, the future of clinical innovation lies not in replacing clinicians with machines, but in designing systems where technology strengthens human judgment, preserves accountability, and supports better patient care.

References

Amann, J., Blasimme, A., Vayena, E., Frey, D., & Madai, V. I. (2020). Explainability for artificial intelligence in healthcare: A multidisciplinary perspective. *BMC Medical Informatics and Decision Making, 20*(1).

Boonstra, A., Versluis, A., & Vos, J. F. J. (2020). Implementing electronic health records in hospitals: A systematic literature review. *BMC Health Services Research, 14*(1). https://doi.org/10.1186/1472-6963-14-370

Porter, M., & Lee, T. (2015). *The Strategy That Will Fix Health Care.* https://www.aerodigestive.us/wp-content/uploads/2020/11/Porter-Lee-2013-The-strategy-that-will-fix-health-care-annotated.pdf

****

ESTONIA | DIGITAL BY DESIGN: HOW TARTU UNIVERSITY HOSPITAL PROVED THAT TECHNOLOGY WORKS BEST WHEN PEOPLE STAY IN CONTROL | SAKSHIKA DHINGRA, EDWARD W. MARX, ADITI U. JOSHI AND ALINE NOIZET

Technology is commonly implemented in healthcare systems in workflows that have never been structured to use it. Clinicians adapt. Patients tolerate friction. Organizations often absorb the cost of these workarounds as an unintended operational expense. Estonia took another direction. Instead of posing the question of how technology can be integrated into healthcare, it posed a question of how healthcare should be designed when digital infrastructure and the judgment of humans are supposed to co-exist in the first place. This philosophy, applied at Tartu University Hospital, the largest academic medical center in the country of Estonia, was turned into something unusual in the field of digital health, an ecosystem where technology enhances human ability without usurping professional autonomy. As the experience of the hospital proves, innovation is not made sustainable when systems are more intelligent; on the contrary, it is crucial that people be firmly in power.

A Small System With No Room for Inefficiency

The image of a digital pioneer that Estonia has created is usually depicted as visionary, yet its actions were driven by practical reasons. Inefficiency was not a luxury with a low population, a lack of clinical workforce, and limited resources. Prior to national digital integration, the challenges Tartu University Hospital clinicians encountered were the following: outdated patient histories, the presence of duplicated diagnostics, slow access to and the inability to share information within the care environment, and so forth (Huang et al., 2022). Patients were known to repeat themselves too often. The clinicians wasted time in their search for information instead of making sense of it. Since the beginning, leaders of the health sector in Estonia understood that technology would not be the only way to address these issues. There had to be trust, transparency, and governance.

Building a Digital Spine, Not a Command Center

The Estonian digital health system, along with the daily activities of Tartu University Hospital, is based on the national electronic health record (EHR). The EHR in Estonia was not meant to be institutional control but a shared infrastructure, unlike most of the centralized systems. There was professional autonomy among clinicians. Hospitals were still responsible in terms of care. The system was connective tissue instead of an upper hand. All citizens received a secure digital identity so that clinicians in Tartu could access longitudinal records regardless of the care setting. Notably, patients were able to view the people who accessed their data and the reasons. This openness built trust, and it was made clear that technology was created to serve people and not spy on them. At the hospital level, this translated to reduced information lapses, shortened time to construct clinical situations, and reduced administrative angst, without loss of independence.

Decision Support That Respected Judgment

With the development of the digital base, Tartu University Hospital offered decision-support tools to help clinicians at the point of care. These involved the use of rule-based alerts, drug interaction verification, and early risk indicators that were supported by AI. More importantly, these systems were advisory. There were permitted, anticipated, and reported overrides. None of the clinicians were compelled to adhere to algorithmic recommendations. This balance mattered. Routine checks and information retrieval were done by automation. Complex decisions, uncertainty, and patient communication were still left to human judgment. Instead of deskilling the clinicians, the technology assisted them in concentrating on the areas that humans excel in: reasoning, empathy, and adapting (OECD, 2019). Clinicians reported using less time to find data and devoting more time to data interpretation.

Clinicians as Stewards, Not End Users

Cultural and not technical: one of the most impactful decisions that Tartu University Hospital made was to place clinicians as the keepers of the digital system. Nurses and physicians were involved in usability tests, priorities on improvement, and digital governance committees. There were visible and responsive feedback mechanisms. In cases where tools were disruptive to work, problems were handled transparently. This collaboration avoided the alienation of massive digital changes. Clinicians knew the reasons behind system change and decision-making processes. Technology teams got to know how the everyday practice was really going on. Innovation also was based on actual delivery of care.

Patients as Active Stakeholders

The Estonia human–technology balance did not leave patients out. In Tartu University Hospital, citizens were able to access their records, prescriptions, referrals, and visit summaries in digital format. They were able to track data transactions and grant sharing. Clinical interactions were altered with this access. Patients came with more knowledge. There was increased collaborative conversation. This improved continuity of care because information was accessible to patients rather than being confined within institutional systems. People made the value of technology possible through participation (DuBois, 2019).

Scaling With Discipline, Not Automation Fever

Due to the growth of digital capacities of Estonia, restraint was a virtue. Each new tool presented at the Tartu University Hospital was checked in relation to one question: Is it something that will make people's work easier? There were pilot projects in AI projects, including early warning systems and population health analytics. Their relevance to clinical practice and integration into existing workflows were considered more important than technical novelty. The tools that did not prove valuable were updated or discarded. This science helped avoid excessive automatization and loss of confidence. Clinicians were not afraid that technology would take away their experience.

Outcomes That Reflected Alignment

The results were systemic. According to the clinicians, there was enhanced coordination of care, increased access to detailed patient history, and minimized redundancy of testing. The documentation has improved, and clinical decision-making has been enhanced. Tartu University Hospital changed as quickly as possible during times of stress-induced situations, the most significant of which was the COVID-19 pandemic. The digital infrastructure brought complexity to a side, which enabled clinicians to take care of patients instead of administration overhead. Knowing that the system was people oriented, the system was effective because it was not rigid.

Leadership That Defended the Balance

The leaders of hospitals and the whole nation were constantly reiterating one point: digital health was not meant to replace human care but to complement it. This philosophy influenced policies, funding decisions, and communication. Clinicians had confidence in the fact that professional identity would not be lost. Patients believed that they would be treated in a personal manner. Protecting coherence instead of following the trends was practiced by leadership.

Lessons in People With IT

The case of Tartu University Hospital, however, remains a vital lesson that healthcare innovations need to be dispersed as the most efficient ones through work allocation, not through robotization. Human beings are highly judgmental, emphatic, and contextual beings. Technology is good in terms of memory, consistency, and scale. When these strengths are strategically incorporated, then innovation is achieved. Healthcare organizations tend to swing both ways, either overwhelming clinicians and excessive reliance on automation. Estonia stayed centered.

Conclusion: The Quiet Power of Balance

Estonia failed to create a digital healthcare system through a system that enables technology to take control of care. It managed to accomplish this by making technology respect it. Tartu University Hospital showed what balanced innovation is going to be in practice by designing systems that maintain autonomy, are transparent, and enhance human capability. As the global healthcare processes embark on the paths of AI, automation, and digital transformation, Estonia provides us with a wake-up call: healthcare of the future is not digital or human. It is digital and human. And when that balance is ensured, then innovation will not be disruptive but sustainable.

References

DuBois, K. N. (2019). Deep medicine: How artificial intelligence can make healthcare human again. *Perspectives on Science and Christian Faith*, *71*(3), 199–201.

Huang, S., Jin, X., Jiang, Q., & Liu, L. (2022). Deep learning for image colorization: Current and future prospects. *Engineering Applications of Artificial Intelligence*, *114*, 105006. https://doi.org/10.1016/j.engappai.2022.105006

Organisation for Economic Co-operation and Development (OECD). (2019). *Health in the 21st Century: Putting Data to Work for Stronger Health Systems.*

*****

GERMANY | AUGMENT, NOT REPLACE: HOW CHARITÉ BERLIN USED AI TO SUPPORT CLINICAL JUDGMENT WITHOUT LOSING IT | SAKSHIKA DHINGRA, EDWARD W. MARX, ADITI U. JOSHI AND ALINE NOIZET

Healthcare innovation tends to fail mostly when technology requires clinicians to relinquish judgment. Algorithms are promising efficiency, accuracy, and scale, but clinical medicine is highly contextual, uncertain, and human (Alanazi, 2023). None of the places where artificial intelligence started to creep into the clinical decision-making practice in Germany showed this tension more prominently than at Charité-Universitaetmedizin Berlin, which became one of the largest academic hospitals in Europe. The case of Charité teaches a very important lesson: digital innovation does not work when people become accustomed to technology but when technology is purposefully designed to collaborate with people. Instead of trying to automate some processes, Charité took a more disciplined stance: AI was implemented as an aid to clinical rationality but not as a replacement for it. It not only allowed for a higher level of efficiency and safety but also clinician confidence in a system that was being progressively mediated by digital tools.

A Growing Cognitive Burden

Charité is a research and high-volume clinical care institution working at the forefront of research and clinical care. Its clinicians treat some of the most complicated cases in Europe with a range of rare, advanced oncology, transplant medicine, and intensive care cases. Along with the spread of clinical knowledge there was an increase in the cognitive load imposed on the physicians. The decision-making process began to involve the integration of laboratory values, imaging, comorbidities, emerging guidelines, and risk factors unique to patients more frequently and with limited time available (Alanazi, 2023). Although records and orders were already digitized in digital systems, it did not eliminate much of the mental burden of interpretation. Knowledge was there but not necessarily to be acted upon. Automation was not in demand among clinicians. They wanted some assistance in seeing.

Early Lessons From Overreach

Similar to most academic centers, Charité tried out experimental use of advanced analytics and algorithmic tools. There were pilots who made promises of predictive insight but did not perform well in practice. Clinicians doubted unclear recommendations, were scared of liability when AI advice went against experience, and were opposed to tools that undermined workflows. The issue was not technological immaturity, as the leadership saw, but misalignment (Downing et al., 2018). Tools had been brought on board as solutions and not as partners. The point was to be made: AI could not be enforced as authoritative. It was forced to earn its spot as an assistant.

Redefining the Role of AI

Charité reformulated its approach by clearly specifying what AI would/would not do. Patterns would be surfaced through artificial intelligence, attention prioritized, and less routine cognitive effort expended, but clinical judgment would always be the last word in each instance. Procurement and design were based on this principle. Transparency, explainability, and integration with clinical workflows were the key factors in selecting AI systems. Black-box models were deliberately avoided because they lacked transparency and explainability (Demaidi, 2023). Instead, decision-support tools that presented contributing factors, ranges of uncertainty, and sources of evidence were prioritized. Clinicians did not receive a directive. Context was provided to them.

Co-Designing With Clinicians

Engaging clinicians early and on an ongoing basis is one of the most significant decisions made by Charité. Internal medicine, intensive care, and radiology physicians were invited to design, not to approve products that were already finished but to influence them. They assisted in determining the decisions that were worth taking a stand on and which ones were not to be interfered with. They recommended the way of framing alerts, the timing of their appearance, and when there should be no alert. Notably, the clinicians enjoyed vetoes. The tools which created friction or confusion were amended or eliminated. Such a partnership repackaged AI as a partner and not an adversary. Trust followed.

Supporting Judgment at the Point of Care

Practically, AI-assisted tools at Charité targeted the domains in which human attention is the most challenged, which include the early identification of any deterioration, prioritization of high-risk patients, and the extraction of complex datasets. As an example, predictive models were applied to identify patients at higher risk of sepsis or clinical deterioration not to initiate automatic action but to allow the patient to be revisited sooner. Clinicians would be able to understand why a patient was flagged, to investigate the variables which contributed, and to determine whether action was justified. Accountability was not compromised by the fact that overrides were anticipated and recorded. AI suggested; humans decided.

Training Humans Alongside Machines

Charité understood that to be successful, it needed to invest in people as much as it put into software. Clinicians were taught in a structured manner about the functionality of AI models with introductory concepts of sensitivity, specificity, and bias. This openness de-mystified the instruments. In this case, physicians got to know when to trust signals and when to question them. AI was no longer viewed as a black box that was impossible to understand but as a probabilistic assistant that can be both powerful and constrained. The more they came to know, the less anxiety they had. It ceased to be defensive use but became thoughtful use.

Governance That Protected Autonomy

This balance was strengthened by good governance. In the case of Charité, AI tools were integrated into the existing clinical accountability models, not developed alongside them. The clinician of record was always held accountable. There were well-established guidelines on how human judgment and algorithmic suggestion disagreements were to be dealt with. Mostly, disagreement was followed by review, not by overruling. To ensure that there was no drift, overreliance, or underuse of the performance, monitoring of performance was done over time. Such a strategy appeased both the clinicians and regulators: innovation was not anarchy.

Measurable Benefits Without Cultural Cost

In the long run, quantifiable gains were achieved. Clinicians have noted that they feel more situational awareness, especially during high-acuity settings. The time spent in search of relevant information reduced. There were opportunities of early intervention with no resultant significant increase in alert fatigue. More importantly, these profits were not at the expense of professional identity. Doctors still felt accountable, respected, and appreciated. Artificial intelligence minimized noise, but it did not usurp logic. It was arguably adoption that was the best gauge of success. The use of tools was done not out of necessity but due to their usefulness.

Leadership That Held the Line

The role of the leadership of Charité was silent but decisive. They did not give in to pressure, both on the part of vendors and others outside the company, to seek complete automation or radical assertions of change. They instead placed importance on sustainability, trust, and progressive improvement. Rollouts were staged. There was protection of feedback loops. Leaders heard, instead of rushing schedules when apprehensions were raised by clinicians. This forbearance paid off. Those innovations that passed through this scrutiny were long term.

Lessons in Balance

The case of Charité highlights a larger fact regarding healthcare innovation: technology does not generate value on its own. The value is created where expertise of humans and digital capability converges. AI did not become successful at Charité due to its advancement but due to its restraint. The hospital has been able to avoid the two pitfalls of overdependence and rejection by honoring clinical judgment, investing in knowledge, and incorporating governance. By so doing, Charité showed that the future of digital health is not in replacing clinicians but rather in assisting them to think more clearly in a more complex world.

Conclusion: When Technology Knows Its Place

At Charité-Universitaetsmedizin Berlin, medicine was not redefined by artificial intelligence. It refined it. The conscious matching of people with IT as opposed to raising one above the other presented the hospital with the model of innovation, which could be trusted by clinicians, maintained by leaders, and benefited from by patients. With workforce issues and increased complexity across healthcare systems in Europe, the lesson of Charité seems both easy and deep: the most effective innovations are those that understand when to get out of the way and let humans take the lead.

References

Alanazi, A. (2023). Clinicians' views on using artificial intelligence in healthcare: Opportunities, challenges, and beyond. *Cureus, 15*(9). https://doi.org/10.7759/cureus.

Demaidi, M. N. (2023). Artificial intelligence national strategy in a developing country. *AI & Society, 40*. https://doi.org/10.1007/s00146-023-01779-x

Downing, N. L., Bates, D. W., & Longhurst, C. A. (2018). Physician burnout in the electronic health record era: Are we ignoring the real cause? *Annals of Internal Medicine, 169*(1), 50. https://doi.org/10.7326/m18-0139

Chapter 3

Create Roadmaps

Develop a plan for the functions required to innovate and encourage effective communication between functional experts for strategic clarity.

There is an unsubstantiated fear that plans and order run counter to the innovation spirit. Effective roadmaps actually serve as beacons or markers that help innovators navigate their way without being distracted and thrown off course. Plans do not stifle innovation but rather provide necessary guardrails to ensure focus and completion. Too many great ideas were never realized as resources and passion dwindled from an unnecessarily long journey.

SPAIN | XR IN PUBLIC HEALTHCARE | JOSÉ FERRER COSTA

Background

Immersive technologies were not entirely new to our organisation when this institutional project began. Virtual reality has already been used in specific clinical contexts, mainly in exposure-based interventions for phobias and addiction. These uses were evidence based, but they remained local. They depended on external tools, small motivated teams, and informal arrangements. There was no shared governance, no internal support structure, and no organisational strategy. VR existed, but only at the margins.

What follows is not the story of a single programme but of how an organisation learned to move immersive technology from the margins into everyday clinical life.

Projecte Benestar emerged within this context as a structured psychoeducational programme for healthcare professionals, focused on stress regulation, attention, and emotional balance. Immersion was used deliberately as a learning medium, not as treatment and not as a technical experiment but as part of a broader educational design. During its implementation, something shifted.

Professionals did not talk about the device. They talked about patients.

"This could help children who are afraid of needles."

"This might be useful in palliative care."

DOI: 10.4324/9781003780175-3

"This could support cognitive work in rehabilitation."

These reflections did not come from strategy sessions or innovation frameworks. They came from practice, from clinicians translating what they had experienced into the needs they encountered every day. That translation, from experience to care, is where this story begins.

Setting the Context. Badalona Serveis Assistencials (BSA) is a public, integrated healthcare organisation spanning primary care, hospital, mental health, and community services, where innovation must coexist with routine care, regulatory constraints, and strong public accountability.

In this type of setting, public healthcare operates under a permanent condition of tension. Demand is high, time is scarce, safety requirements are non-negotiable, and resources are constantly scrutinised. Every new element introduced into the system competes with something else, usually time, attention, or legitimacy. Innovation is broadly welcomed but only so far as it does not destabilise what already holds the system together.

This tension becomes particularly visible with technologies that do not map neatly onto existing clinical categories. The effects of XR are often indirect and experiential: reduced anxiety, improved engagement, increased tolerability, enhanced learning. These outcomes matter clinically and ethically, but they are difficult to capture within traditional performance indicators or budgeting frameworks.

As a result, XR tends to enter public healthcare through the margins, as a pilot, a research project, or a time-limited innovation grant. It is protected while the project lasts and frequently disappears when it ends. The issue is not technical failure but structural externality. These initiatives remain outside routine care.

At BSA, this pattern was recognisable early on. The challenge was therefore not whether XR could be useful. In specific contexts, that was already evident. The question was how to prevent it from remaining a collection of fragile pilots, dependent on individual enthusiasm rather than institutional capacity.

Defining the Innovation

What we developed was not an XR programme, a software platform, or a single clinical pathway. It was the gradual construction of institutional capacity to work with immersive technologies in a way that could be clinically meaningful, ethically acceptable, and operationally sustainable.

Over time, this capacity came to be referred to as the BSA VR Hub. Not because a hub was planned from the outset but because the accumulation of initiatives made a shared structure necessary. The hub is not a physical space or a discrete team but a set of functions: coordination, clinical alignment, ethical oversight, technical support, training, and evaluation. These functions allowed immersive tools to move from exception to routine practice.

As this capacity developed, four practical principles took shape.

Ideas originated in care. XR initiatives began with concrete questions raised by professionals, patients, and families, not with technology exploration or vendor proposals.

Design was co-created. Content, workflows, and clinical logic were built iteratively with those who would use them, making co-creation a condition for relevance, safety, and adoption.

Evaluation extended beyond efficacy. Alongside clinical outcomes, feasibility, usability, organisational fit, and sustainability were treated as primary criteria. An intervention that could not survive routine care was not considered successful.

Technology was framed as augmentative rather than substitutive. Immersive tools were introduced to support professional judgement, therapeutic relationships, and patient agency, helping to avoid both unrealistic expectations and defensive resistance.

Together, these principles shifted how immersive technologies were understood inside the organisation. XR stopped being "something we use sometimes" and became "a capacity we are building." The central question moved from "can we run this project?" to "can the organisation hold this practice?" That shift defines the innovation described in this chapter.

The Roadmap in Action

Benestar, a Structured Entry Through Professional Wellbeing

Benestar was the first immersive intervention at BSA to be intentionally designed, implemented, and evaluated as a structured programme rather than as a local or exploratory use of virtual reality.

It was conceived as an eight-week psychoeducational programme for healthcare professionals, focused on mindfulness, emotional regulation, and self-compassion. Short immersive experiences were integrated into weekly facilitated sessions as a pedagogical resource rather than as a technological trial. Following an initial research pilot, the programme was later integrated as an institutional initiative across several centres.

From a scientific perspective, Benestar demonstrated that an immersive intervention could be delivered safely and acceptably within routine organisational settings, with high adherence and no relevant adverse effects, as reported in the associated publication. From an organisational perspective, however, its most relevant effect was different.

Benestar created a shared, embodied reference point for immersive technology within the institution. Professionals encountered XR through their own experience, in a context of care, reflection, and institutional support. This shifted how XR was understood internally, away from novelty or external provision and toward wellbeing, learning, and organisational responsibility.

At the same time, the programme showed that immersive interventions could be scheduled, facilitated, and sustained within everyday operations. Its implementation required coordination across innovation, occupational risk prevention, centre management, and clinical teams, making visible the structures and roles later required for other XR initiatives.

In this sense, Benestar did not only demonstrate that XR works as an intervention but that it can be integrated in a legitimate and manageable way. This normalisation, more than its specific outcomes, enabled subsequent clinical projects to emerge, gain trust, and become part of routine practice rather than remaining isolated experiments.

Further Reading

Ferrer Costa, J., Morán, N., García Martí, C. et al. (2024). Immediate impact of an 8-week virtual reality educational program on burnout and work engagement among health care professionals: Pre-post pilot study. *JMIR XR and Spatial Computing*, 1, e55678. https://xr.jmir.org/2024/1/e55678

REDOCVR, Chronic Pain in Primary Care

REDOCVR did not begin as a technology initiative but as an extension of existing group-based chronic pain programmes in primary care.

Psychologists and physiotherapists already delivering these groups, and who had previously participated in *Projecte Benestar*, identified persistent gaps in engagement, emotional regulation, and self-management. Together with the innovation team, they explored whether immersive tools could support these dimensions without disrupting established routines.

From the outset, REDOCVR was co-designed by clinicians, patients, and the innovation team. Therapeutic goals and session structure were defined by professionals, while patients contributed to pacing, sensory tolerability, and relevance. XR was introduced as a brief module within existing group sessions, using the same professionals, schedules, referral pathways, and spaces, rather than as a separate service.

The programme was implemented in three primary care centres during phases 1 and 2 and evaluated through a real-world implementation study focused on feasibility, usability, and acceptability. These phases showed that routine teams could deliver the intervention, patients could accept it, and centres could sustain it.

On this basis, REDOCVR received institutional support and funding from the Spanish Ministry of Health and has entered phase 3, focused on expansion. It is currently being implemented across all BSA primary care centres and piloted in two external groups in other institutions.

REDOCVR showed that a co-designed, professionally anchored, and organisationally integrated intervention can stabilise and scale within public primary care.

Further Reading

Integrating extended reality into primary care chronic pain programs via the REDOCVR intervention. (2025). *JMIR XR and Spatial Computing*. https://xr.jmir.org/2025/1/e82858

Cognitive Rehabilitation, Shared Leadership in Practice

The cognitive rehabilitation programme emerged from collaboration between the rehabilitation team and the innovation unit, rather than being initiated by either side alone.

Several members of the rehabilitation team had previously participated in *Projecte Benestar*, so immersive technologies were already familiar to them as experiences rather than abstractions. When limitations in existing cognitive training became apparent, particularly around engagement and ecological validity, they approached the innovation team to explore whether immersive tools could meaningfully extend their practice.

From that point, the programme was co-designed and co-led. Clinicians defined therapeutic goals, session structure, and patient selection. The innovation team supported content development, technical integration, and evaluation. Patients and families contributed to pacing, sensory load, and task relevance.

This arrangement allowed immersive exercises to be embedded within routine rehabilitation sessions rather than implemented as a parallel activity. No new referral pathways or external facilitators were required. The intervention became part of daily workflow, sustained through shared responsibility between clinical and innovation teams.

Here again, the relevance lies less in the technology than in the working model it revealed. Innovation did not sit outside care or attempt to replace it. It operated alongside routine practice and supported incremental change from within.

Further Reading

Virtual reality in cognitive rehabilitation: A pilot study on usability and preliminary clinical outcomes in seniors with mild cognitive impairment. (2024). *Journal of Medical Extended Reality*. https://www.liebertpub.com/doi/10.1089/jmedxr.2024.0051

Shared Immersive Spaces, Institutional Infrastructure for Presence and Care

Not all patients can, or should, use head-mounted displays. In sociosanitary and long-term care settings, factors such as frailty, dizziness, cognitive impairment, or sensory sensitivity can make individual devices unsuitable.

To address this, BSA implemented an immersive projection room at the intermediate care Centre El Carme. From the outset, the room was conceived as an institutional, non-pharmacological resource, with defined objectives in cognitive stimulation, functional rehabilitation, and emotional wellbeing. Inaugurated in 2023, it uses a 360-degree projection system (MK360+ by BROOMX) to create immersive environments without individual headsets.

The immersive room is embedded in routine activity at the centre. It is used for group-based cognitive stimulation adapted to different levels of impairment, as a support space for physiotherapy and speech therapy sessions, and for guided relaxation with professionals as part of the institutional wellbeing plan. Because the experience takes place in a shared space, patients, professionals, and, when appropriate, family members remain present with one another rather than isolated by a device.

The room has also been used to recreate familiar environments for patients who cannot leave the centre, including culturally meaningful settings during festive periods. In these moments, immersion is not experienced as an intervention but as part of the everyday environment of care.

This use of a shared immersive space reflects a broader shift in how immersive technologies are approached within the organisation. Rather than functioning as discrete tools applied to individuals, immersive environments operate as part of the care setting itself, supporting presence, connection, and dignity within routine practice.

XR in Everyday Care Moments

As immersive tools became familiar within the organisation, they began to be used in specific, time-limited moments of care rather than as standalone programmes. These moments were characterised by anxiety, discomfort, or anticipatory distress that interfered with clinical processes, such as venipuncture, minor procedures, preoperative preparation, endoscopy, chronic wound care, or blood donation.

In these contexts, XR was introduced as a brief, non-pharmacological support to reduce pain and anxiety and to facilitate cooperation. It was framed as complementary rather than substitutive, supporting existing care practices without displacing them. Several of these uses were explored through small pilots and feasibility studies, including preoperative anxiety reduction and immersive support during digestive endoscopy. These initiatives were documented through case series and conference presentations that focused on feasibility, acceptability, and workflow integration rather than on efficacy claims.

What matters here is less the outcome of each individual pilot than the pattern they reveal. Clinicians did not ask whether XR should become a new service but whether it could help at this moment, with this patient, without disrupting routine care. That shift was only possible because XR was already familiar, trusted, and supported. Devices were available, support structures were in place, and professionals knew whom to contact when issues arose. XR had stopped belonging to projects and started belonging to care.

Further Reading

Ferrer Costa, J., Muñoz Cociña, Z., Ciudad, M. J. et al. (2024). Virtual reality in preanesthetic care: A case series on feasibility and usability. *Journal of Medical Extended Reality.* https://www.liebertpub.com/doi/10.1089/jmedxr.2024.0061

NutriVRTEA, Transferring the Co-Creation Model

NutriVRTEA is an ongoing programme supporting nutrition education and reducing food-related anxiety in children and adolescents with autism within nursing consultations.

The programme was built through co-creation involving child mental health nurses, a community nurse, a primary care nutritionist, families, a child with autism, the innovation team, and developers. Content, session structure, sensory load, and pacing were defined jointly before implementation.

This ensured integration into routine nursing consultations rather than the creation of a parallel intervention. NutriVRTEA illustrates how the organisational and methodological capacity developed in earlier projects is now being reused in new domains. The same design logic, co-creation, professional ownership, and early workflow integration are being transferred rather than reinvented.

It marks a shift from building projects to building a way of building projects.

Professional Education and Sensitive Topics

Immersive environments were also adopted for professional learning and reflection. Beyond simulation, XR supported training in sensitive areas such as recognising and responding to gender-based violence. In these contexts, immersion functioned less as procedural rehearsal and more as perspective-taking and reflective space.

Here again, XR worked best when embedded within existing training structures and aligned with recognised educational goals rather than positioned as a disruptive alternative.

Technical Partners as Enablers

This work relied on technical and content partners who supported development, maintenance, and day-to-day reliability. Alongside head-mounted displays, immersive projection systems were incorporated to improve accessibility and enable shared experiences with patients, families, and professionals. Their role was not to showcase technology but to ensure it functioned consistently and safely, allowing care, relationships, and professional judgement to remain central.

Barriers and Lessons Learned

As the work moved beyond isolated pilots, two constraints became increasingly visible.

One was practical. Several initiatives that were clinically compelling proved difficult to sustain once they encountered everyday realities such as staffing patterns, time pressure, or unclear responsibility for delivery. This gradually changed how proposals were examined. Alongside clinical plausibility, greater attention was paid to operational viability, whether an intervention could realistically be delivered, supported, and maintained under routine conditions.

The second constraint was organisational. Most innovation mechanisms are designed to support beginnings rather than continuities. They tend to fund acquisition or launch phases but rarely cover coordination, training, maintenance, or the professional time required to integrate a new practice into everyday care. Without clear institutional anchoring, initiatives tended either to fade out or to concentrate the burden on the same small group of motivated individuals.

Responding to this required a change in framing. Immersive interventions were no longer presented as technological experiments but as contributions to care quality and safety. This made it possible to discuss them within existing governance and accountability structures, rather than treating them as exceptional projects operating at the margins.

The Human Dimension

Acceptance developed gradually. Some professionals were cautious, and in some cases openly sceptical. This was not approached as resistance to be overcome but as a reasonable response to novelty in a safety-critical environment.

Rather than relying on persuasion, trust emerged through experience. When professionals encountered immersive environments directly, they were able to judge for themselves whether these tools were useful, tolerable, and relevant to their work.

For patients, involvement took a different form. Participation meant actively shaping interventions rather than simply using them. Patient feedback influenced not only interface details but also session structure, pacing, and framing. This changed both how the interventions functioned and how responsibility for them was shared.

Vision and Repeatability

Over time, this work began to resonate beyond the organisation. Inclusion within National Health System programmes concerned with clinical practice appropriateness signalled that immersive interventions were being recognised as part of routine care rather than as exceptional initiatives. Publications and awards did not drive this process, but they reflected it. They indicated that what had been developed locally could be understood, communicated, and assessed within broader professional contexts.

This recognition created space for collaboration with other institutions, not through the replication of a fixed model but through shared experimentation under different organisational and clinical conditions.

Conclusion

Nothing described in this chapter was implemented according to a prior plan. A programme created space. Professionals articulated needs. Structures adapted. Practices accumulated.

What emerged was not a predefined system but a way of working with uncertainty, constraint, and complexity. In this sense, innovation was less about introducing something new and more about learning how to take care of something until it could be integrated into everyday work.

Selected Outputs and Evidence

The following section presents a selection of institutional materials that document the initiatives described in this chapter, and how they were evaluated, communicated, and progressively integrated over time.

Institutional project pages (Badalona Serveis Assistencials)

- Virtual reality with therapeutic and educational purposes at BSA
https://www.bsa.cat/ca/r+d+i/rdi_projecte/realitat-virtual-amb-finalitat-terapeutica-o-docent

Public dissemination videos

- *Projecte Benestar*
https://youtu.be/-dwQ8HeAxNs?si=h4OGEj2R2Geh9nPg
- REDOCVR programme
Video phase 1: https://www.youtube.com/watch?v=5ODuj5DqFgk
Video phase 2: https://youtu.be/iFHLFaCnPAs?si=kOjbeLypBIWAr1vO
- Application of Virtual Reality in Mental Health and Addictions at BSA
https://youtu.be/rpFJWebmok4?si=r-4H0c-Xbm5QOs3y
https://www.youtube.com/watch?v=1T6QLJ3SCcg
- Virtual reality and surgery care
https://youtu.be/tK_8mNex3vU?si=A6UdWvy5dal9IcWv
- BSA Continues Committed to Virtual Reality to Improve Cognitive Stimulation
https://youtu.be/4AlfYePoSl4?si=QgeuOWsXY3lNPFPO
- Virtual reality in Autism+
https://www.youtube.com/watch?v=9-A07-QKq_s

*****

GERMANY | FROM SLIDES TO STRATEGY: HOW CHARITÉ BERLIN USED ROADMAPS TO TURN DIGITAL PATHOLOGY INTO REALITY | SAKSHIKA DHINGRA, EDWARD W. MARX, ADITI U. JOSHI AND ALINE NOIZET

Ambition in healthcare comes quite quickly, even before alignment. Technology has the power to drive change, but without shared alignment among stakeholders, even the most sophisticated systems remain underutilized. This conflict was evident in the process of achieving digital pathology in Germany. The technology was ready. The clinical need was urgent. The uptake was slow, however, not due to opposition but fragmentation. In the case of Charité-Universitaetmedizin Berlin, which is one of the largest academic medical centers in Europe, leaders realized that digital pathology would fail as an IT project. It needed a multi-year, conscious plan, such as one that streamlined clinical practice, infrastructure, governance, and regulation. Development was not achieved by moving fast but by structure.

A Fragmented Starting Point

Pathology has been a traditional part of German diagnostic medicine, especially oncology. By the mid-2010s, the pathology departments of Charité were experiencing increasing pressure. The number of cases grew, subspecialization intensified, and the problem of the lack of workforce was amplified. Digital pathology was not an innovation. Image management systems and whole-slide imaging were present and only used in isolated incidences, mainly during research or in isolated pilot studies. Scanning of slides was done digitally and stored and reviewed, but this was not often combined with regular diagnostics. The issue was not an immature technological situation. It was a lack of a concerted course of action.

Recognizing the Necessity to Have a Roadmap

Charité leaders came to a very important conclusion: digital pathology has touched almost every corner of the organization. There was an involvement of clinical workflows, IT infrastructure, procurement, training, quality assurance, and regulatory compliance. The need to approach it as an easy technology implementation would ensure failure. Charité took time to create a multi-year roadmap of digital pathology as opposed to making a rush in procurement. This plan also demystified not only what was to be implemented but also when, why, and who. The following questions were used to drive the process:

- What subspecialties would be transferred initially?
- What would be the life of the analog and the digital workflow through the transition?
- What would define clinical success, beyond purely technical performance?
- What would the training and validation entail?

The early response to these questions minimized ambiguity and harmonized the expectations among the departments as a result of leadership.

Aligning Clinical and Technical Timelines

Deliberate pacing was a characteristic attribute of the roadmap of Charité. Clinical readiness was aligned to technical deployment timelines. Digital scanning infrastructure was introduced at a slow pace; the first use case involved situations with clear value on-hand: consultation cases, second opinion, and tumor boards. This enabled clinicians to have gains without wholesale interference. The use of artificial intelligence was postponed intentionally until the digital workflow settled down. Pathologists had time to evolve, develop, and gain confidence (College of American Pathologists, 2013). The adoption of traditional microscopes did not happen suddenly, but clinicians increased modalities as they became more comfortable. This gradual process helped to save trust and avoid change fatigue.

Governance as a Guiding Rail

The regulatory climate in Germany is said to be a hindrance to innovation. It stabilized at Charité. The roadmap explicitly included the governance structures that included data protection, clinical validation, and quality assurance. It was made clear that AI algorithms would never be independent diagnostic agents but only decision-support tools. The definition of performance monitoring and validation protocols was pre-established (Berwick, 2016). Clinician judgment was not overridden but rather triggered a check of the artificial intelligence output. Such clarity was a reassurance to both regulators and clinicians and ensured there was no ambiguity as far as accountability was concerned. The government did not retard innovation; it made it permanent.

Technology in Service of Strategy

Technology decisions at Charité were guided by the strategic roadmap rather than by vendor enthusiasm. Whole-slide scanners, image management systems, and AI tools were chosen according to their interoperability, scalability, and regulatory readiness and not novelty. The capabilities were activated one by one. Features that were not in line with the clinical priorities were delayed. This science avoided overextension and made sure that the focus was on the results and not the checklists. Technology was a follower of strategy and not vice versa.

Successful Early Wins That Created Momentum

Tangible benefits came along with roadmap milestone accomplishments. Digital tumor boards were able to use real-time site-to-site collaboration without the need to physically move slides. The consultation response times were reduced. Smaller partner hospitals would have access to subspecialty knowledge. The introduction of AI tools was eventually supported by pre-screening and pointing at areas of concern during high-volume cancer diagnostics. Pathologists said that they had better attention and efficiency, especially in repetitive jobs. These initial victories boosted belief in the roadmap and enhanced institution commitment (Porter & Lee, 2015).

Leadership That Stayed the Course

It is not much harder to create a roadmap than to follow it. The leadership of Charité was extremely important in keeping the focus in the face of staffing, budget constraints, and external interference. Leaders did not give up on the roadmap but reconsidered it when there was a lull. Changes were instituted, but the overall direction was not lost. This consistency mattered. Clinicians were confident that their work would not be nullified with changing priorities. The process of innovation became predictable, and thus attainable.

Teaching How to Make Roadmaps

The experience of Charité proves that planning does not limit innovation; on the contrary, it facilitates it. Roadmaps are not rigid or inflexible, but they are clear. With the expression of an overlapping course, Charité put stakeholders on one page, minimized doubt, and turned desire into long-term action. Innovation stopped being made by individual pilots and turned to systematic advancement.

Conclusion: When Direction Makes the Difference

The idea of digital pathology did not achieve success in Charité due to the acceleration of scanners or the advancement of algorithms. It was successful because leadership focused on direction other than getting distracted. Charité managed the complexity and did not lose its momentum by means of intentional road mapping. The hospital celebrated clinical reality and progressive movement towards a digital future. Healthcare innovation is hardly a race. It is a long path of constraint, uncertainty, and change. These challenges do not disappear with the use of roadmaps; they only make organizations aware of the next steps to take when they occur. And in such clarity is innovation achieved.

References

Berwick, D. M. (2016). Era 3 for medicine and health care. *JAMA*, 315(13), 1329. https://doi.org/10.1001/jama.2016.1509

College of American Pathologists. (2013). *Validating Whole Slide Imaging for Diagnostic Purposes in Pathology*. Northfield: College of American Pathologists.
Porter, M., & Lee, T. (2015). *The Strategy That Will Fix Health Care*. https://www.aerodigestive.us/wp-content/uploads/2020/11/Porter-Lee-2013-The-strategy-that-will-fix-health-care-annotated.pdf

*****

ICELAND | CLOSING THE LOOP ACROSS EUROPE FROM VISION TO EXECUTION: THE ASCLEPIUS PROJECT AS A CLMM EXCELLENCE PLATFORM | FRANCINE DE STOPPELAAR

"Medication is where clinical risk, operational complexity, and financial reality collide."

Medication as a Strategic Reality

Across Europe, healthcare systems are under unprecedented pressure to deliver better outcomes while managing finite, and in many cases shrinking, resources. Few domains expose this tension as clearly as medication therapy. Medicines touch almost every hospitalized patient, influence nearly every clinical pathway, and represent one of the most significant and fastest-growing cost categories in healthcare.

European healthcare expenditure now exceeds €1.7 trillion annually,[1] roughly 10% of GDP. Medical goods, including medicines, account for close to one-fifth of total healthcare spending, while hospitals themselves represent more than one-third of overall expenditure. In many European countries, hospital pharmaceutical spending alone represents between 20 and 50% of all reimbursed drug costs, driven by high-cost oncology treatments, biologics, and increasingly personalized therapies.[2]

These numbers matter—not simply because they are large but because they reveal a fundamental truth: medication management is no longer only a clinical safety concern; it is a strategic economic responsibility.

Digitization without orchestration is just faster chaos.

And yet, despite the financial and clinical significance of medication therapies, the processes that govern it inside hospitals remain fragmented. Prescribing may be digital, dispensing partially automated, administration barcode-enabled, and monitoring documented. Yet these elements often operate as loosely connected islands rather than as a coherent system.

Closed loop medication management (CLMM) promises to address this fragmentation. But too often, CLMM is approached as a technological destination rather than an organizational journey. Technology is purchased, systems are connected, and go-live dates are celebrated—only to discover that the loop, in practice, remains open.

Europe Is Not One Hospital

CLMM is frequently discussed as if it were a single, universally applicable model. In reality, Europe presents a mosaic of healthcare systems shaped by different regulatory frameworks, reimbursement mechanisms, professional cultures, and levels of digital maturity.

Some countries mandate unit-dose dispensing. Others rely predominantly on whole pack ward stock. Some hospitals operate fully integrated enterprise EHR environments; others manage a patchwork of best-of-breed systems connected through custom interfaces. Even within the same country, hospitals differ widely in governance structures, decision-making autonomy, and appetite for change.

Attempting to apply a single "ideal" CLMM blueprint across this diversity almost inevitably leads to over-customization, inflated costs, and implementation fatigue. Projects stall not because the vision is flawed but because the path toward it is unrealistic.

> Hospitals do not struggle with CLMM because they lack technology. They struggle because they lack a shared roadmap.

Defining the Innovation: Roadmaps as the Missing Operating System

The Asclepius Project[3] was established as a pan-European excellence platform with a clear and pragmatic ambition: to help hospitals design, test, refine, and share realistic roadmaps for closed loop medication management.

This is not a vendor initiative, nor a theoretical framework detached from practice. It is a practitioner-led effort grounded in lived experience across academic medical centers, regional hospitals, and cross-border collaborations.

Rather than promoting specific solutions, the Asclepius Project focuses on decision logic: which steps to take, in which order, under which conditions, and with which trade-offs.

This approach aligns directly with the HIMSS Innovation Pathway "Create Road Maps," which recognizes that innovation requires structure, sequencing, and communication. Roadmaps do not constrain innovation; they protect it. They provide guardrails that keep complex transformation efforts focused and achievable.

Three principles consistently underpin the Asclepius Project roadmap philosophy. First, maturity before complexity: hospitals must stabilize foundational processes before layering advanced automation. Second, meaning before movement: interoperability must ensure shared understanding, not merely technical connectivity. Third, people before platforms: sustainable CLMM depends as much on trust, roles, and culture as on software.

> A roadmap does not tell you how fast to go. It tells you where not to skip steps.

CLMM as an Orchestrated Workflow, Not a Collection of Tools

One of the most important contributions of the Asclepius Project has been reframing CLMM as an orchestrated workflow rather than a stack of technologies.

Prescribing, verification, dispensing, distribution, administration, and monitoring are often optimized independently. In a closed loop, however, each step derives its value from being digitally and operationally connected to the next. A flawless bedside scan cannot compensate for ambiguous prescribing data upstream, just as advanced pharmacy automation cannot deliver safety benefits if administration remains manual or poorly documented.

The Asclepius Project deliberately presents CLMM as a circular process rather than a linear chain. Medication therapy is inherently dynamic. Prescriptions change, therapies are paused, doses are adjusted, medications are returned, and waste must be managed. A closed loop therefore requires continuous traceability and feedback, enabling medication to re-enter the system safely at any point.

This cyclical perspective fundamentally alters how roadmaps are designed. The focus shifts away from one-time go-live events toward sustainable operational states that can absorb change without breaking.

Closing the loop is not about finishing a project. It is about sustaining control.

Sequencing the Journey: Why "Big Bang" CLMM Rarely Works

Across European CLMM implementations, one lesson recurs with striking consistency: attempts to implement everything at once rarely succeed. Hospitals face understandable pressure to accelerate transformation, budget cycles, political momentum, and leadership expectations all push toward comprehensive solutions. Yet experience shows that overly ambitious scope often overwhelms systems and staff alike.

Successful implementations instead follow a phased roadmap, even when the end vision is comprehensive. Early phases focus on establishing a reliable digital backbone: structured electronic prescribing, consistent medication data, and clear governance across pharmacy, IT, nursing, and medical leadership. Without this foundation, downstream automation merely amplifies existing inconsistencies.

Subsequent phases address the physical medication flow. Barcode availability, pharmacy automation, and inventory governance are introduced selectively—where they reduce risk and variability rather than simply increasing throughput.

When upstream processes are robust and reliable, bedside verification can fully realize its safety potential. Barcode medication administration becomes a clinical safety instrument rather than a compliance burden.

Finally, mature environments shift toward optimization. Data is used to drive continuous improvement, validate return on investment, reallocate workforce capacity, and support sustainability goals such as waste reduction and shortage mitigation.

These phases are not rigid steps but decision zones. Hospitals may pause, recalibrate, or revisit earlier stages as context evolves. The roadmap provides direction, not dogma.

Interoperability Reframed: From Interfaces to Shared Meaning

Interoperability is often cited as the most complex technical challenge in CLMM. Yet the Asclepius Project consistently observes that the greatest obstacles are conceptual rather than technological.

Hospitals frequently ask whether systems can exchange data. The more fundamental question is whether all systems interpret that data in the same way.

Semantic interoperability—the consistent understanding of medication identity, dose, route, timing, and patient context across systems—is what truly enables closed-loop functionality. Without it, automation accelerates assumptions rather than reducing risk.

A single medication may be prescribed under a generic name, verified using a clinical knowledge base, dispensed using a product identifier, and scanned at the bedside using yet another coding logic. Technically connected systems can still fail clinically if they do not share meaning.

In the European context, addressing this challenge increasingly depends on the deliberate use of shared standards. IDMP-based medicinal product identification provides a common structure for describing medicines across regulatory, clinical, and logistical systems. Clinical terminologies such as SNOMED CT support the prescribing context, while GS1 standards enable physical traceability at the level of packaging and barcodes. Data exchange standards such as HL7 FHIR facilitate communication between systems but do not define meaning by themselves.

Other medical domains have already navigated this challenge. Radiology only became scalable and safe once DICOM standardized not just image transfer but interpretation. Laboratory medicine followed a similar path with LOINC. CLMM now stands at a comparable inflection point.

Roadmaps that defer semantic governance inevitably accumulate technical debt—debt that later phases cannot easily repay.

> Interoperability is not solely about moving data. It is about agreeing on what the data means.

ROI as a Roadmap Driver, Not a Retrospective Calculation

Financial justification is often treated as a parallel exercise to CLMM implementation, addressed after technical decisions have already been made. The Asclepius Project challenges this sequencing.

Experience across multiple European implementations demonstrates that return on investment is rarely determined by the price of technology itself. Instead, ROI is shaped primarily by workflow choices: central versus decentralized distribution, the scope of unit-dose coverage, inventory models, and the level at which verification occurs.

By embedding ROI thinking directly into the roadmap, hospitals gain a powerful decision framework. Early phases may prioritize patient safety and workforce resilience over immediate financial return. Later phases unlock tangible economic benefits through inventory reduction, waste prevention, and labor optimization.

This staged value realization is essential for sustaining executive commitment over multi-year transformation journeys, particularly in environments where capital investment must compete with other strategic priorities.

> The strongest business cases are built before the first interface is designed.

The Human Dimension: CLMM as a Trust System

Technology can enforce rules, but it cannot create trust.

CLMM fundamentally reshapes professional roles. Pharmacists evolve from dispensers into system stewards. Nurses transition from memory-based work to verification-based practice. Physicians encounter greater transparency and standardization in prescribing behavior.

These shifts are profound. Without deliberate leadership, communication, and engagement, resistance is not only predictable, it is rational.

The Asclepius Project therefore treats human connection as a core component of roadmap design. Monthly webinars normalize challenges. Field trips allow peers to observe CLMM in operation rather than in slide decks. White papers are written by implementers for implementers. Workshops focus on shared decision-making rather than product demonstrations.

This collective learning environment reduces isolation and reframes setbacks as part of a shared journey rather than individual failure.

> Closed loops are built with systems. They are sustained with trust.

From Isolated Projects to a European Learning Ecosystem

The long-term ambition of The Asclepius Project extends beyond individual hospital implementations. By sharing roadmaps, KPIs, lessons learned, and even failures across borders, European hospitals can dramatically reduce duplication of effort and implementation risk.

In doing so, CLMM evolves from a competitive differentiator into a shared standard of care, supporting patient safety, workforce sustainability, and financial resilience at scale.

Innovation accelerates when organizations stop working in isolation and begin learning together.

Closing the Loop on "Create Road Maps"

Innovation rarely fails because organizations lack vision. It fails because vision lacks structure.

The Asclepius Project demonstrates that creating roadmaps, grounded in realism, sequencing, and shared learning, is itself a powerful innovation. In medication management, where clinical risk and economic impact intersect daily, this structured approach is not optional.

Closed loop medication management does not arrive all at once. It closes deliberately, step by step, when people choose to walk the road together.

> The future of medication safety will not be invented. It will be implemented, one well-designed roadmap at a time.

DENMARK | PRINCIPLES AND KEY LESSONS FROM SUCCESSFUL ATTEMPTS AND LESS FORTUNATE ONES | MEHDI KHALED

The Roadmap Paradox

Here's something that'll sound familiar: every digital health transformation starts with a roadmap. Yet, in my twenty-five years of globetrotting across national digital health ecosystems, success is mitigated at best. The details are there. The problem lies elsewhere—somewhere between their foundation and their cultural maze.

Roadmaps are optimised for technology deployment rather than care transformation. They prioritise vendor timelines over organisational readiness. They measure progress in systems implemented rather than lives improved.

The patterns we see in successful digital health implementations at scale reveal an uncomfortable truth: the roadmap itself is the problem. Most roadmaps answer the wrong question entirely.

They ask 'How do we implement this new technology?' rather than 'How do we ensure technology is used to serve our patients better?'

This essay explores personally identified patterns of effective roadmap lifecycles. It draws on what actually works in digital health transformation. The lessons come from less-documented failures and over-marketed successes across healthcare systems worldwide.

The Foundational Error: Buying the App Before Fixing the Process

The most common digitisation roadmap failure happens before you've even drawn the first line. Organisations rush to digitise. They skip the fundamental readiness assessment. This is building a skyscraper on a shallow layer of bricks.

The Maturity Assessment Principle

Diligent organisations start with brutally honest assessments. They examine five critical dimensions: outcome variability, workflow optimisation, technical infrastructure, management capability, and governance structures. They may compare their physical capacity to their actual ability to deliver. This isn't about ticking boxes on a political deliverable scorecard. It's about one question: would you invest your own money in your organisation at its current state?

The Estonia model demonstrates this perfectly. Before their digital transformation, they didn't jump to implementation. They assessed. They identified gaps. They systematically addressed foundational issues. Their roadmap was a capability-building journey, pure and simple.

Singapore's Healthier-SG initiative offers a more recent example. Following its implementation in mid-2023, hospital length of stay decreased from 3.8 to 3.5 days. In-hospital mortality dropped from 3.7% to 2.9%. But these outcomes emerged only after years of systematic capability building across Singapore's healthcare clusters. The groundwork came first. The results followed.

Failed roadmaps skip this step entirely. They assume readiness. Worse, they believe new technology will somehow fix underlying organisational dysfunction. It doesn't. It amplifies it. Digital systems deployed on broken processes create digitised dysfunction at scale.

The lesson is clear: the roadmap must explicitly map the journey from current maturity to required maturity. Do this before any major technology investment occurs.

The Technical Debt Reality

Technical debt isn't just an IT problem. It's a roadmap-killer. Most roadmaps treat it as background noise, something to 'address alongside' the transformation. This is a critical error.

The UK's NHS provides a sobering example. The British Medical Association estimated that clinicians lose more than 13.5 million hours annually. The cause? Inadequate or malfunctioning IT. The system's £37 billion capital investment shortfall compared to peer countries since 2010 has left providers struggling. They work with outdated systems that don't connect to each other. This creates exactly the kind of unstable foundation that dooms digital initiatives before they start.

Consider the infamous NHS National Programme for IT. Launched in 2002 with roughly £6 billion in contracts. Scrapped after nine years. Final cost to British taxpayers: more than £10 billion. The failure stemmed largely from attempting to build on an unstable technical foundation whilst ignoring organisational readiness. A spectacular, expensive lesson.

Successful roadmaps put technical debt reduction on the critical path. They recognise a simple truth: you can't build modern digital health infrastructure on legacy systems held together with patches and workarounds. The Netherlands' heart failure telemonitoring success wasn't just about implementing new technology. It was about ensuring the underlying infrastructure could support it reliably.

A proper roadmap explicitly phases technical debt reduction before major new implementations. This means telling stakeholders what they don't want to hear: 'We need six months of infrastructure work before we can deploy this new patient portal.' This honesty prevents the cascade of failures. It stops new systems being built on unstable foundations.

The Patient-Centred Principle: Inverting the Design Process

The second major failure pattern in roadmaps? Starting with technology rather than patient need. This seems obvious. Yet roadmap after roadmap begins with 'Deploy EHR System X' or 'Implement AI Solution Y.' The right starting point is 'Reduce patient wait times' or 'Eliminate care coordination gaps.'

Journey Mapping Before Technology Mapping

Smart roadmaps begin with patient journey mapping. They map the actual experience patients have navigating the healthcare system. Not the idealised version administrators imagine. This means following patients like Amal through every touchpoint. Identify every friction point. Note every moment of confusion. Document every breakdown in care coordination.

Only after this deep journey mapping should you consider technology solutions. Here's the critical insight: often the right solution isn't new technology at all. It might be fixing a broken referral process. Simplifying communication protocols. Eliminating unnecessary steps that technology was previously implemented to 'optimise.'

The roadmap must reflect this sequence. Phase One isn't 'Select Patient Portal Vendor.' It's 'Map Top Five Patient Journey Pain Points and Root Causes.' Phase Two isn't 'Deploy Portal.' It's 'Pilot Process Improvements and Determines Which Actually Require Technology.' This reordering prevents the common trap. It stops you implementing technology solutions to problems you don't fully understand.

The Simplification Filter

Every item on a roadmap should pass through a simplification filter. Ask one question: 'Will this make things simpler for patients and caregivers, or more complex?' If the honest answer is 'more complex, but in ways we believe will eventually pay off—say if we fix other foundational organisational roadblocks,' that item needs serious reconsideration.

Failed roadmaps are filled with initiatives that add complexity. They promise theoretical future benefits. Successful roadmaps ruthlessly eliminate complexity. They recognise that healthcare is already overwhelmingly complex. Any digital transformation that doesn't actively reduce that complexity moves in the wrong direction.

This means rejecting technically impressive solutions sometimes. It means saying no to AI-powered tools that require five new workflows. It means choosing simple, intuitive interfaces over feature-rich platforms. The roadmap should explicitly identify complexity metrics. Require each major initiative to demonstrate net complexity reduction.

The Workflow Integration Imperative: Designing for Reality, Not Policy

The third critical failure pattern? Creating roadmaps that exist in parallel to actual clinical workflows rather than being designed around them. This disconnect creates what digital health experts call 'interoperable fragmentation.' Systems technically talk to each other. Practically, they create more work.

The Provider-Designed Principle

Successful roadmaps are designed with caregivers. Not for them. This means engaging frontline clinicians as co-designers who understand the reality of clinical work. Not as stakeholders to 'get buy-in from.'

The difference is profound. A roadmap designed for caregivers might include 'Train all staff on new EHR features.' A roadmap designed with caregivers might include 'Reduce documentation time by 30% through workflow redesign and selective automation of repetitive tasks.' See the difference?

This principle requires building protected time for caregiver engagement into the roadmap itself. Not token representation in steering committees. Meaningful involvement in design sprints. Workflow analysis sessions. Prototype testing. The roadmap should explicitly allocate resources and time for this engagement. Recognise it as essential work, not optional consultation.

The Parallel Workflow Problem

Failed roadmaps create parallel workflows. Systems exist alongside existing processes rather than replacing them. Caregivers end up documenting in the EHR and maintaining their paper systems 'just in case.' Patients get information through the portal and still call the office 'to make sure.'

Australia's My Health Record offers a cautionary tale. A$1.15 billion invested between 2012 and 2016. The result? The system was accessed in only 19.6% of emergency department presentations in 2021. Caregivers continued to rely on their local systems. Why? The national system hadn't fully replaced existing workflows. It had simply been added on top of them. Studies reported that 25% of clinicians' time was spent collecting information about the patient rather than actually treating them. The new system failed to reduce this burden.

Successful roadmaps explicitly plan for workflow convergence. They identify parallel systems. They plan their sunset. They ensure new systems fully replace old processes, not supplement them. This requires uncomfortable conversations. Forcing cutover. Removing safety nets. Accepting short-term disruption for long-term simplification.

The roadmap must include—and communicate—specific sunset dates for legacy processes. It must include explicit plans for preventing parallel workflow emergence. This means being willing to delay new system launches. Wait until they're truly ready to fully replace existing processes.

The Measurement Framework: Knowing If You're Actually Succeeding

Perhaps the most insidious roadmap failure? Measuring the wrong things. Roadmaps filled with technology deployment milestones. 'Go-Live Achieved.' 'Training Completed.' 'System Adopted.' These tell you absolutely nothing about whether you're actually improving healthcare delivery.

The Balanced Metrics Principle

Successful roadmaps employ balanced metrics across four categories: patient outcomes, caregiver experience, operational efficiency, and technical performance. Notice the order. It's not accidental.

Patient outcomes—and more importantly outcome variability—must be the primary measures. Not satisfaction surveys, though those matter. Actual health outcomes. A German hospital CEO once told me: 'I can raise patient satisfaction rates by 50% overnight by hiring a good chef.' He implied it's cheaper and way more efficient on that 'metric' than hiring a good Doctor. The real metric questions are these: Are chronic disease patients achieving better control? Are preventable hospitalisations declining? Are care gaps closing?

Caregiver experience shall be at the same priority level as the patient metric. Care professionals shall never be considered second-grade citizens. Burnt-out caregivers can't deliver excellent care. The technology quality doesn't matter. Ask: Are documentation burdens decreasing? Is time spent with patients increasing? Are caregivers able to focus on clinical judgement rather than data entry?

Operational efficiency and technical performance matter. They're supporting metrics. A system that runs perfectly but doesn't improve care *is* a failure. Even if it hits all its technical milestones.

The roadmap should establish baseline measurements for all four categories before beginning. Set realistic improvement targets. Explicitly plan measurement points. Define data collection methods. Adopt data format standards. Create data persistence layers that are 100% decoupled from system vendors' databases. Create response protocols for when metrics move in the wrong direction.

The Early Warning System

Smart roadmaps include early warning indicators. Signals that something's going wrong before it becomes a crisis. These might include caregiver work-around behaviours. Patient portal abandonment rates. Increasing help desk tickets for specific functions.

Denmark offers a striking example. They achieved a 99% digitalisation rate. They exchange over 6 million healthcare messages monthly between provider organisations. Impressive technical metrics. Yet patient feedback revealed something troubling: over 60% of Danish citizens felt more coherence was needed between hospitals, GPs, and municipalities. This early warning signal revealed a critical gap. Interoperability alone doesn't equal integration. The roadmap had been optimised for data exchange. It failed to ensure the right information reached the right recipient at the right time.

The roadmap should explicitly identify these indicators. Establish regular review cadences. Not annual strategic reviews. Monthly or even weekly operational reviews that can catch problems early. Prioritising and monitoring progress must always come before seeking perfection. No system is. This pragmatic approach requires building feedback loops and rapid response capabilities into the roadmap itself. Not treating them as separate maintenance activities.

The Incentive Architecture: Making Success Individually Rational

Even well-intentioned roadmaps fail if their milestones are aligned with the organisation's incentive structure. This is where many technically sound roadmaps come unstuck. They assume people will adopt new approaches simply because they're 'better.' They ignore the reality of institutional inertia. They ignore individual incentives.

The Short-Term Win Principle

Human beings and organisations operate on short-term incentives. Even when they intellectually understand long-term benefits. Successful roadmaps explicitly engineer short-term wins throughout the transformation journey.

This means structuring the roadmap to deliver tangible, visible benefits early and often. Not 'benefits that will accrue once the entire system is implemented.' Real improvements that caregivers and patients experience within weeks or months of each phase.

Singapore's ActiveSG health promotion programme demonstrates this effectively. The government preloaded S$100 onto each citizen's account. This incentivised initial engagement with digital health platforms. An immediate, tangible benefit that drove adoption. As one user noted, 'If you don't learn . . . it's forfeited from you. Then you are forced to learn.' This short-term incentive created the momentum for longer-term behaviour change. One might claim people would be doing the right things for virtually the 'wrong' reasons, but hey—this moved the needle. Whatever is culturally accepted must be right.

Consider an alternative to a three-year EHR implementation that promises some stated benefits 'once everything is connected.' Break it into phases where each phase delivers standalone value. Maybe Phase One focuses solely on reducing medication reconciliation time. A concrete, immediate benefit caregivers experience daily. Phase Two might tackle appointment scheduling friction. Each phase builds momentum. Each demonstrates that this transformation actually makes work life better, provided it doesn't create other problems.

A 30-60-90-day target-setting cadence worked well in most large scale projects I've been part of. It makes people see and feel the time boundaries. It migrates teams to work together. It's not a target that's lost in an invisible future.

The Governance Reality

A good governance shall aim at creating the ability to look back into the repertoire of every past decision, and intuitively understand why and how those decisions have been made.

Failed roadmaps assume a level of organisational coordination, accountability and decision-making that simply doesn't exist. They require departments to collaborate seamlessly. Data flows freely. Everyone prioritises transformation work despite competing demands.

The UK-NHS Public Accounts Committee found something striking. Despite eighteen years of attempts to digitally transform, none of the components essential to successful delivery were in place. Largely due to poor governance and accountability structures. The National Audit Office noted that the government lacked a reliable understanding of funding requirements. It had no strong governance. No accountability for delivery.

Successful roadmaps acknowledge governance reality. They plan around it. They explicitly map power structures. They identify potential resistance points. They design transparent accountability mechanisms that actually work in the organisation's culture.

This might mean giving individual departments some level of control over their implementation phases. Not imposing rigid, centralised mandates. It might mean tying leadership compensation to transformation milestones. It might mean empowering a transformation office with real authority and resources. Not just coordinating responsibility.

The roadmap should explicitly address governance structures needed at each phase. Plan for establishing these structures before they're needed. Don't create them reactively when problems emerge.

The Adaptive Principle: Planning for Uncertainty

The final lesson from both failures and successes? Perhaps the most important. Rigid roadmaps fail in complex healthcare environments. The world changes. Technologies evolve. Pandemics happen. Regulations shift. A roadmap that can't adapt is a roadmap that will become obsolete.

The Rolling Wave Approach

Smart roadmaps employ rolling wave planning. Detailed plans for the near term. Directional plans for the medium term. Vision-level plans for the long term. They're updated regularly based on lessons learnt and changing conditions.

This means structuring roadmaps in 90-day cycles. Clear, measurable objectives for each cycle. At the end of each cycle, replan the next three cycles. Base replanning on results, learning, and changed circumstances. Long-term vision remains stable. The path to reach it remains flexible.

This approach prevents the common trap. Multi-year implementation plans that become increasingly disconnected from reality as time passes. It allows course corrections before small problems become major failures.

The Pilot With Purpose

Successful roadmaps embrace purposeful piloting as a core principle. Not an optional preliminary step. Major initiatives begin as focused pilots in controlled environments before scaling. Here's the key: these pilots must be designed to genuinely test whether something should scale. Not just to tick a box before inevitable rollout.

The UK's Global Digital Exemplar (GDE) programme demonstrated this approach effectively. It used a phased strategy to fund relatively digitally mature organisations first. Then paired them with less mature partners. Most participating organisations achieved a substantial boost in their digital transformation pace. Though a few struggled with the ambitious goals.

This means creating honest success criteria before pilots begin. Being willing to kill initiatives that don't meet them. No matter how much has been invested. It means designing pilots that can fail safely. Without catastrophic consequences. It means learning from failures and iterating before scaling.

The roadmap should explicitly identify pilot phases. Define assessment criteria and success metrics. Mark decision points. Map alternative paths if pilots reveal problems. This creates permission to learn and adapt. Rather than pressure to proceed regardless of results.

Conclusion: The Roadmap as Living Strategy

Creating effective roadmaps for digital health transformation requires inverting many traditional planning assumptions. It means assessing readiness before planning deployment. It means starting with patient needs rather than technology capabilities. It means designing around actual workflows rather than ideal processes. It means measuring what matters rather than what's easy to measure. It means engineering incentives and adapting to reality.

Most importantly? Recognising that the roadmap isn't a static blueprint to be executed. It's a living strategy to be continuously refined. Success doesn't come from perfectly predicting the future. It comes from building capacity to learn and adapt as you go.

The organisations that succeed in digital health transformation don't have better initial roadmaps. They have better processes for continuously improving their roadmaps based on real-world results. They stay focused on the true goal: serving patients better. They're willing to change any plan. Abandon any technology. Challenge any assumption in service of that goal.

That's the fundamental difference between roadmaps that lead to transformation and those that lead to expensive disappointment. Roadmaps in health and care are about being better at planning, learning, and iterating. At a time where the digital noise is louder than the signal, 'roadmaps for what' matters most: better care and less burden for patients.

*****

SWITZERLAND | STRATEGIC EVIDENCE GENERATION FOR DIGITAL HEALTH AND AI | KIMBERLY NOEL AND ROCHE PHARMA

Conviction: To Set Strategy, Know the Problems, the Stakes, and the Crowd

Ruth Bader Ginsburg is quoted for saying 'Fight for the things that you care about. But do it in a way that will lead others to join you." In all of the environments I have led in my career, this quote reminds me that conviction is an essential aspect of innovation and *how* you engage determines success. As the Global Lead of AI advocacy and Digital health at a pharmaceutical giant in Medical Affairs, I was tasked to bring the insights of the "outside world" to enhance our portfolio of medicine in development. Due to my background in digital health, AI and a board certification in clinical prevention and public health, I can be drawn into many different directions, representing teams for many different assets each with distinct challenges. In these many collaborations, being an "outsider" to a tried and tested industry requires great adaptation to be effective, even if one is respected for experience. In order not to be considered and subsequently promptly ignored, a great deal of stakeholder buy-in is required. Many innovators know that setting effective strategy is through teamwork. Without strong and influential early adopters, strategy roadmaps become obsolete. However, often little emphasis is given on the "how" in early stages of innovation, where conviction garners allies based on thoughtful problem definitions and strong alignment of purpose.

In the high-stakes pharmaceutical race of chronic weight management, the molecule is only half the story. My experience in the clinical "trenches" managing challenging patients with multimorbid disease made it clear to me that even the most life saving drugs do not work in a vacuum. I believe that the context of care, behaviors, cultures, relationships with food, societal pressures, mental health, finances, and more make up the web trapping those in poor health despite the prescriptions I could write as a physician. It is due to this intrinsic "messiness" of chronic disease that AI and digital health tools show great promise in helping patients in helping clinicians and patients "see" through the complexity. But for those in my company whose precise mission above all else is to focus exclusively on developing pharmaceutical molecules, how can innovation strategy, especially in volatile times, be relevant to them? What is the role of Big Pharma in this space? How much did we as a company need to pay attention to artificial intelligence, digital endpoints and telehealth? And even for those who believe in the company's role to address comprehensive care needs of patients, what exactly does that mean for clinical development and evidence plans? For many, innovation is demarcated by the "beyond the molecule" strategy, and in the rush to bring these miraculous new drugs to market, focus is emphasized not to slow progress nor complicate studies.

In my view, these questions can pose a trap if one rushes to address these challenges from the innovation perspective alone. My experience has led me to bring co-ownership of these problems with relevant stakeholders, so that I can effectively translate my insights to build strategy together. Strategic leadership in these new times requires upskilling most colleagues, fostering preparedness, and radical resilience to adopt digital and AI tools. The solutions for future hangups in adopting digital health tools will likely not be in the "beyond the molecule" space but rather within the core business itself. So without the early conviction of joint problems to tackle, ample energies need to be redirected to create the alliances of early adoptership. This is very true when there is no precedence. In setting pioneering innovation roadmaps one needs to require teamwork, scenario planning, agility and trust.

When time for relationship building is not sufficient for deep rooted lived experiences and/or when one is an actual or perceived outsider, accurate problem definition has been a helpful tool in accelerating buy-in. Intensive listening to understand, capturing the top priorities of the common challenges allows for meaningful insights and trust building. It is when people can see their challenges relate to the innovation that defenses are more manageable to the change management process. It is this initial step in "knowing the problems, the stakes and the crowd" that the roadmapping can begin.

Sharing the Problem: The Integrated Evidence Gap

Healthcare tech innovation has historically languished compared to other sectors, necessitating practical guides that improve innovation capabilities. Drafting the Digital Health (DH) CVRM Strategy was a comprehensive effort designed to fulfill this promise. Early in our integrated evidence planning (IEP) process, the life cycle team (LCT) identified a significant strategic void: a lack of clarity on how to integrate digital tools into our clinical development programs (CDPs) to achieve meaningful product differentiation. This problem was not an innovation problem per se but a process issue.

As a team, we identified several "high-priority" evidence gaps, specifically a lack of data on how digital trackers (i.e., wearables) can improve adherence to lifestyle programs in our CDPs and a lack of evidence regarding digital engagement leading to better adherence and results in the real world. Furthermore, while artificial intelligence has emerged as a transformative force for diagnosis and personalized treatment, the broader industry has struggled with hurdles in standardization, ethical considerations, and data privacy. Without a structured roadmap, we risked falling behind competitors who were already engaging with the FDA to capture digital endpoints. Roadmaps serve as essential beacons, providing necessary guardrails to ensure focus and completion.

Embrace the Gaps: The DH Evidence Strategy Work Packages

An important realization in developing strategy for Big Pharma, was an obvious need to understand how innovation work is actually done when translated to action. In my latest organization, the boots on the ground work is organized into work packages, where aims are clear, endorsed and executed in alignment with guidance from asset strategies and integrated evidence plans. For digital health tools, especially those driven by AI, clear strategic alignment with the trusted foundational guidance. The next step in garnering early buy-in was to go to the source of influence, drafting digital health into the integrated evidence plans, and asset strategies directly. This early work de-risks adoption of digital health evidence strategies to enable digital health technology (DHT) integration into clinical programs allowing for more effective results. The process of addressing foundational guidance highlights the many stakeholders essential to build alliances with, who may not be on the innovator's radar until much later in the process. In working to bridge common understanding with this wider community this often may be perceived time intensive, however I have found that this is the "going slow to go fast" move that allows for effective scaling of solutions later.

I have found that the following strategies in early engagement of stakeholders have helped with essential buy-in:

The "Shared Map": Identify a common need that others are addressing. Garner lessons learned and join the effort. For the obesity teams, keeping them abreast of the clinical validations of wearable and AI use in obesity was helpful to help create a common effort.

"No-Regret" De-Risking: Identifying the "safe path" is often the obvious step overlooked in many strategies. At times to identify this strategy, it is sometimes helpful to envision inaction. Most of the time inaction poses a threat to standard processes. In this exercise of envisioning inaction, sometimes the de-risk solution is better iterated. For example, for the obesity teams, the use of passive, closed-label monitoring with research-grade wearables allowed for consideration as a non-confounding interventional trial solution for data collection.

Future-Proofing (The "Expressway"): Clearly depicting scenarios and new regulatory, geopolitical or emerging realities enables planning and enhances visibility for stakeholders who are less able to envision change. For example, educating the obesity stakeholders on the FDA's Prescription Drug Use-Related Software (PDURS) framework to enable software to be optionally prescribed alongside the drug was a novel consideration for many stakeholders. Furthermore, understanding the changes in AI adoption for diagnosis and management of obesity, the rise of direct to consumer telehealth and changing geopolitical pressures on access to obesity medicines enabled adoption of digital health strategies for certain obesity assets.

Case Study: The DECODE-Obesity Consortium

An example of the "Create Roadmaps" theme is Roche's participation in the Ametris DECODE-Obesity consortium. Clinical validation of digital endpoints is notoriously expensive and lengthy. By collaborating with industry peers, Roche gains access to validated digital measures for physical activity and physical functioning years before the 2028 launch.

This strategy allows us to ensure that the digital measures being validated support the claims where molecules are most likely to outperform competitors. Furthermore, it provides competitive insight into the populations and measures regulators care strongly about, such as FDA's perspectives on physical function endpoints. Participating in these discussions helps us understand which arguments resonate most with health authorities (FDA/EMA) to increase the likelihood of success in future interactions.

Barriers & Lessons Learned: Navigating the EU AI Act

Creating this roadmap required navigating several institutional and technical barriers. Plans do not stifle innovation but provide the focus needed to overcome unnecessarily long journeys:

- **The EU AI Act & Classification:** We anticipated the EU AI Act (2024/1689) by recognizing that many DHTs used in clinical settings are classified as high risk. Our roadmap addresses this by emphasizing transparency and explainability to satisfy both regulators and clinicians, as AI systems used in medical technology rely on processing sensitive health data.
- **Separating Strategy From Execution:** A key lesson was that the work package must guide evidence needs and considerations first, without detailing the full breadth of operationalization, which requires different cross-functional collaboration.
- **The "No-Regret" Philosophy:** To avoid the risk of a digital tool influencing behavior and thus confounding trial results, we promoted "closed-label passive monitoring." This allows for data collection on physical functioning while keeping efficacy data "clean."

The Human Aspect: Restoring Meaningful Life

Innovation must never rely solely on technology; the best outcomes result from a strong balance at the intersection of people and technology. Our roadmap prioritizes meaningful aspects of health (MAH) that matter to patients: reduction in limitations of physical functioning and improved sleep quality. By validating these endpoints, we address the "human factor"—ensuring digital solutions are usable and meaningful to the patient's daily experience. This aligns with the EU AI Act's principle of human oversight, ensuring technology remains a servant to clinical judgment and patient well-being.

Vision for the Future: The Integrated Solution

The ultimate destination of our roadmap is a differentiated label claim about the benefit of a medicine from data collected from a digital health or AI tool. The future may bring clinically impactful insights from data collected by research-grade tools. Furthermore there are interesting perspectives in meaningful correlation with consumer-grade wearables, or integration with a validated companion app. Although the future is bright with examples of pioneering efforts for new integrated solutions of drugs, early adoption for scale requires the commitment of efforts discussed previously.

Wrap Up: Fulfilling the Promise

By "creating roadmaps," the DH Evidence Strategy Work Package has provided a structured, de-risked path to digital excellence even in environments of high volatility and high stakes. Roadmaps help innovators navigate without being distracted and thrown off course. We have moved from identifying gaps to prioritizing mitigations, ensuring our digital investments are compliant with evolving standards like the EU AI Act and focused on the ultimate goal: superior clinical benefit for the patient.

*****

SPAIN | WHEN PHARMACEUTICAL MARKETING WORKS FOR AI, NOT THE OTHER WAY AROUND | JANET CARDOZA CALDERON

Designing Innovation by Listening to the Healthcare System

Artificial intelligence has become a board-level priority within pharmaceutical organizations. Significant investments have been made in advanced analytics, omnichannel orchestration, and AI-enabled decision engines. However, despite the sophistication of these technologies, many initiatives have failed to deliver sustainable impact at scale. The root cause is rarely technological.

In practice, AI does not fail due to model performance but because the operating model surrounding it was never designed for intelligence to thrive. Marketing functions remain structured around channel execution, campaign calendars, and fragmented data ownership. As a result, AI systems are fed with inconsistent signals, low-quality behavioral data, and misaligned inputs between commercial and medical teams undermining trust, adoption, and value creation.

This challenge reveals a critical insight for executive leaders: AI transformation in pharma should not be viewed as a technology program but as an organizational redesign. For AI to succeed, marketing must evolve from an activation engine into a strategic architecture—one that curates consistent, high-value data; orchestrates coherent journeys; and translates human behavior into actionable intelligence.

This essay seeks to analyze how redefining marketing as an AI-enabling operating mode supported by deliberate roadmaps, governance, and leadership becomes a decisive innovation pathway for pharmaceutical organizations undergoing end-to-end AI-driven transformation (HIMSS, 2019; HIMSS, 2023; HIMSS, 2025), and may represent the new way we understand pharmaceutical marketing in the post-AI era.

The Context

Pharmaceutical organizations operate at the intersection of unprecedented complexity and rapidly accelerating expectations. Regulatory pressure continues to intensify, driven by evolving data privacy requirements, emerging AI governance frameworks, and increasing demands for transparency, explainability, and ethical accountability. At the same time, healthcare professionals are experiencing growing fatigue with omnichannel engagement models that prioritize volume, metrics, and dashboards over relevance and the true value of pharmaceutical marketing eroding trust and reducing returns across both digital and in-person interactions (Epstein & Street, 2011; Sinsky et al., 2016).

In parallel, artificial intelligence has rapidly evolved from an experimental capability into a strategic imperative. Executive agendas are filled with promises of next-best-action engines, predictive targeting, and personalization at scale. However, the operational reality inside many pharmaceutical organizations tells a different story. AI initiatives remain stuck in pilot phases, disconnected from daily workflows, or underutilized due to poor data quality and limited organizational readiness.

This disconnect is further amplified by the historical evolution of marketing functions. Omnichannel expansion has often resulted in fragmented channel ownership, duplicated content strategies, and disconnected performance metrics that merely fill PowerPoint presentations. Rather than generating clarity, this complexity has diluted signal quality and overwhelmed both internal teams and external stakeholders. In this environment, AI is expected to compensate for a structural incoherence it was never designed to solve when in reality, AI requires coherence in data to reach its full potential.

The result is a growing gap between ambition and execution. AI is positioned as the solution to scale personalization and efficiency, yet it is deployed within operating models that were never designed to support intelligent decision-making in a fragmented data environment. Closing this gap requires a fundamental re-examination of how marketing, data, governance, and leadership interact not as parallel initiatives but as an integrated roadmap toward sustainable transformation, providing the coherence that both organizations and AI critically need.

Innovation

Marketing as an AI-Enabling Operating Model

The innovation presented in this essay is not a new algorithm, platform, or artificial intelligence solution. It is a fundamental redefinition of the pharmaceutical marketing operating model, intentionally designed to allow AI to function with relevance, trust, and scalability fully leveraging the potential and simplicity that AI offers today.

Historically, pharmaceutical marketing has been organized around execution: campaign planning, channel activation, content deployment, and performance reporting. While effective in a pre-AI environment, this structure generates fragmented data, inconsistent behavioral signals, and disconnected decision cycles. When AI is introduced downstream into this model, it is expected to optimize outcomes without the ability to influence the quality or coherence of the inputs it depends on. Under this data disconnection, organizations expect AI to generate clarity, yet the more disconnection is introduced, the more disconnection AI ultimately produces.

Repositioning marketing as an AI-enabling operating model reverses this dynamic. Marketing assumes responsibility not for activating channels but for designing the conditions under which intelligence can emerge. Its role evolves into that of a signal architect curating meaningful data, defining standardized behavioral taxonomies, orchestrating coherent journeys, and ensuring that human insight is embedded from the outset.

This shift also requires new governance models and cross-functional alignment. Marketing becomes the integrator across commercial, medical, digital, analytics, and field teams aligning engagement strategy, data design, and AI use cases under a shared roadmap. Rather than treating AI as an add-on capability, intelligence becomes a natural extension of how the organization plans, executes, and learns.

Case Study

Spain & Southern Europe: From Listening to AI-Orchestrated Healthcare Engagement

The turning point occurred when a European pharmaceutical organization recognized that its AI initiatives were not failing due to a lack of analytical capability but due to the absence of a governance system that structured decision-making. AI had been deployed as a recommendation tool, rather than as a structural framework to help determine what to prioritize, when to act, and under which ethical and regulatory criteria.

In this context, marketing was redefined as the function responsible for designing the signal system that would feed both internal AI and external generative AI systems. In parallel, AI ceased to be viewed as an automation engine and instead became a support mechanism for informed human decision-making.

Step 1: Reframing AI as a Decision Support Layer, Not Automation

The first shift was conceptual. Aligned with the European human-centric AI approach (European Commission, 2021), the organization redefined the purpose of AI: not to decide on behalf of the organization but to structure the information required for people to make better decisions.

This required establishing clear principles consistent with ethical frameworks for trustworthy AI (Floridi et al., 2018):

- AI does not replace human judgment
- No decision with clinical or commercial impact is automated
- Every recommendation must be explainable, traceable, and reversible (Doshi-Velez & Kim, 2017)
- AI acts as a coherence layer across functions

Step 2: Positioning Marketing as the Architect of the Signal System

Inspired by Amazon and Netflix where recommendations are the result of well-designed signals (Gomez-Uribe & Hunt, 2016), marketing assumed a new role: architecting the inputs that govern intelligence.

In practice, this meant shifting from optimizing campaigns to optimizing:

- signal quality
- semantic consistency of content
- journey coherence
- alignment between clinical context, intent, and timing

These signals did not describe individuals but aggregated behaviors—fully compliant with GDPR (European Commission, 2016) and avoiding invasive profiling.

Step 3: Redesigning Omnichannel as a Decision System, Not an Impact Calendar

Omnichannel was re-architected to answer a different question:

> *What does the organization need to know in order to decide better?*

Each touchpoint was assigned a clear function within the system:

- generating context
- validating hypotheses
- detecting friction
- identifying value opportunities

As a result, omnichannel evolved from an impact calendar into a structured observation system (Linden et al., 2003) closely aligned with how recommendation systems generate insights.

Step 4: Standardizing Content and Journeys for Coherent AI Governance

To enable AI to function as a governance system, marketing redesigned content following AI-readable principles:

- clear semantic structures
- reusable modularity
- consistent metadata
- explicit medical validation
- clear separation between scientific information and promotion

This allowed internal AI systems to:

- compare scenarios
- prioritize options
- identify value patterns without relying on automated decision-making

Step 5: Integrating AI Into Decision Committees, Not Just Dashboards

A critical shift involved bringing AI into the spaces where decisions are made—not just into reporting tools.

AI outputs were integrated as:

- inputs for brand strategy committees
- support for omnichannel planning
- evidence for investment decisions
- early signals of regulatory risk or HCP fatigue

AI thus became a layer of cognitive governance similar to how Netflix uses data to decide what to produce or how Amazon prioritizes initiatives always with final human decision authority.

Step 6: Positioning the Organization as a Trusted Source for Generative AI

As a natural consequence, marketing also began working outward. By structuring clear, validated, and semantically consistent content, the organization became legible and referenceable by generative AI systems.

The objective was not to "optimize for ChatGPT" but to:

- act as an expert, verifiable, and ethical source
- answer real healthcare system questions
- build traceable scientific authority

This strengthened visibility in AI-mediated search environments without breaching promotional regulations.

Step 7: Human-in-the-Loop as an Operating Principle

Aligned with the European AI Act (European Commission, 2024), field, medical, and compliance teams were integrated as permanent validators of the system. AI suggested, contextualized, and prioritized, but people decided. This approach proved essential for building trust, adoption, and long-term sustainability.

The organization did not "implement AI." It built an intelligence-based governance system in which:

- marketing designs the signals
- AI orders complexity
- leaders make better, more ethical decisions
- the organization becomes visible and trusted by external generative AI systems

In the era of generative AI, the true differentiator is not the algorithm but who governs intelligence and how.

Organizations that understand marketing as the architect of the cognitive system, and AI as a governance support layer, will be the only ones capable of scaling value without losing control, ethics, or trust.

Barriers & Lessons Learned

What Listening Revealed Beyond the Technology

The transition toward marketing as an AI-enabling operating model revealed barriers more decisive than any technical limitation. The first challenge was organizational resistance. AI was often perceived as an external imposition, generating uncertainty around ownership and accountability.

Governance emerged as a second critical barrier. Existing decision frameworks were optimized for campaigns and channels, not intelligence. Data ownership was fragmented, approval processes were sequential, and AI use cases lacked clear escalation paths. Without explicit governance, AI recommendations risked being ignored or applied inconsistently.

Field trust represented another inflection point. Initial skepticism was not driven by rejection of technology but by lack of transparency and clinical context. Trust improved when AI outputs were repositioned as decision support and when field feedback was systematically integrated upstream.

Compliance considerations also constrained momentum. Legal and regulatory teams raised legitimate concerns regarding data traceability, explainability, and ethical boundaries. This reinforced a critical lesson: AI cannot be added retrospectively to compliance frameworks; it must be embedded from the design of the marketing operating model.

Elaborate on the Human Aspect: When Innovation Starts (and Succeeds) With People

While technology and governance provide structure, leadership and human behavior determine success. Reframing marketing as an AI-enabling operating model required a profound mindset shift, challenging long-standing assumptions around control, expertise, and value creation.

Leadership was essential in redefining AI as a learning process rather than a technology initiative. This created psychological safety and enabled teams to address data and process gaps without personalizing failure.

Capability development focused on building AI fluency rather than technical specialization. Teams learned to critically interpret insights, ask better questions, and apply professional judgment. AI ceased to be viewed as a black box and became a shared capability that amplifies human expertise (Topol, 2019).

Vision for the Future/Repeatability for Readers

A Model That Scales Beyond Technology

The relevance of marketing as an AI-enabling operating model will continue to grow. As regulatory frameworks mature and healthcare systems demand greater accountability, organizations will compete not on who adopts AI first but on who enables it most responsibly.

This model is inherently repeatable. It does not depend on a specific technology stack or level of digital maturity. Any organization can begin by redesigning its marketing roadmap around signal quality, governance, and human judgment.

AI transformation must be governed as an enterprise capability. When marketing roadmaps align with data strategy, compliance, and field execution, AI becomes a durable organizational asset rather than a series of disconnected pilots.

Closing: Creating Roadmaps for AI-Enabled Marketing Transformation

This experience reinforces a fundamental truth: AI does not succeed through acceleration but through deliberate design. Creating roadmaps is the discipline that transforms ambition into sustainable execution.

By positioning marketing as an enabler of intelligence rather than its consumer, organizations create the conditions for AI to be ethical, interpretable, and scalable. The question for leaders is no longer whether to adopt AI but whether they are willing to design the roadmap that allows it to work.

Although this transformation is articulated through marketing, its ultimate impact is realized where it matters most in healthcare: the experience and outcomes of oncology patients. In oncology, where decisions are complex, time is critical, and scientific knowledge evolves rapidly, the way information flows through the system can materially influence quality of care. By repositioning marketing as an AI enabler and AI as a governance layer for decision-making, organizations reduce one of the most significant sources of friction in oncology: fragmented and poorly contextualized information.

When omnichannel journeys are designed to generate coherent signals and AI organizes complexity in an explainable way, healthcare professionals gain earlier and more relevant access to scientific knowledge. Instead of receiving disconnected messages or redundant content, clinicians are supported with information aligned to clinical context, disease stage, and real-world questions emerging in daily practice. AI does not replace medical judgment; rather, it helps prioritize what information matters most at each moment, reducing cognitive overload in high-pressure oncology environments and enabling more informed, timely decisions.

From the patient perspective, the benefits are tangible even without direct interaction with AI or marketing systems. Better-aligned information flows reduce inconsistencies in clinical communication, improve coordination across care settings, and support more empathetic, human-centered interactions. By structuring access to up-to-date scientific knowledge and supporting decision-making through aggregated, explainable signals, this model helps reduce unwarranted variability in care and promotes greater equity across regions and institutions, an essential principle in European healthcare systems. Anchored in strong governance, compliance, and human-in-the-loop principles, AI becomes a trusted support for ethical, transparent decision-making. Ultimately, designing marketing to work in service of AI is not a technical or commercial exercise but a powerful indirect lever to improve equity, experience, and outcomes for oncology patients ensuring that intelligence, when governed with purpose, delivers value to those who need it most.

Notes

1 Eurostat News 17 November 2025; OECD Health at a Glance 2023–2024.
2 Ibid
3 The Asclepius Project is a pan-European, practitioner-led excellence platform focused on the development and implementation of closed loop medication management (CLMM) in hospital settings. It brings together hospital pharmacists, clinicians, digital health experts, and system architects from multiple European countries to share real-world experience, develop decision-oriented roadmaps, and support context-sensitive CLMM implementation across diverse healthcare systems.

References

HIMSS Framework and Digital Transformation in Healthcare.

HIMSS. (2019). *Voices of Innovation: Fulfilling the Promise of Information Technology in Healthcare*. Taylor & Francis.

HIMSS. (2023). *Voices of Innovation, 2nd Edn.: Post-pandemic Healthcare Transformation*. Taylor & Francis.

HIMSS. (2025). *Voices of Innovation: AI Edition*. Taylor & Francis.

HIMSS. (n.d.). *Innovation Pathways Framework*. Healthcare Information and Management Systems Society. https://www.himss.org

Gobernanza de IA y marco regulatorio europeo

European Commission. (2016). Regulation (EU) 2016/679 of the European Parliament and of the Council (General Data Protection Regulation). *Official Journal of the European Union*. https://eur-lex.europa.eu/eli/reg/2016/679/oj

European Commission. (2021). *Ethics Guidelines for Trustworthy AI*. High-Level Expert Group on Artificial Intelligence. https://digital-strategy.ec.europa.eu

European Commission. (2024). Artificial Intelligence Act (AI Act): Proposal for a regulation laying down harmonised rules on artificial intelligence. *Official Journal of the European Union*. https://artificial-intelligence-act.eu

Human-centric AI and decision support

Floridi, L., Cowls, J., Beltrametti, M. et al. (2018). AI4People—An ethical framework for a good AI society: Opportunities, risks, principles, and recommendations. *Minds and Machines*, 28(4), 689–707. https://doi.org/10.1007/s11023-018-9482-5

Topol, E. (2019). *Deep Medicine: How Artificial Intelligence Can Make Healthcare Human Again*. Basic Books.

Omnichannel, decision-making y information overload en healthcare

Epstein, R. M., & Street, R. L. (2011). The values and value of patient-centered care. *Annals of Family Medicine*, 9(2), 100–103. https://doi.org/10.1370/afm.1239

Sinsky, C., Tutty, M., & Colligan, L. (2016). Allocation of physician time in ambulatory practice. *Annals of Internal Medicine*, 165(11), 753–760. https://doi.org/10.7326/M16-0961

Recommendation systems y signal-based decision models (Amazon / Netflix—conceptual alignment)

Gomez-Uribe, C. A., & Hunt, N. (2016). The Netflix recommender system: Algorithms, business value, and innovation. *ACM Transactions on Management Information Systems*, 6(4), 1–19. https://doi.org/10.1145/2843948

Linden, G., Smith, B., & York, J. (2003). Amazon.com recommendations: Item-to-item collaborative filtering. *IEEE Internet Computing*, 7(1), 76–80. https://doi.org/10.1109/MIC.2003.1167344

Explainable AI and decision governance

Doshi-Velez, F., & Kim, B. (2017). Towards a rigorous science of interpretable machine learning. *arXiv* preprint arXiv:1702.08608. https://arxiv.org/abs/1702.08608

European Parliament. (2020). *The Ethics of Artificial Intelligence: Issues and Initiatives*. https://www.europarl.europa.eu

Oncology, decision complexity and equity

European Society for Medical Oncology (ESMO). (2023). *ESMO Clinical Practice Guidelines*. https://www.esmo.org

World Health Organization. (2022). *Cancer Control: Knowledge into Action*. WHO Press. https://www.who.int

*****

SPAIN | BUILDING THE FRAMEWORK FOR SCALABLE HEALTHCARE INNOVATION | JORDI PIERA-JIMÉNEZ

Background

Catalonia (northeast Spain) is one of Europe's most vibrant healthcare innovation ecosystems. According to the 2024 BioRegion Report, the life sciences and healthcare sector represents 7.6%

of Catalonia's GDP, employs over 280,000 people, and encompasses more than 1,500 companies, 90% of which are SMEs [1]. With 470 active startups and scaleups, 93 research institutions, and over 1,200 clinical trials (ranking 6th in Europe), we are not short on innovation. However, the COVID-19 pandemic exposed significant limitations in our healthcare infrastructure dramatically. When we needed to rapidly deploy telemedicine, coordinate vaccination campaigns, and share real-time epidemiological data, we discovered how much our fragmentation constrained our response [2]. The urgency of these challenges highlighted the critical need for integrated systems as digital consultations surged from 2% to over 25% of primary care visits, yet the underlying infrastructure strained under demands it was never designed to handle [3, 4].

And yet, we face a paradox every day. When we visit our hospitals and primary care centres, we see remarkable innovations: AI algorithms detecting diabetic retinopathy, predictive models for hospital readmissions, and digital tools streamlining chronic disease management. Brilliant solutions developed by brilliant teams. But here's the problem: these innovations rarely leave the walls of the institutions that created them. Hospital A creates a strong falls prediction model. Meanwhile, Hospital B, just 30 kilometres away, develops a similar tool from the ground up. Primary care centre C designs a diabetes management app that patients appreciate, but if those patients move to a different area, they lose access. Innovation is alive in Catalonia, but it happens in isolated pockets. Some people benefit, while others are left waiting. In a public healthcare system that promises universal coverage, this fragmentation is not only inefficient, but it is also unfair. Take Maria, a 75-year-old living in Hospital A's catchment area. She benefits from that falls prediction model, which alerts her doctor to high-risk situations and helps prevent serious injuries. When Maria moves to a nearby town served by Hospital B, she loses access to this service. This is more than inconvenient. It puts her at greater risk. In a public healthcare system committed to universal coverage, this fragmentation isn't just inefficient. It's inequitable.

This chapter describes how we built the foundation to solve this problem: not by stifling or putting barriers to local innovation but by creating the framework conditions to scale it systematically.

Setting the Context: Innovation Without Infrastructure

Spain's healthcare system is organised around seventeen autonomous regions, each with full authority over healthcare delivery and funded through general taxation. This decentralised model means that while the central government sets basic standards, regions design and manage their own health services independently. Catalonia, with 8 million residents, operates one of the most complex regional systems. The Catalan Health Service (CatSalut) acts as the single public insurer providing universal coverage, but unlike regions that deliver care primarily through public facilities, Catalonia contracts with over seventy diverse provider organisations: the public Catalan Institute of Health (serving approximately 30% of the population), private non-profit foundations, hospital consortia, municipal providers, and religious organisations [5]. This diversity emerged from historical circumstances and deliberate political design, creating a quasi-market model that fosters local responsiveness and competition on quality but also fragments the digital landscape significantly.

This same diversity drives innovation. Each organisation controls its own IT systems, employs its own technical teams, and pursues its own digital strategy. The result: thirty different electronic medical record (EMR) systems, countless homegrown applications, and pockets of genuine excellence scattered across the territory [5]. A 2024 inventory identified 168 AI tools deployed across Catalan hospitals [1]. Impressive, but largely uncoordinated.

The COVID-19 pandemic exposed these limitations dramatically. When we needed to rapidly deploy telemedicine, coordinate vaccination campaigns, and share real-time epidemiological data, we discovered how much our fragmentation constrained our response [3]. Digital consultations increased from 2% to over 25% of primary care visits, yet the underlying infrastructure strained under demands it was never designed to handle [3,4].

The issue is not a shortage of innovation. Instead, there are three main problems. First, organisations duplicate efforts because they lack visibility into what others are developing. Second, scaling is nearly impossible because a solution that works in one health IT system often does not work in another, with EMRs being the most significant barrier. Third, equity suffers: people in areas with digitally advanced providers get better tools, faster service, and more personalised care, while others are left behind.

The Strategy: From Fragmentation to Shared Capability

The Digital Health Strategy of Catalonia draws its fundamental direction from the Catalonia Health Plan 2021–2025 [6], ensuring that technological innovations support broader healthcare goals rather than exist as independent initiatives. A structured strategic planning process involving multiple stakeholders was implemented following the approach in Ward and Peppard's *Strategic Planning for Information Systems* [7].

The process consisted of four phases: analysing the current situation through focus groups, surveys, and interviews; envisioning the desired future scenario aligned with the Health Plan's objectives; defining strategic initiatives through gap analysis; and proposing a strategic plan with key performance indicators, an implementation roadmap, and a communication plan. More than 300 individuals participated in defining the initial strategy, including healthcare professionals from various disciplines and care levels, health system managers, IT specialists, patient representatives, academic institutions, and industry partners.

The analysis phase revealed what Beale and Hovenga describe as the "symptoms that indicate when the time has come for a major renovation" [8]. Those in charge of managing any healthcare delivery organisation's IT environment recognise these symptoms well: growing size and complexity of system maintenance backlogs; changes taking longer to implement; rising costs of maintaining and adding data integrations; and difficulties in scaling systems to support more users and transactions [8]. Our fragmented landscape of thirty EMRs exhibited all of these.

But one symptom stood out above all others: semantic incoherence. For nearly two decades, Catalonia addressed interoperability through a pure data exchange approach. The Shared Electronic Health Record of Catalonia (HC3), established in 2008, pools information from thirty different EMRs into a central repository. Information is collected locally following each provider's own standards, then normalised according to international messaging standards (HL7-CDA, SNOMED-CT, LOINC) when transferred to the central record [5]. This approach was innovative for its time and has delivered significant value, enabling professionals to access clinical documents across organisational boundaries.

However, this document-based interoperability model carries substantial costs. Every new data element, every new integration, and every new use case requires custom development work to map local concepts to shared standards. When one provider records a diagnosis using their local terminology and another uses different codes, the semantic reconciliation happens at exchange time through complex transformation rules. The meaning remains locked inside each source system, defined implicitly in software and database schemas rather than explicitly in shared, governable knowledge artefacts [8]. This explains why innovations couldn't scale across our ecosystem. A clinical decision support tool built for one EMR cannot simply read data from another, because the underlying semantics are incompatible. It wasn't just technical incompatibility. It was semantic incompatibility.

The strategic analysis led us to a clear conclusion: incremental improvements to our current architecture would never address these fundamental limitations. We needed a paradigm shift in how we conceive, build, and manage health information systems. The answer that emerged was what Beale and Hovenga call the knowledge-driven platform approach, also known as the open platform paradigm [8, 9].

A knowledge-driven platform differs fundamentally from traditional health IT architectures. It is a platform "whose domain semantics are explicitly defined by knowledge artefacts rather than being implicitly expressed in software and database schemas" [8]. This means separating the vast majority of semantic definitions from software and databases, moving them to an independent representation with a single authoritative definition. Domain experts and clinicians become direct actors in defining how clinical information is structured, rather than having IT vendors make these decisions buried inside proprietary products. The Apperta Foundation characterised this approach through eight fundamental principles: use of open standards, common shared information models, application portability, federation capability, vendor and technology neutrality, open data support, open APIs, and operability supporting DevOps principles [9].

From a business perspective, a knowledge-driven platform represents a set of conformance criteria held by the procurement side, rather than a secret architecture hidden inside a vendor product. It makes the buyer the owner of the solution, and the industry a supplier of well-defined components rather than total solutions. A successful platform results in what Beale and Hovenga call a "platform economy of plug-and-play vendors competing on application quality rather than data lock-in" [8].

This is precisely what our fragmented ecosystem needed. Rather than asking seventy provider organisations to replace their systems, we would build shared platform services that any organisation could connect to through standardised interfaces. The platform would provide clinical data repositories, terminology services, and identity management built once at system level. Provider organisations would retain their existing applications but gain the ability to read and write clinical data using common, explicitly defined models. An innovation developed by one organisation could be deployed across the ecosystem because all participants share the same semantic language. The goal was not to centralise control but to create the infrastructure that enables distributed innovation to scale.

The Governance: Participatory Decision-Making at Scale

The platform is only useful if people trust it and use it. Good governance is not merely a support mechanism but a fundamental condition for project success. When we talk about governance, we refer to the distribution of decision-making authority within an organisation or across a system involving multiple entities.

We established the Digital Health Strategy Office with seven specialised units: Services (administrative, legal, financial, and communication support), Implementation and Evaluation (deployment and real-world evidence analysis), Project Portfolio Management Office (centralised coordination aligned with strategic objectives), Clinical Informatics (healthcare professionals defining digital products based on clinical needs), Product and Design (user experience and service design), Clinical Knowledge Modelling (semantic interoperability and data quality), and Technology (architecture, development, security, and deployment).

We identified seven main stakeholder groups: government institutions; healthcare providers, including mental health and social care; healthcare professionals, managers, and their associations; the technology industry; standardisation and information security bodies; patients, caregivers, and patient associations; and universities and digital health research centres.

To promote participatory governance, we rely on formal governance structures and engagement processes. At the strategic level, a strategic committee controls execution and budget, managing communication and resource mobilisation. An advisory council provides guidance on programmes and products. A steering committee handles operational decisions, standards approval, and risk management. An operational committee manages day-to-day execution. Finally, programme committees support local resource mobilisation and regional implementation.

Within a digital health strategy that serves the public interest, industry providers are not included in formal governance bodies. This separation safeguards neutrality, fairness, and decision-making guided by long-term sustainability. However, maintaining continuous dialogue with the industry is essential to ensure it understands the system's vision and future needs.

The Technology: Architecture for a Knowledge-Driven Platform

Having identified the knowledge-driven platform as our strategic direction, we committed to specific open standards: openEHR for clinical data modelling (enabling two-level modelling that separates reference models from clinical archetypes), HL7 FHIR for data exchange, and SNOMED CT and other vocabularies for clinical terminology [10]. The main idea around these choices is to directly address the semantic incoherence problem. When every organisation stores data using the same clinical models, innovations built in one context can read and process data from any other.

The architecture is organised in three layers. The data layer includes the central clinical data repository built on openEHR standards, an FHIR-based terminology server, a demographics server, and additional structured data sources. The services and orchestration layer comprises microservices and micro frontends that support application development, with a process engine that orchestrates system-wide workflows and enables the modelling and reuse of clinical pathways. The third layer is the marketplace, which encompasses governance tools, development environments (sandboxes, testing frameworks, synthetic data generators), and validation services.

This marketplace layer is essential for opening the platform to the ecosystem. The use of a platform entails the emergence of a "platform economy" whereby small and large vendors can build components according to published specifications and offer them into a common market [8]. This differs fundamentally from the mega-suite approach to health IT, which effectively locks other vendors out of provision. A vibrant marketplace of interoperable applications and services emerges, allowing competition based on functionality and user experience rather than proprietary data access. This environment enables smaller innovators to compete alongside established vendors, and healthcare organisations can confidently select best-of-breed solutions knowing they will work seamlessly within the broader ecosystem.

The conformance model makes this possible. Platform specifications serve as conformance points for procurement purposes. The interfaces, information models, and knowledge definitions that define platform components are known to the customer organisation and used as requirements to which vendors must comply. This puts the customer and user community in the driving seat operationally and financially. A platform specification can be used to purchase component implementations incrementally rather than in a big-bang fashion; to establish component-level formal conformance within tender documents; to escape vendor lock-in, since any offering that conforms to a particular API and information model could be provided by more than one vendor; and to enable data ownership by the provider and citizens, not product vendors [11].

This transition establishes a "mixed development economy" where new modes of development coexist with legacy approaches [8]. Platform-based development will not instantly replace current systems. Instead, critical data (medications, allergies, health problems) are synchronised across systems during transition, new clinical capabilities are implemented exclusively on the platform, and existing systems are gradually migrated or replaced as they reach technological obsolescence [10].

This approach allows providers to focus their resources on clinical innovation rather than infrastructure maintenance. It creates the conditions where good applications can spread.

The Guiding Principles: Equity by Design

Numbers and architectures matter, but the roadmap ultimately serves people. To ensure the strategy reflected the needs of those it would affect, we conducted one of the largest participatory human-centred design processes documented in healthcare information systems. The process involved 265 participants representing citizens and informal caregivers, healthcare professionals, healthcare managers and leaders, and experts in digital health innovation. Through twenty-four sessions across Catalan geography and seven topic-specific expert sessions, we used design thinking methodologies and cocreation tools to develop a collective vision for Catalonia's future healthcare model [12]. This was not consultation as an afterthought. It was participation as a deliberate strategy to build the buy-in necessary for system-wide transformation. When stakeholders help create the principles that guide implementation, they become invested in the outcome.

Participants identified critical barriers to digital health equity, including digital literacy gaps, fragmented information systems, and insufficient consideration of vulnerable populations' needs. The cocreation process yielded ten fundamental principles published in a dedicated whitepaper [13]:

1. **The person and their care circle at the centre**: Holistic patient journeys, family inclusion, clinical-life data integration, coordinated logistics, user-friendly interfaces.
2. **Health for everyone, everywhere**: Universal digital access, digital skills adaptation, disability-language inclusion, plain language use, multi-channel availability.
3. **Tools for more compassionate care**: Empathetic, accessible communication, comprehensive contextual view, administrative task automation, enhanced human care.
4. **A better professional experience**: Quick visual access, simplified cross-device registration, integrated decision tools, adaptable coordinated workstations, and cross-sector data sharing.
5. **An active role of the population**: Personal data control, visual health tools, self-monitoring cocreation, community resource access, innovation participation.
6. **Personalised and proactive care**: Individualised care tailoring, contextual risk detection, experience-based adjustment, automated personalised communications.
7. **Systematic use of data for decision-making**: Population needs identification, data-driven decisions, behavioural prevention guidance, intervention evaluation, and equitable resource management.

8. **Integrated quality data working for health**: Strategic data alignment, cross-level accessibility, real-time open sharing, holistic data inclusion, standardised data management.
9. **An information system that builds trust**: Authorised data use, confidentiality protection, clinical data management, data accuracy verification, and role-based access.
10. **Collaboration as a driver of innovation**: Shared governance innovation, rapid tech scaling, internal entrepreneurship, and co-created solutions.

These principles ensure that digital transformation serves equity goals. When evaluating implementation sequence, deployment priorities, and feature development, we ask: "Does this reduce or widen the gap between best-served and worst-served populations?" This question doesn't answer itself, but asking it consistently changes decisions.

Vision for the Future and Repeatability

By establishing this framework, we have created the conditions for systematic innovation deployment. An AI model developed at one hospital can be deployed across the ecosystem through configuration, not reconstruction. A patient engagement tool that improves medication adherence can become available system-wide within months, not years. Researchers can query a single standardised repository rather than negotiate with thirty separate organisations. And when citizens move between territories, their care continues seamlessly.

If you are dealing with similar fragmentation, our approach may help. Focus on scaling rather than standardising, since organisations are more open to infrastructure that supports their work than to losing autonomy. Build governance before technology, so stakeholders trust the process and are more likely to adopt the results. Involve them in decisions from the beginning. Set the technology direction early and choose open standards that allow systems to work together without forcing specific applications. Most importantly, base everything on principles created with the people who will use and be affected by these systems, making equity a core part of the design.

Conclusion: From Scattered Brilliance to Shared Capability

Catalonia doesn't lack innovation. What we lacked was infrastructure to transform scattered brilliance and efforts into shared capability. The framework we have built aims to address that gap by centralising the foundations (standards, infrastructure, governance) while keeping innovation decentralised. Providers retain autonomy over their applications and local developments but build on common ground that makes their innovations portable, scalable, and equitable.

The HIMSS Innovation Pathway emphasises creating roadmaps because innovation without direction dissipates. In complex, fragmented ecosystems like ours, roadmaps serve a specific function: they coordinate independent actors toward shared benefit without suppressing the diversity that generates creativity.

We have established the strategy, built the governance, defined the technology architecture, and cocreated the principles that will guide implementation. The foundation is now set. The roadmap lives. That's the innovation: not controlling what gets built but enabling what gets built to be transferred into real life settings.

References

1. Biocat. (2024). *2024 BioRegion Report* [Internet]. https://www.biocat.cat/sites/default/files/content/file/2025/02/21/4/2024_catalonia_bioregion_report_0.pdf. Consulta 15 gen 2026
2. Pérez Sust, P., Solans, O., Fajardo, J. C. et al. (2020). Turning the crisis into an opportunity: Digital health strategies deployed during the COVID-19 outbreak. *JMIR Public Health and Surveillance*, 6, e19106. https://doi.org/10.2196/19106
3. Saigí-Rubió, F., Vidal-Alaball, J., Torrent-Sellens, J. et al. (2021). Determinants of catalan public primary care professionals' intention to use digital clinical consultations (eConsulta) in the post-COVID-19 context: Mixed methods study. *Journal of Medical Internet Research*, 23, e28944. https://doi.org/10.2196/28944
4. Solans, O., Vidal-Alaball, J., Roig Cabo, P. et al. (2021). Characteristics of citizens and their use of teleconsultations in primary care in the catalan public health system before and during the COVID-19 pandemic: Retrospective descriptive cross-sectional study. *Journal of Medical Internet Research*, 23, e28629. https://doi.org/10.2196/28629
5. Piera-Jiménez, J., Carot-Sans, G., Ramiro-Pareta, M. et al. (2024). A 25-year retrospective of health IT infrastructure building: The example of the Catalonia region. *Journal of Medical Internet Research*, 26, e58933. https://doi.org/10.2196/58933
6. Direcció General de Planifcació en Salut. (2021). *Pla de salut de Catalunya 2021-2025* [Internet]. [citat 19 de abril de 2025]. https://scientiasalut.gencat.cat/handle/11351/7948. Consulta 19 abr 2025
7. Ward, J., & Peppard, J. (2011). *Strategic Planning for Information Systems, 3rd Edn.*, repr. Chichester; Weinheim: Wiley.
8. Beale, T., & Hovenga, E. (2022). The knowledge-driven platform: Strategic technologies for a platform ecosystem approach. In: *Roadmap to Successful Digital Health Ecosystems* [Internet]. Elsevier [citat 19 de abril de 2025]. p. 115–141. https://doi.org/10.1016/B978-0-12-823413-6.00006-9
9. Apperta Foundation. (2017). *Defining an Open Platform* [Internet]. [citat 18 de abril de 2025]. https://apperta.org/assets/Apperta_Defining_an_Open_Platform.pdf. Consulta 18 abr 2025
10. Piera-Jiménez, J., & Carot-Sans, G. (2025). Catalonia's journey to the open platform paradigm in healthcare. En: Scheuer, A., & Studzinski, J., editors. *Digital Maturity in Hospitals* [Internet]. Cham: Springer Nature Switzerland [citat 17 de abril de 2025]. p. 111–127. https://doi.org/10.1007/978-3-031-80704-6_8
11. Hammond, W. E., Bent, B., & West, V. L. (2022). Goodbye electronic health record? En: Scott, P., Mantas, J., Benis, A., et al., editors. *Studies in Health Technology and Informatics* [Internet]. IOS Press [citat 10 de desembre de 2025]. https://doi.org/10.3233/SHTI220917
12. Piera-Jiménez, J., Vilarasau Creus, N., Maymó Costa, A. et al. (2025). Co-creating principles for digital health equity: A cross-sectional, qualitative study for participatory human-centred design in Catalonia (Preprint). *Journal of Medical Internet Research* [Internet]. [citat 15 de gener de 2026]; https://doi.org/10.2196/84129
13. *Visió col·lectiva per al futur de la salut: Bases per a un nou model assistencial i de sistemes d'informació.* (2025, juny) [Internet]. https://doi.org/10.62727/DSalut/13197

*****

SPAIN | BUILDING ROADMAPS FOR IMMERSIVE, MULTIMODAL COGNITIVE REHABILITATION ACROSS CLINICAL POPULATIONS | MAITE GAROLERA, NEUS CANO, OLGA GELONCH, YEMILA PLANA, MARTA CASALS-COLL AND PAULA GOMEZ-MANYES

Introduction

I became infected during the first wave of COVID-19, at a moment when uncertainty shaped both clinical practice and daily life. Among the many unanswered questions of that period, one emerged as critical from a neuropsychological perspective. Could the virus affect the brain, and if so, would its effects be limited to the acute phase or continue over time? As early cases accumulated, reports of diminished sense of smell, cognitive fog and difficulty concentrating suggested that SARS-CoV-2 might affect the nervous system.

As the lead of the Brain, Cognition and Behavior Research Group (C3-CST) and head of the Neuropsychology Unit at the Consorci Sanitari de Terrassa, I approached these emerging cases with both a research and clinical perspective, which helped shape the early questions that guided our work.

Within C3-CST (https://www.neuropsicologiacst.cat), this initial concern soon became a structured line of inquiry. Our dual role as a research group and the clinical team responsible for neuropsychological assessment allowed us to observe these patterns directly and begin to shape a roadmap linking patient experience with systematic evidence.

Setting the Context

As the pandemic progressed, persistent symptoms became increasingly common among individuals who had recovered from the initial infection. Across ages, professions and levels of acute severity, people described experiences that interfered with everyday functioning. Fatigue emerged as one of the most consistent complaints. Many reported shortness of breath after minimal physical effort, while others described physical and mental exhaustion that limited their capacity to manage routine tasks and responsibilities.

Cognitive and emotional symptoms also became increasingly prominent. Individuals with no prior neurological or psychiatric history noticed memory lapses, difficulties sustaining attention, slower thinking and challenges in planning or organizing daily activities. Some found it harder to follow conversations or multitask as easily as before, while others experienced heightened anxiety or reduced tolerance to stress. These patterns appeared repeatedly across diverse groups and could not be explained by prolonged rest or emotional distress alone. Together, they pointed toward a broader and persistent condition affecting cognitive, emotional, and functional domains after COVID-19 that required systematic scientific examination.

These clinical presentations led our C3-CST research group to initiate and coordinate the NAUTILUS project (https://project-nautilus.github.io/), one of the earliest large-scale studies focused on the cognitive impact of post-COVID condition (PCC). NAUTILUS enrolled more than 600 participants across nineteen health institutions in Catalonia, Madrid, the Canary Islands and Andorra. Using a standardized neuropsychological assessment, the project examined attention, memory, processing speed, executive function, emotional state, functional capacity and quality of life using a unified methodology.

The NAUTILUS multicenter study provided a detailed and empirically grounded characterization of PCC. One of its clearest outcomes was that cognitive impairment stood at the core of the condition. Many individuals experienced difficulties in processing speed, executive functioning, memory and global cognition months after the acute infection. These difficulties appeared both in people who had gone through a severe acute phase requiring hospitalization and in those whose initial illness had been mild and managed at home (Ariza et al., 2022; doi: https://doi.org/10.3389/fnagi.2022.1029842; Ariza et al., 2023; https://doi.org/10.1007/s00415-023-11587-4).

The findings also revealed a marked impact on quality of life. Compared with people who had not experienced COVID-19, individuals with PCC reported lower physical and psychological well-being, more limitations in daily routines and a reduced ability to participate in social and community life. This pattern was consistent across both severe and mild cases. Remarkably, those with mild PCC often had among the lowest well-being levels, suggesting that persistent difficulties could not be explained solely by the severity of the acute infection (Ariza et al., 2023; doi: https://doi.org/10.1002/acn3.51952).

The NAUTILUS project also revealed important functional and occupational consequences. Many people with PCC experienced changes in their employment status, and those working in cognitively demanding roles often found it harder to maintain their previous pace and performance. Some needed to adapt their responsibilities or reduce their workload, reflecting the impact that persistent cognitive and emotional symptoms had on their day-to-day functioning (Ariza et al., 2024; doi: https://doi.org/10.1007/s00406-023-01748-x).

Taken together, these findings show a clear progression from early clinical observations to a precise scientific characterization of PCC. The initial reports of fatigue, cognitive difficulties, emotional distress, sleep disruption and functional limitations are systematically confirmed and quantified in the NAUTILUS multicenter study. The evidence converges on a coherent conclusion: PCC is a multifaceted condition in which persistent cognitive deficits interact with emotional and sleep disturbances, leading to significant impairments in daily, social and occupational functioning. This integrated understanding underscores the need for an intervention capable of addressing these cognitive, emotional and functional challenges in a coordinated and accessible way.

Define Your Innovation

Building on the understanding developed through NAUTILUS, C3-CST led the development of RehabCOVID (https://www.neuropsicologiacst.cat/rehabcovid/), a multimodal, immersive intervention model created within our research group and enriched by collaboration with patients who contributed their lived experiences and with the technical team responsible for the immersive platform. The model was refined to align with established principles of neuropsychology and contemporary cognitive rehabilitation while remaining closely connected to real clinical needs and user-reported challenges. This coordinated, multidisciplinary process enabled the team to translate scientific evidence into a coherent, clinically meaningful approach to address the complexity of post-COVID conditions.

RehabCOVID was created with a clear purpose: to offer a coordinated response to the cognitive, emotional and functional challenges observed in PCC, drawing on principles that support brain plasticity. Each session weaves together three complementary components that prepare the mind, train key cognitive skills and strengthen functional capacity. Mindfulness-based practices help regulate emotional and physiological activation, supporting clarity of thinking and cognitive engagement. Cognitive training exercises strengthen functions such as attention, memory, processing speed and executive skills. Functional physical activation promotes body awareness, balance and graded effort and is known to benefit cognitive functioning by supporting regulation, energy management and overall brain health. Together, these elements create the conditions needed to support recovery and the reorganization of abilities affected by PCC.

A defining feature of RehabCOVID is its use of immersive environmental technology developed by BroomX Technologies. By employing the MK360 system (https://broomx.com), participants are surrounded by naturalistic, dynamic scenes that create a panoramic, engaging environment. This immersive approach produces a strong sense of presence without the need for head-mounted displays, ensuring that the experience remains comfortable and inclusive for individuals with PCC. The immersive setting helps sustain attention, promotes emotional calm and increases engagement throughout the session. Up to five people take part in each session, enabling a group format that encourages peer support and improves adherence.

The program places a strong emphasis on connecting rehabilitation activities with everyday life. The scenes used for cognitive exercises recreate daily situations such as walking through city streets, entering a market or carrying out routine tasks like preparing a meal. Practicing cognitive strategies within these realistic contexts supports generalization, making it easier for participants to apply what they learn during the sessions to real-life situations. For the mindfulness and physical activation components, immersive scenes of natural environments, such as beaches, forests or open fields, are used. These blue and green spaces offer a calm and restorative atmosphere that supports emotional balance, concentration and body awareness. In this immersive setting, mindfulness focuses on breathing, sensory grounding and present-moment awareness, while physical activation involves gentle, functional movements that promote balance; body awareness; and safe, graded effort. This integrated approach strengthens the connection between emotional regulation, physical engagement and cognitive practice, helping the skills developed during the sessions transfer naturally into daily functioning.

RehabCOVID offers an intervention model that reflects the complexity of post-COVID conditions and the need for accessible, engaging and evidence-based rehabilitation. It connects scientific understanding with practical strategies for recovery.

Case Study

RehabCOVID sessions were delivered in a structured, one-hour format that integrated mindfulness, cognitive training and functional physical activation within the immersive environment. Each session began with a brief grounding exercise that helped participants settle into the present moment and regulate emotional activation. This was followed by the cognitive component, in which participants practiced attention, memory, processing speed and flexibility while interacting with everyday immersive scenes. The final part of the session involved gentle functional movements that supported body awareness and gradual effort. Each session concluded with a short reflection to consolidate learning and reinforce the sense of progress.

Over eight weeks, people with PCC engaged in this immersive multimodal group-based intervention. The shared virtual environment contributed to a motivating and supportive atmosphere that encouraged participation and continuity. By the end of the program, neuropsychological assessments showed clear improvements: global cognition, attention, processing speed, episodic memory and executive function had increased, and depressive symptoms had decreased (Cano et al., 2024; doi:https://doi.org/10.3389/fpsyg.2024.1441018).

Alongside these objective changes, participants rated the experience very positively. Session after session, they reported high levels of enjoyment and a strong sense of improvement, and these positive evaluations remained stable from the first to the last session. Fatigue was recorded after every session, allowing researchers to track how this central symptom of PCC evolved throughout the intervention and confirming that the pace of the program was manageable for participants (Cano et al., 2024, https://doi.org/10.3389/fpsyg.2024.1441018).

To better understand how the body responded to this type of training, heart-rate variability was also monitored during the intervention. At the beginning, some physiological indicators shifted, suggesting an initial response to the effort and novelty of the sessions. As participants became more familiar with the immersive environment and the weekly routine, these values returned to levels like those observed at the start of the program. This pattern offered useful insight: rather than generating sustained physiological stress, the program appeared to trigger an early adjustment that later stabilized as people adapted to the demands of the sessions (Cano et al., 2025; doi: https://doi.org/10.3390/app15084111).

Taken together, all these findings, the cognitive and emotional improvements, the positive subjective experience, and the gradual physiological adjustment, pointed in the same direction. The RehabCOVID program was stimulating but manageable, well-accepted by participants and capable of producing both objective benefits and meaningful changes in how individuals with PCC experienced their own progress over time.

Barriers and Lessons Learned

The deployment of the immersive multimodal program revealed several barriers that were especially relevant from a technological and operational perspective.

The first challenge was the strong day-to-day variability of PCC symptoms. Participants' cognitive, emotional and physical states shifted considerably, influencing their capacity to interact with the environment and the pace at which they could progress through each session. This required ongoing monitoring and dynamic adaptation of task demands, without losing the structural clarity needed to maintain orientation in the immersive space.

Fatigue was another key factor that directly affected cognitive load. On lower-energy days, participants found it more difficult to sustain attention or engage with complex tasks. A consistent session structure proved essential here: predictable sequencing reduced the mental effort needed to navigate the environment and made real-time adjustments smoother and less disruptive.

A more technology-specific barrier was the design and selection of immersive environments. Creating scenes that were realistic enough to feel meaningful yet not so visually dense as to cause overload required careful tuning. Some users were more sensitive to environmental richness, necessitating simplifying visual elements or adjusting pacing. At the same time, working with familiar everyday settings became one of the program's strengths, as it supported the transfer of trained skills to real-world situations and increased the ecological validity of the experience.

Accessibility and interaction design also played an important role. Using projection-based immersion without wearable devices reduced physical discomfort and simplified the user interface, enabling participants to stay focused on the content. The group-based format added another operational advantage by fostering motivation, continuity and a sense of shared progress.

Taken together, these barriers highlighted the need to balance structural clarity with adaptive flexibility. Aligning session flow, environment design, cognitive demands and user comfort was essential to ensure feasibility and stability while respecting the fluctuating nature of PCC.

Human Aspect

Although the objective data provided valuable evidence, the participants' voices offered the clearest expression of the program's impact. Many described RehabCOVID as a meaningful turning point in their recovery. They often noted that setting aside one hour per session, twice a week, for focused engagement helped restore a sense of mental clarity and calm. The immersive environment created a unique balance of cognitive challenge and emotional regulation, and the mindfulness components helped many reduce anxiety and reconnect with a sense of internal stability.

Several participants reported improvements in their ability to follow conversations, organize daily tasks and manage cognitive load. Others highlighted the usefulness of the strategies they practiced during the program. Techniques for managing attention, regulating cognitive effort and sustaining presence became part of their everyday routines. Many noted that they finished sessions feeling more centered and grounded. The combination of noticeable improvements and practical tools, allowing them not only to feel better but also to understand how to maintain that progress, was often described as one of the most meaningful aspects of the experience.

Vision for the Future and Repeatability

The evolution of RehabCOVID is ongoing and informed by both clinical experience and scientific evidence. C3-CST is currently analyzing data comparing the immersive intervention with an online version developed by our research group. This analysis aims to clarify the specific contributions of the immersive environment relative to a digital format. In parallel, we are studying neuroimaging data, markers of brain plasticity, and eye-tracking measures to explore the mechanisms underlying the improvements observed during the intervention.

A priority for the next phase is to validate the RehabCOVID program in a larger, multicenter and potentially multinational study to strengthen generalizability across different healthcare contexts and ensure that the approach can be confidently extended beyond the initial setting.

A significant milestone has been the integration of RehabCOVID into primary health care centers within our public health institution. The program is now used in routine clinical pathways for individuals with persistent cognitive symptoms after COVID-19. This demonstrates its feasibility and value outside of a research context and confirms that the model can be implemented in everyday clinical practice.

Although the model originated as a response to the specific challenges of PCC, the process of defining cognitive symptoms, establishing functional impact criteria and creating a structured pathway for intervention revealed a broader principle: RehabCOVID is, in essence, a model for managing cognitive vulnerability. The same indicators, communication structures, and functional goals that proved effective for PCC naturally extend to other conditions in which cognitive symptoms affect daily functioning.

Based on the experience gained through RehabCOVID, the model has been adapted for other populations with cognitive vulnerabilities. Several programs have been developed by C3-CST in collaboration with partner institutions. OncoBRAIN is designed for individuals experiencing cognitive difficulties related to cancer. VirtualMETS supports those with metabolic syndrome and cognitive challenges. VirtualDONA focuses on older women in vulnerable situations. REVIVE is an adaptation for individuals with mild cognitive impairment or early dementia. Each program maintains the core structure of RehabCOVID while adjusting the content and intensity to fit the specific characteristics of each population.

RehabCOVID's modular structure and flexible delivery formats enhance its scalability and adaptability. The model offers a foundation for integrating new technologies, supporting additional clinical populations, and developing personalized rehabilitation pathways. Its evolution reflects a commitment to evidence-based, patient-centered innovation.

Tie-Back to Create Roadmaps

The evolution of RehabCOVID shows how a well-structured roadmap can guide an innovation from early clinical uncertainty to a scalable and evidence-based immersive solution. The process began with frontline observations of persistent cognitive, emotional and functional symptoms after COVID-19, which were later characterized through the NAUTILUS multicenter study. This evidence provided a clear problem definition and clarified the functional components required for an effective response.

Each part of the program was developed using a sequential, evidence-informed logic. The immersive design, the structure of the sessions, the ecological environments and the focus on cognitive and emotional self-management all reflected needs identified through research. Pilot implementation generated objective outcomes and user feedback that supported iterative refinement, allowing adjustments in pacing, task complexity and usability based on participants' fluctuating symptoms.

This trajectory aligns with the HIMSS Create Roadmaps process, providing a clear structure that supported the transition from initial observation to implementation and scale.

A key milestone was the integration of RehabCOVID into routine primary care. Applying the model within real-world care pathways demonstrated that an innovation born from research and immersive design could be operationalized sustainably in frontline practice.

Beyond validating the program for PCC, the roadmap enabled its evolution into a broader intervention model applicable to other forms of cognitive vulnerability. The structured indicators, shared communication framework and modular session architecture created a transferable foundation that has already been adapted for other clinical populations. The same core principles, ecological immersive stimulation, structured progression, adaptive pacing and group-based delivery, have been applied to individuals living with cancer-related cognitive impairment, people with metabolic conditions affecting cognition and emotion, older women in vulnerable circumstances and individuals with mild cognitive impairment or early-stage neurodegenerative conditions.

For each population, a rigorous adaptation methodology has been followed. This process begins with identifying specific cognitive, emotional and functional needs and includes direct participation of representative users to ensure ecological relevance. It continues with the adaptation of the intervention framework; the selection or creation of tailored cognitive, physical and emotional regulation exercises; and expert validation of content. The corresponding clinical trials, currently underway, are assessing feasibility, usability and preliminary efficacy according to established research standards. This systematic approach ensures that each adaptation maintains the scientific rigor, functional objectives and immersive logic established in RehabCOVID.

In this sense, RehabCOVID has progressed from a targeted intervention to a reproducible and scalable model of immersive, multimodal cognitive rehabilitation. The roadmap enabled innovation to advance reliably from initial insight to clinical efficacy, from efficacy to integration in primary care pathways and from a single clinical target to meaningful scale across diverse patient populations.

*****

KOSOVO | BUILDING KNOWLEDGE-DRIVEN INNOVATION IN NURSING AND ALLIED HEALTH EDUCATION IN KOSOVO | BESARTA TAGANOVIQ

Healthcare innovation is often described through the lens of advanced technologies, mature systems, and substantial financial investment. My experience in Kosovo has taught me a different lesson. In environments shaped by post-war recovery, limited resources, and evolving institutional standards, innovation cannot rely on isolated pilots or individual enthusiasm. It must be intentional, structured, and embedded in how institutions function. Innovation, in such contexts, is less about introducing what is new and more about ensuring that change can take root, survive, and grow within fragile systems.

Working at the intersection of nursing education, healthcare management, and institutional reform in Kosovo, I have learned that sustainable innovation emerges not from tools alone but from aligning knowledge, people, and governance around a shared long-term direction. This alignment is particularly critical in systems where education and health reforms are still consolidating in parallel, and where institutional memory is short due to frequent restructuring, donor cycles, and leadership changes. Without such alignment, even well-designed initiatives risk remaining temporary solutions rather than becoming part of everyday practice. Kosovo represents a distinctive innovation environment. As a young country emerging from war, its healthcare and higher education systems were built under conditions of urgency and scarcity, requiring simultaneous system building and service delivery. Unlike mature systems that can refine established structures, Kosovo has had to develop foundational standards while responding to immediate population needs. At the same time, Kosovo has one of the youngest populations in Europe, creating both opportunity and responsibility. A large share of the population is entering the workforce, placing pressure on higher education to provide future-oriented competencies, while health services must simultaneously adapt to long-term demographic needs. These pressures are further amplified by strong diaspora dynamics. Seasonal return of diaspora communities increases demand on already stretched health services, while exposure to healthcare systems abroad raises expectations for care quality, accessibility, and digital responsiveness. Innovation is therefore not optional; it is a survival strategy. It becomes the means through which institutions attempt to bridge the gap between rising expectations and constrained resources.

These challenges, however, are unevenly distributed. Urban–rural and regional imbalances continue to shape access to healthcare services, specialized professionals, and digital infrastructure. Municipalities outside the capital face more pronounced capacity gaps, fewer specialized services, and limited opportunities for professional development. This uneven landscape reinforces the need for approaches that can adapt to local realities while maintaining national coherence.

In this context, private higher education institutions and private healthcare providers play an increasingly important system-building role. While public institutions remain the backbone of regulation and service delivery. Private HEIs offer agility in curriculum development, interdisciplinary experimentation, and piloting innovative educational models, particularly in emerging fields where public capacity is constrained. Similarly, private hospitals complement the public system by expanding service availability, introducing specialized care, and serving as important practice-based learning environments. Together, public and private actors form a hybrid ecosystem in which innovation can be tested, refined, and scaled.

Despite this potential, innovation in Kosovo has often taken the form of short-term, donor-funded initiatives that struggle to endure once external funding ends. The missing element has rarely been motivation or creativity but institutional continuity. In post-war contexts such as Kosovo, innovation also carries a dimension of trust and legitimacy. Past experiences with short-lived reforms have made stakeholders cautious, underscoring the importance of transparent, predictable, and institutionally anchored approaches that rebuild confidence over time. Alongside implementation, research is conducted on a day-to-day basis, allowing institutions to continuously reflect on practice, generate evidence from real settings, and adjust innovation efforts in real time rather than retrospectively. In response to these realities, innovation was reframed not as experimentation but as capability building. This meant strengthening how knowledge is identified, shared, and applied; investing in human capacity and leadership; introducing digital solutions only where institutional and pedagogical readiness existed; and embedding outcomes into governance and quality assurance structures. Evidence from healthcare organizations in Kosovo and other transition economies shows that digital innovation is effective only when supported by human, cognitive, cultural, and organizational readiness. In contrast, the uncritical integration of legacy technologies can undermine progress and reduce organizational readiness for change (Taganoviq et al., 2022).

A concrete illustration of this approach is the introduction of innovative study programs that had not previously existed in Kosovo. Through Heimerer College, speech therapy and occupational therapy were established as formal academic programs, addressing long-standing gaps in rehabilitative and developmental care. These professions had previously been largely absent from the system, despite clear population needs among children, older adults, and persons with disabilities. Their introduction required not only curriculum development but also alignment with health institutions, regulatory bodies, and clinical environments unfamiliar with these roles. Advanced nursing practice at the master's level represented another critical shift. Nursing education in Kosovo had traditionally been framed through a task-oriented lens. By embedding advanced clinical reasoning, leadership, research literacy, and evidence-based practice into graduate education, nurses were repositioned as autonomous professionals and contributors to system-level innovation. Digital health was introduced as a dedicated master's program—the first of its kind in the region—integrating technology with ethics, governance, data literacy, and clinical workflows rather than treating digitalization as an end in itself. These academic developments were complemented by participation in Erasmus+ Capacity Building in Higher Education projects, which enabled structured multidisciplinary collaboration across nursing, speech therapy, occupational therapy, healthcare management, and digital health. Student-led health services emerged as a particularly impactful outcome, allowing students to address real community needs within supervised, quality-assured environments. These services were not simulations; they operated within institutional governance structures and contributed directly to service delivery.

The "Coffee & Care" initiative illustrates this approach. In a country where formal geriatric services remain limited, Coffee & Care provided daily low-threshold support, social engagement, and basic health monitoring for older adults. At the same time, it functioned as a multidisciplinary learning environment integrating nursing, speech therapy, occupational therapy, and psychosocial care. Its innovation lay not in complexity but in cultural sensitivity, feasibility, and alignment with educational objectives. Building on these experiences, the Future Care Lab was established as an advanced learning environment exploring how robotics and intelligent systems can support basic care services while transforming teaching practices. Rather than replacing human care, the lab enables students and educators to explore human–technology collaboration, ethical considerations, and workload optimization in a controlled, reflective setting. It also serves as a bridge between education, research, and practice, reinforcing innovation as an ongoing process rather than a one-time intervention.

In Kosovo, innovation does not struggle because ideas are scarce but because systems and people are often expected to change faster than conditions allow.

Technology-first approaches remain fragile without human and governance readiness, and donor-driven timelines risk undermining sustainability. Addressing these challenges requires approaches that are predictable, shared, and grounded in people's everyday work. When educators, healthcare professionals, and managers understand the direction of change, resistance decreases and ownership increases. At the heart of this transformation are people. Healthcare professionals in Kosovo operate in environments that demand constant adaptation and problem-solving. Educators have increasingly become facilitators of reflective practice rather than transmitters of static knowledge, while managers have shifted from administrative oversight toward enabling professional capability. Innovation gained traction when it was recognized not as an additional burden but as a pathway to professional legitimacy and system improvement.

While rooted in Kosovo, these lessons are transferable. Many European systems face workforce shortages, aging populations, fragmented services, and growing digital pressure. Navigating these challenges sustainably requires aligning innovation with people, practice, and institutional realities. In Kosovo, innovation became meaningful only when it was guided with care, informed by daily practice, and allowed to mature over time. Ultimately, the most powerful innovation was not a new program or technology but the collective decision to move forward together—learning, adapting, and building systems that can endure.

References

Ariza, M., et al. (2022). Cognitive impairment in post-COVID condition: Results from the NAUTILUS multicenter study. *Frontiers in Aging Neuroscience*, *14*, 1029842. https://doi.org/10.3389/fnagi.2022.1029842.

Ariza, M., et al. (2023). Neurocognitive and functional outcomes in post-COVID condition: Findings from the NAUTILUS study. *Journal of Neurology*. https://doi.org/10.1007/s00415-023-11587-4.

Ariza, M., et al. (2024). Occupational and functional consequences of post-COVID condition: Results from the NAUTILUS multicenter cohort. *European Archives of Psychiatry and Clinical Neuroscience*.

Cano, M., Ariza, M., et al. (2024). Immersive virtual reality–based cognitive rehabilitation for people with post-COVID condition: Results from a multimodal group intervention. *Frontiers in Psychology*, *15*, 1441018. https://doi.org/10.3389/fpsyg.2024.1441018.

Cano, M., Ariza, M., et al. (2025). Heart rate variability responses during immersive virtual reality cognitive rehabilitation in people with post-COVID condition. *Applied Sciences*, *15*(8), 4111. https://doi.org/10.3390/app15084111.

Taganoviq, M., Spahic, L., & Kurti, A. (2022). Digital transformation and organizational readiness in healthcare systems of transition economies: Lessons from the Western Balkans. *International Journal of Medical Informatics*, *162*, 104738. https://doi.org/10.1016/j.ijmedinf.2022.104738.

Chapter 4

Collaborate and Listen

Listen for ideas that will potentially solve a problem or present an opportunity to collaborate with stakeholders and galvanize your network.

Many innovations started by listening, observing, and then communicating ideas and solutions to problems. When you listen, people are more likely to share ideas and provide encouragement. The more you engage others, the more ideas you are likely to catch. Great innovations are typically a result of multiple iterations by numerous individuals invited to participate in ideation and execution. Inviting others to share in your innovation will galvanize support and engagement necessary for success.

One is too small a number for innovation. Innovation is largely a result of a team of teams' approach to solving a problem or exploiting an opportunity. It can be an ego challenge to have a great innovation and allow others to modify and edit your dream. We can take innovation too personally and become captive to the potential and miss out on something greater. Leveraging others actually frees the innovation to grow and expand beyond what you initially envisioned. There is strength in seeking the wisdom of others.

CROATIA | HOW TO BUILD HEALTH INNOVATION WHEN NO SYSTEM EXISTS TO SUPPORT IT | MAJA MIMICA

Innovation Without a System

The first hospital pilot we ever tried to launch did not fail because of technology. It failed because no one knew who was responsible. The solution worked. The startup team was motivated. The clinicians were curious. Yet after six months, the project quietly disappeared, not with conflict or formal rejection but with silence. Emails went unanswered. Meetings were postponed. The IT department changed priorities. The clinical champion was reassigned to another ward. There was no formal "no," only institutional entropy.

DOI: 10.4324/9781003780175-4

This experience was not an exception. It was the rule. In Croatia, health innovation rarely collapses because ideas are weak. It collapses because there is no system designed to carry ideas from intention to implementation. This chapter shares how NetHub, a private non-profit health innovation hub and business accelerator, learned to operate in that reality by placing collaboration and listening at the center of everything we do.

Fragmentation as the Default State

Croatia's healthcare system is universal, centralized on paper, and fragmented in practice. Hospitals are publicly owned and chronically underfunded. Clinicians are overworked. Digital infrastructure varies dramatically between institutions. Procurement processes are slow and risk-averse. Research, clinical practice, and entrepreneurship operate in parallel worlds that rarely intersect. Beyond structural challenges, there is a deeper social layer.

Science and technology are culturally separated from business. Universities focus on publications. Hospitals focus on care delivery. Entrepreneurs are often viewed with suspicion—an echo of the 1990s privatization period, when corruption and opaque ownership structures shaped public perception. To this day, "entrepreneur" is frequently associated with exploitation rather than value creation. Patenting activity is low. Technology transfer offices exist but are understaffed and underpowered. Public funding for applied research is inconsistent and bureaucratic. Private investment in health innovation remains minimal, as much of the private sector prioritizes tourism as the fastest route to profit growth. Trust between public and private sectors is fragile.

In such an environment, healthcare innovation does not fail because people lack talent. It fails because no one owns the space between institutions.

NetHub as an Ecosystem Connector

NetHub did not begin as a business accelerator. It emerged organically from publicly funded healthcare and research and innovation projects, where different organizations were required to collaborate but had no practical mechanism to do so effectively. What began as project coordination gradually evolved into something more structural: an informal bridge between silos. Today, NetHub operates as a private non-profit organization dedicated to health innovation and ecosystem building. Its credibility was not built through capital but through continuity.

Key milestones include:

- A strong institutional partnership with the University of Split School of Medicine and University Hospital of Split, which became foundational assets—not only as research and development collaborators but as a cultural translator between clinicians, researchers, and innovators.
- Implementation of multiple pre-acceleration programs focused on early-stage healthtech innovation.
- Continuous connection of clinicians, researchers, technology experts, students, policymakers, and patients into mixed, cross-functional teams.
- Direct involvement in the development of more than twenty health innovations, ranging from digital health tools and medical devices to pharma products.

- Organization and co-creation of the Health Tech Adria Conference, now a regional platform connecting researchers, startups, investors, healthcare professionals, policymakers, and other opinion leaders in Southeast Europe and beyond.
- Active collaboration with other health innovation hubs across Southeast Europe.

None of this was achieved through a traditional top-down innovation model. It required something simpler, slower, and more fragile: listening.

Collaboration as an Operating System

In mature ecosystems, collaboration is supported by structure. In Croatia, structure is what collaboration must replace. Early on, NetHub discovered three uncomfortable truths:

1. Stakeholders rarely articulate their real constraints in formal meetings, often due to skepticism shaped by past failed initiatives.
2. Most innovation projects fail before they begin—not technically but socially, driven by fear of the unknown and institutional risk aversion.
3. Trust is the primary currency of innovation, and it cannot be imported.

As a result, our core function became orchestration rather than execution. We learned to operate as:

- translators between clinical language and technical language,
- voices of end-users, most often patients,
- mediators between public institutions and private companies,
- neutral conveners in politically sensitive environments, and
- long-term partners rather than short-term project coordinators.

Our innovation was not a product or a platform. It was the ability to bring the right people into the same room and keep them there long enough to understand each other.

Barriers and Lessons Learned

Lesson 1: Innovation Starts With Listening, Not Pitching

Startups arrive with solutions. Health payers, healthcare providers, and patients live with problems. Most innovation programs invert this order. In Croatia, our methodology grew not from formal design frameworks but from living inside the same system we are trying to improve. We are not external observers entering hospitals with checklists and sticky notes. We sit in corridors because our family members are waiting for test results. We listen to conversations during night shifts because someone we care about is working them. Over coffee in overcrowded staff rooms, we hear not "user feedback" but exhaustion, shortcuts, quiet fears, and small acts of resilience. These everyday exposures shape our understanding far more deeply than structured interviews ever could. Formal needs assessments rarely capture this reality. Clinicians do not ask for "AI tools." They ask for fewer clicks, fewer duplicated forms, fewer phone calls, fewer interruptions during procedures, and more time with their family. By reframing innovation as problem discovery rather than solution promotion, resistance decreased. Stakeholders felt seen rather than targeted. Listening became our first deliverable.

Lesson 2: In Small Systems, Relationships Outweigh Processes

Formal memoranda of understanding matter far less than personal credibility. In fragmented systems, projects move forward not because a contract exists but because someone is willing to answer the phone at 9 p.m. NetHub invested deliberately in human continuity:

- staying present after project funding ended,
- attending clinical meetings even when no immediate opportunity existed,
- supporting researchers with no commercial agenda, and
- inviting policymakers into technical discussions without public pressure.

Over time, this created an informal trust network. When new projects emerged, such as Horizon Europe consortia or regional initiatives, this network functioned as invisible infrastructure. Innovation followed relationships, not the other way around.

Lesson 3: Shared Ownership Is More Important Than Intellectual Property

Many early projects failed because innovation was treated as someone else's responsibility:

- "the startup's product,"
- "the university's research,"
- "the hospital's pilot," or
- "the ministry's strategy."

We gradually shifted toward co-creation models:

- clinicians involved from ideation,
- students embedded in development teams,
- IT experts participating in clinical validation, and
- patients contributing to usability testing.

Ownership became collective. Once ownership became shared, formal intellectual property discussions became easier, not harder.

The Human Dimension

Health innovation in Croatia is not primarily constrained by technology. It is constrained by fatigue. Clinicians working double shifts. Researchers navigating unstable funding cycles, usually overloaded with teaching. Young professionals leaving the country. Patients are learning to expect delays as normal. Against this background, collaboration is emotionally demanding. It requires patience, humility, and the willingness to absorb institutional frustration without becoming cynical.

NetHub's role often extends beyond coordination into quiet emotional labor: reassuring clinicians that their ideas matter, convincing startups that public institutions are not inherently hostile, reminding policymakers that innovation is built by people, not reports. Innovation, in this context, is not a product. It is a behavior, slowly but steadily becoming a new mindset.

Vision for the Future—Repeatability Beyond Croatia

Croatia is not unique. Across the Adriatic region and the Western Balkans, health innovation faces similar conditions:

- limited funding,
- regulatory complexity,
- institutional mistrust,
- risk-averse mindset,
- talent outflow, and
- political instability.

The dominant European innovation narrative: venture capital, rapid scaling, and technological acceleration, does not translate well into these environments.

What does translate:

- ecosystem stewardship,
- trust engineering,
- patient institutional diplomacy, and
- long-term presence.

In regions where infrastructure is weak, collaboration becomes the infrastructure. The model is replicable not as a blueprint but as a mindset: start with listening, invest in relationships, and design innovation around real human constraints.

Wrap-Up

NetHub has not produced unicorns. It has produced something less visible but more durable:

- clinicians who now collaborate with startups,
- researchers who understand regulatory pathways,
- students who see healthcare as a field of innovation rather than bureaucracy,
- policymakers who consult stakeholders before drafting programs, and
- institutions willing to pilot together.

In high-income innovation hubs, technology is the driver. In fragmented healthcare systems, collaboration is the technology. Listening is the interface. Trust is the platform.

NetHub's experience in Croatia suggests that innovation does not begin with funding, policy, or even ideas. It begins when institutions learn to hear each other again. In environments where no formal system exists to support innovation, *collaboration is not a soft skill. It is the system.*

SPAIN | COLLABORATE AND LISTEN—DESIGNING HEALTH SYSTEMS WITH SOCIETY | ANDREA BARBIERO

Healthcare systems have historically been built on a paternalistic model: professionals decided, patients complied, and institutions defined what was considered best. Over time, this model began to fracture. Greater access to information, the emergence of patient advocacy movements, and the growing prevalence of chronic conditions gave way to a more deliberative model, in which patients were informed, consulted, and occasionally involved.

Yet deliberation still preserves an imbalance of power. Voices may be heard, but decisions often remain centralized.

Across different regions of the world, healthcare systems are now transitioning toward a participatory model. This shift is not exclusive to any single geography. However, it has found particularly fertile ground in contexts where health is understood not merely as the absence of disease but as a state of wellbeing—shaped by social, environmental, and relational determinants.

In systems grounded in welfare-state traditions, participation aligns naturally with broader notions of collective responsibility, social cohesion, and shared value. Patients, professionals, caregivers, and citizens are no longer positioned as external stakeholders but as active contributors to how health services are designed, governed, and transformed.

This transition is neither linear nor complete. Paternalistic, deliberative, and participatory logics frequently coexist within the same organizations. Yet the direction of travel is clear. As healthcare systems confront growing complexity, legitimacy and sustainability depend less on authority and more on shared responsibility.

Listening, in this context, is not a courtesy. It is a redistribution of influence. Collaboration is not consensus-building; it is co-ownership. When people experience participation as meaningful—when they see their contributions shaping priorities, decisions, and outcomes—they develop a sense of responsibility for what is being built. This sense of ownership transforms innovation from something that must be implemented into something that is actively sustained.

From Patients to Citizens

The move toward participation reflects a more in-depth transformation in how health is conceived. Patients are no longer seen solely as users of services but as carriers of experiential knowledge. Citizens are not passive beneficiaries of systems; they are co-producers of health outcomes.

This evolution challenges traditional hierarchies of expertise. Clinical, managerial, and technological knowledge remain essential, but they are no longer sufficient on their own. Lived experience—of illness, care, caregiving, and system navigation—adds a form of intelligence that cannot be replicated through data, modeling, or simulation.

Participation acquires meaning only when it influences decisions. When people are invited to speak but not to shape outcomes, participation becomes ritualistic. When their contributions alter priorities, designs, or rules, participation becomes transformative.

Co-Designing a New Home-Based Care Service

The design of a new home-based care service in Parc Tauli Hospital, a public hospital in Catalonia, Spain, illustrates how collaboration reshapes both services and relationships when participation is embedded from the outset.

The service was conceived as a new model of care rather than a reconfiguration of an existing one. From its earliest stages, it incorporated the voices of patients, informal caregivers, healthcare professionals, managers, and digital teams. The objective was not merely to optimize workflows but to understand what truly matters when care moves from hospital walls into private homes.

Patients and caregivers played a central role in identifying critical points of contact, moments of vulnerability, and sources of uncertainty that rarely surface in formal clinical pathways. Their insights highlighted aspects of care that are often underestimated by organizations, such as the need for continuity, clear communication, and recognition of the caregiver's role as part of the care ecosystem.

This participatory process allowed the service to be designed around real-life care dynamics rather than institutional assumptions. Decisions regarding roles, coordination mechanisms, and support structures were shaped by lived experience, ensuring greater alignment between professional practice and everyday realities.

A pilot was implemented with positive results, confirming that integrating patient and caregiver perspectives into service design contributes to greater coherence, usability, and acceptance of new models of care. Beyond outcomes and indicators, the experience demonstrated that when people are involved meaningfully in shaping services, they are more likely to trust, support, and sustain them over time.

Listening as a Form of Governance

Participation also plays a decisive role at the level of system strategy and public policy. Digital transformation initiatives frequently fail when they are designed as technocratic exercises, disconnected from the realities of care delivery and the people who sustain it.

Also in Catalonia, the definition of a collective vision for the future of the health system marked a significant shift in how digital health strategies are conceived and governed. Rather than being developed through closed expert processes, the strategy was shaped through an unprecedented community-based participatory design process, involving more than 3,400 people across the territory.

Patients, caregivers, health and social care professionals, managers, and technology experts participated in a large-scale collective effort to reimagine both the healthcare delivery model and the role of information systems in supporting it. The process combined rigorous design thinking methodologies, twenty-eight participatory workshops across ten health regions, and data collected from more than 3,200 healthcare professionals, ensuring that evidence and lived experience informed decision-making.

The outcome was not merely a strategic document but a shared framework where science, policy, and societal voices converged. The process led to the definition of ten design principles for a person-centered health and social care model, articulating a clear transition from fragmented, episode-based care toward integrated, longitudinal models rooted in communities and well-being.

Digital transformation was framed as an enabler of this shift rather than an end in itself. The roadmap moved away from top-down technology deployment toward open, knowledge-driven platforms, with the ambition of converging toward a single, interoperable system centered on the Catalan Health Record as a shared backbone.

At the national level, a complementary expression of participatory governance can be found in the public consultation process launched by the Ministerio de Sanidad for the future Digital Health Law. Rather than limiting regulatory design to institutional or expert circles, the ministry opened the drafting process to organizations, professional associations, patient groups, and the wider public through a formal consultation mechanism.

The proposed legislation seeks to regulate the use of digital and emerging technologies—such as big data, biometrics, and neurotechnologies—while establishing a robust framework for the ethical, secure, and scientifically responsible use of clinical data. A central pillar of the law is the guarantee that all citizens, across public and private systems, will have access to an interoperable digital health record, enabling continuity of care throughout Spain and across the European Union.

By inviting participation at this early stage, the consultation acknowledges that decisions about data governance, digital rights, and technological use in health are not merely technical or legal matters. They are societal choices that require transparency, debate, and collective input.

Together, these experiences reinforce a critical lesson: pushing technology and regulation from the top down does not work. When communities participate meaningfully in shaping strategies and legal frameworks, digital transformation gains legitimacy, trust, and durability. At this scale, listening becomes a form of governance.

Innovating With Insured Members and Professionals

Participation is not confined to public systems. Private organizations also benefit when innovation is approached as a collaborative endeavor.

The Spanish insurer DKV created *Comunidad Amiga*, a participatory space where insured members and healthcare professionals collaborate to test and shape new digital health solutions. Technologies are assessed not only for usability but also for relevance, ethical implications, and integration into real care practices.

This approach reduces innovation risk and increases adoption. It recognizes that relevance cannot be designed in isolation and that listening is a strategic capability rather than a reputational exercise. Here, collaboration strengthens both trust and organizational resilience.

Citizen Science and Shared Knowledge

The most transformative expressions of collaboration and listening emerge in citizen science, where knowledge is co-produced rather than extracted.

The European cooperative Salus.coop enables citizens to voluntarily donate well-being and health data for scientific research under a cooperative governance model. Participation extends beyond data contribution to include the rules that govern its use.

Data donation operates under a specific data-sharing license, inspired by the logic of Creative Commons. This license was co-created through a participatory process, involving citizens, researchers, legal experts, and other stakeholders. Together, they defined the conditions under which data can be shared, reused, and protected, ensuring transparency, purpose limitation, and collective benefit.

In this framework, data donation becomes a conscious civic act rather than a passive extraction. The license functions not only as a legal instrument but also as a social contract grounded in trust.

A complementary experience can be found in participatory research initiatives in Parkinson's disease promoted within the Vall d'Hebron Research Institute (VHIR). The institute has created a dedicated *Research and Innovation Responsibility* area to open research processes to society and embed citizen participation as a structural component of innovation.

One concrete example is the project *Tejiendo Ciencia*, developed around Parkinson's disease. Through participatory processes, the concerns and lived experiences of patients, caregivers, healthcare professionals, and researchers were incorporated into the definition of new research questions. The initiative also resulted in a public exhibition designed to make Parkinson's visible to society, transforming research into a shared cultural narrative.

In these experiences, collaboration transcends consultation. Knowledge is created through dialogue, and science becomes a space of shared meaning-making.

What Collaboration Demands

Across these contexts, common patterns emerge. Participation must be intentional rather than symbolic. Listening without influence erodes trust. Ownership drives adoption more effectively than persuasion. Interoperability challenges are as social as they are technical. Collaboration requires time, resources, and organizational humility.

Above all, collaboration and listening are cultural capabilities that determine how systems learn, adapt, and endure.

Health as a Shared Endeavour

As healthcare systems navigate profound transformation, participation can no longer remain at the margins. It must be embedded in service design, policy-making, innovation strategies, and research governance.

The future of healthcare innovation depends less on asking better questions and more on sharing power. "Collaborate and Listen" is not about amplifying voices; it is about changing how decisions are made.

*****

SPAIN | DESIGN THINKING FOR ADOPTION IN HEALTHCARE—HOW HOSPITALS CAN INNOVATE THROUGH LISTENING, CO-CREATION, AND ITERATION | LORENA PINEDA

Why Design Thinking Belongs in Hospitals

Design thinking is often associated with startups and consumer products, yet some of its most valuable applications are emerging inside hospitals. In healthcare, innovation rarely fails because teams lack ideas. It fails because solutions are introduced without deep listening, without co-creation, and without a realistic path to adoption.

Despite constant references to innovation, many initiatives are still designed as if hospitals were traditional markets: a solution is built, presented, and expected to scale. Hospital environments are complex systems shaped by multiple stakeholders, strict operational constraints, and emotional realities that directly influence outcomes. When innovation is designed outside that system, adoption becomes the main bottleneck.

Design thinking offers a different path. It treats the hospital as a living environment to understand, not a place to "deploy" into. It relies on empathy, observation, rapid prototyping, and iteration. In practice, this means building minimum viable solutions, validating them with real stakeholders, improving them through feedback, and scaling only what proves useful.

This chapter is grounded in a clear conviction: innovating in hospital environments requires the same disciplined process used in other complex contexts, with one crucial difference. Listening and co-creation are not optional. They are both an ethical and an operational requirement. Using a real hospital case developed with Pallapupas, this essay shows how design thinking principles, translated into an explicit method of collaboration and listening, can turn human-centered ideas into solutions that are actually adopted.

From Service Provider to Hospital Partner

The case presented here comes from Pallapupas, an organization with more than two decades of experience working in hospitals to support emotional care through humor-based interventions and professional training. Over time, this organization has demonstrated that emotional experience is not peripheral to care. It shapes how patients and professionals move through the system, how procedures are tolerated, and how trust is built.

As with many mature organizations operating in complex environments, a strategic question emerged: how to evolve without losing focus, how to grow without fragmenting efforts, and how to respond to new challenges in healthcare without relying on isolated or reactive initiatives.

The ambition shifted from delivering individual interventions to becoming a true partner for hospitals. This required a fundamental change in how innovation was approached. Rather than starting from what Pallapupas could offer, innovation needed to start from what hospitals, professionals, and patients needed.

To enable this shift, the Pallapupas Experience Lab was established. It functions as a living R&D system designed around systematic listening, cross-functional collaboration, and validation in real hospital conditions.

The Innovation: A Co-Creation Model Built on MVPs and Iteration

The innovation described in this chapter is not a single product or service. It is an innovation model embedded in the way this company develops new solutions with hospitals through the Pallapupas Experience Lab.

At its core, it is a structured co-creation process that captures real needs from hospitals and care environments, translates them into minimum viable proposals, and through validation and iteration turns them into solutions that deliver tangible value.

Innovation is treated as a continuous process rather than a final output. Value lies not only in the solution itself, but in the method that allows solutions to evolve through real use. The model connects functions that often operate separately, including commercial, strategic, and artistic roles, into a shared innovation process. Responsibility for innovation is distributed rather than centralized.

Most importantly, innovation is built through co-creation with hospitals. Hospitals are not passive recipients. They actively shape what is designed and how it evolves. Solutions are treated as living systems, built with users, for users, and refined through experience. In this approach, design thinking becomes operational and innovation becomes a sustained capability rather than a one-off project.

A Concrete Case: Reducing MRI Sedation Through Co-Designed Experience

A clear example of how the Pallapupas Experience Lab operates in practice comes from an MRI unit facing a recurring and costly challenge: a high proportion of patients requiring sedation to complete the scan.

For patients, sedation often means additional stress, longer recovery times, and a heavier emotional burden around an already uncomfortable procedure. For the hospital, it creates operational complexity, higher costs, longer appointment slots, and greater clinical involvement. While sedation enables the exam, it is far from an ideal solution for either patients or the system.

Instead of requesting a predefined intervention, the hospital proposed a collaborative process with Pallapupas. The request was explicit: to analyze the situation together and explore whether an experience-based intervention could reduce anxiety and potentially reduce reliance on sedation.

Understanding the Real Drivers of Anxiety

The work began with listening. Sedation was treated not as the core problem but as a symptom. Together with hospital stakeholders, the Pallapupas team examined the patient journey and identified factors driving anxiety: fear of confined spaces, uncertainty about what would happen, sensory stressors such as noise and lighting, loss of perceived control, and emotional escalation that often begins well before the patient enters the scanning room.

To deepen understanding beyond meetings, the artistic team spent time on-site observing the MRI unit. They studied patient flow, waiting areas, transitions between moments, and details that shape experience but rarely appear in clinical reporting: how information is delivered under time pressure, where anxiety peaks, what patients hear, and how the environment amplifies vulnerability.

Prototyping an MVP the Hospital Could Validate

Based on these insights, a first minimum viable intervention was designed to reduce anxiety and create emotional containment throughout the MRI experience. It was intentionally lightweight and hypothesis driven. The question was not whether the solution was perfect but whether the direction was useful enough to test.

The proposal was shaped collaboratively with commercial and strategic stakeholders to ensure coherence, feasibility, and alignment with operational constraints in a highly scheduled unit. It was then presented to the hospital explicitly as an MVP: something to test, adjust, or reject.

Iterating Until the Solution Fit the Workflow

Hospital feedback led to multiple iterations. Small-scale trials were conducted to assess whether the intervention addressed the real drivers of anxiety. Some elements proved effective quickly, while others required refinement. The process moved back and forth between proposal, validation, and redesign.

Over time, the intervention evolved from a single action into a structured experience covering the full patient journey: from arrival, to preparation, to the moments immediately before the scan, during the scan itself, and the exit experience afterward. Anxiety was no longer addressed as a single moment but as an accumulation across touchpoints.

Early Signals and Ongoing Evaluation

Once the intervention reached a stable version, it was tested with real patients. Initial evaluation focused on experience outcomes compared to the previous baseline: perceived anxiety, sense of safety, clarity of information, and overall satisfaction.

Only after early improvements in patient experience did the team begin exploring a larger operational question: whether the intervention could reduce the need for sedation in certain cases. While evaluation is ongoing, early signals suggest strong potential impact, both in patient satisfaction and hospital efficiency.

What Prevents Adoption and What Makes Innovation Stick

One of the most significant barriers to innovation in healthcare is the absence of co-creation. When solutions are not designed for the people who use them, rejection is almost inevitable. In healthcare, this rejection is amplified by system complexity, time pressure, and the difficulty of adopting new processes or technologies.

Another recurring barrier is innovation disconnected from strategy. Creative initiatives without a clear link to growth, sustainability, or tangible benefit tend to stall. Knowing why you innovate and what measurable value is expected is essential.

The process also highlights the importance of accepting discards. Exploring ideas that do not progress is not failure but a necessary part of responsible innovation. Normalizing discards reduces internal friction and improves decision quality.

Finally, innovation requires governance. Without cadence, clear roles, and stable spaces for collaboration, innovation is easily overtaken by day-to-day urgencies. Structure, not inspiration, is what sustains innovation.

The Human Layer: Experience as a Clinical and Operational Lever

The human dimension is central to this model. Humanizing healthcare does not mean adding emotional layers onto existing processes. It means redesigning those processes from lived experience.

Listening to professionals means acknowledging emotional load, limited time, and real operational constraints. Listening to patients means understanding fear, vulnerability, and uncertainty beyond clinical indicators. Designing without this understanding leads to solutions that may be technically sound but practically unworkable.

This model also humanizes organizations internally. A stable co-creation space reduces friction between teams and reinforces shared purpose. When collaboration is structured, innovation becomes a collective discipline rather than an isolated effort.

How Others Can Replicate This Approach

The true value of this approach lies in its repeatability. Any organization operating in complex systems can adopt a similar co-creation model by integrating structured listening, MVP design, early validation, iteration, and ongoing strategic alignment.

When innovation becomes habitual rather than exceptional, organizations are better equipped to respond to evolving needs without losing focus. In practice, this approach encourages hospitals and partners to treat solutions as living products: built with users, refined through use, and improved through measurable learning.

Why This Is "Collaborate and Listen" in Practice

This case demonstrates what Collaborate and Listen looks like when translated into a design thinking practice inside hospitals. Collaboration begins at the start of the process, connecting disciplines and organizations that rarely co-create. Listening goes beyond collecting feedback. It becomes the decision-making mechanism that determines what advances, what evolves, and what is discarded.

When innovation is built on this foundation, adoption becomes a natural outcome. Humanization in healthcare stops being an aspirational label and becomes the result of designing with the system rather than for it.

Within the Collaborate and Listen framework, the lesson is clear: healthcare innovation does not fail due to a lack of ideas. It fails due to a lack of real space for co-creation and listening.

Creating those spaces is not symbolic. It is essential.

*****

NETHERLANDS | AUGMENT, DON'T AUTOMATE: HOW ERASMUS MC USED TECHNOLOGY TO STRENGTHEN CLINICAL JUDGMENT | SAKSHIKA DHINGRA, EDWARD W. MARX, ADITI U. JOSHI AND ALINE NOIZET

Automation is often confused with the development of healthcare systems. It is a very thinly veiled, yet strong, notion: when something can be done by technology, it must be. As a matter of practice, this reasoning often undermines professional judgment, deluges clinicians with alerts, and takes care out of context. Erasmus MC in the Netherlands went in another direction. Instead of asking how much of medicine could be put under the control of machines, it posed the question of where technology could enhance human expertise. Instead of creating or inventing a single platform or a breakthrough algorithm, it created a philosophy of digital design in which clinicians were seen as the backbone of the system and technology as the support system. At Erasmus MC, IT was not used to replace thought, but instead, it guarded it.

A Highly Advanced Hospital Facing a Familiar Risk

Erasmus MC is a highly developed international academic medical center in Europe, which integrates tertiary care, research, and medical education on a large scale. Its clinicians deal with some of the most complicated cases in oncology, intensive care, and rare disease. There is a high level of data density, decisions are subtle, and uncertainty is inevitable. With the increasing digital capabilities, electronic records, predictive models, and decision support, the hospital realized an increasing risk. Better decisions were not always accompanied by more information. Clinicians were using more and more cognitive energy on systems instead of patients. The problem was not that of digitization. It was an imbalance.

Reframing the Role of Technology

Erasmus MC reframed its objective to be that technology should absorb routine cognitive load so that clinicians can concentrate on irreducible judgment rather than aiming for maximal automation. Every digital project now uses this idea as a design filter:

- Does this cut down on pointless thinking?
- Does it make things clearer instead of more complicated?
- Does the clinician retain ultimate authority?

The tool was either redesigned or not built at all if the response was negative.

Clinical Judgment as a Scarce Resource

Clinical informaticians and hospital administrators reached a consensus that clinical judgment is fragile and restricted, and it is simple to avoid it. When it comes to receiving notifications, checklists, automatic suggestions, and attention, they are all in competition. They damage trust and serve as distractions when they are underdeveloped (Boonstra et al., 2020). Erasmus MC made the decision to draw attention to a unique resource that needed to be protected. As a result, decision support technologies were designed to step in, not continuously. Signals took precedence over noise. Instead of being seen as a failure, its stillness was seen as one of its qualities.

Designing With Clinicians, Not for Them

Deep physician engagement in system design was a distinctive feature of Erasmus MC's methodology. Physicians, nurses, and pharmacists took part in:

- Determining which decisions actually benefited from assistance
- Establishing alert levels
- Developing the way uncertainty was expressed

Systems provided context—trends, deviations, and pertinent history—instead of making suggestions. Instead of complying, clinicians were asked to interpret. This strengthened confidence in the technology and maintained professional autonomy.

Decision Support That Knows When to Step Back

Erasmus MC applied deterioration risk and resource strain predictive tools in critical care units. Notably, these tools never gave out orders. Instead, they came up with questions:

- This trend is unlike auspicious recovery.
- The pattern of this patient is similar to past complications.

Clinicians said that the tools were a second pair of eyes—helpful but not authoritative. No punishments were given when forecasts were disregarded. The learning opportunities were anticipated and examined through overrides. Such a feedback loop enhanced the models without compromising clinical confidence.

Using IT to Standardize the Routine, Not the Complex

Erasmus MC created a clear differentiation between routine and complex work. Aggressive standardization was done by use of technology:

- Documentation templates
- Medication reconciliation
- Scheduling and coordination.
- Data retrieval

This relieved clinicians of monotonous work, which is not amenable to creativity, whereas complex decisions like diagnostic ambiguity, ethical tradeoffs, and individualized treatment were not overstructured (Porter & Lee, 2015). In this case, the technology was used to reflect as opposed to resolving. This subdivision of labor made medicine human in the places where it was needed the most.

Training Clinicians to Use IT Critically

Education was also another key factor. Erasmus MC educated clinicians not only to employ the digital tools but to challenge them. Training emphasized:

- Knowing the model constraints.
- Being aware of bias and blind spots.
- Reading between the lines and not taking the conclusions.

This resulted in a digitally literate yet digitally non-submissive workforce. Technology was not a substitute for reasoning but became a collaborator.

Governance That Protected Autonomy

Good governance enhances people-first thinking. Significant deployments of the digital realm were assessed by clinical councils. The clinicians could veto the tools that interfered with workflow or judgment. The clinical leadership was responsible to the IT teams and not vice versa. This hierarchy did not allow a gradual shift towards automation as an end in itself. Notably, it also increased adoption (Demaidi, 2023). The level of resistance also reduced when clinicians believed that systems did not interfere with their professional judgment.

Patients Benefiting From Better Judgment

The impacts were felt by the patients even indirectly. Clinicians noted better concentration in the consultation. More deliberate discussion was given to cases that were complex. The decisions were more relaxed and stable. Patients had fewer conflicting messages, unneeded interruptions, and patient explanations. Technology had become the background, where it belonged.

Resilience During Periods of Stress

COVID-19 put the Erasmus MC philosophy to the test. Capacity planning and risk monitoring with the help of predictive models were aided, yet ultimate control was left to clinicians. When models failed to be effective in light of such unprecedented circumstances, the teams were able to adapt without crisis since judgment was never outsourced. The complexity was assimilated by technology; humans dealt with uncertainty. This strength confirmed the design decisions several years ago.

Lessons in "Collaborate & Listen"

Erasmus MC shows that successful digital health does not lie in doing more through technology but the right things through it. Meaning, morality, and adjustment are the elements people are good at. Technology is also good with regularity, magnitude, and recollection. It is when these strengths are strategically correlated that innovation occurs. Excessive automation undermines systems. Considerable augmentation fortifies them. Working with others is the key to success. One is too small a number for innovation to happen. Seek first to understand.

Conclusion: When Technology Knows Its Place

Erasmus MC failed to achieve success since it possessed the best tools. It worked out since it was disciplined to make choices of what technology should not do. The hospital created a digital ecosystem that clinicians and patients could rely on by securing clinical judgment and applying IT to assist and not replace human intelligence. They collaborated and listened. With healthcare sprinting to the future of AI, Erasmus MC gives a down-to-earth reminder: smarter machines are not the objective, improved decisions are. And more advantageous resolutions start—and end—with people. Collaboration is key.

References

Boonstra, A., Versluis, A., & Vos, J. F. J. (2020). Implementing electronic health records in hospitals: A systematic literature review. *BMC Health Services Research*, *14*(1). https://doi.org/10.1186/1472-6963-14-370

Demaidi, M. N. (2023). Artificial intelligence national strategy in a developing country. *AI & Society*, *40*. https://doi.org/10.1007/s00146-023-01779-x

Porter, M., & Lee, T. (2015). *The Strategy That Will Fix Health Care*. https://www.aerodigestive.us/wp-content/uploads/2020/11/Porter-Lee-2013-The-strategy-that-will-fix-health-care-annotated.pdf

*****

ITALY | HOW THE EUROPEAN INSTITUTE OF ONCOLOGY IN MILAN COLLABORATED AND LISTENED TO MAKE AI WORK IN CANCER CARE | SAKSHIKA DHINGRA, EDWARD W. MARX, ADITI U. JOSHI AND ALINE NOIZET

Healthcare innovation is hardly ever a failure due to absent technology. In a greater number of cases, it fails due to the burden of the incompatibility of cultures. Clinicians, researchers, technologists, and administrators all have different languages, incentives, and assumptions. Innovation requires the intersection of these worlds, which is exactly the case with artificial intelligence in oncology: the progress is not limited by algorithms but rather by the ability of cultures to coexist. Sometimes the ideas of collaboration and effective listening are lost. Leaders at the European Institute of Oncology (IEO) in Milan, which is one of the major comprehensive cancer centers in Italy, realized this early. Their oncology experience of AI-supported clinical decision tool implementation proves that success has not come out of centralized requirements or technical innovation alone but rather a conscious mix of academic rigor, clinical judgment, digital entrepreneurship, and institutional governance into one common way of working: collaboration and effective listening.

A System Rich in Expertise, Fragmented by Design

The oncology environment in Italy is one of the most advanced in Europe. The decentralized health system has high-specialized cancer centers, university hospitals, regional providers, and research institutes. It is a structure that encourages excellence and strengthens silos. Clinicians in IEO are confronting the growing complexity at a fast rate. Precision oncology has increased the number of diagnostic markers, treatment pathways, and clinical trials. Italian cancer care has always excelled at multidisciplinary tumor boards, which are now overwhelmed with huge amounts of data. It is becoming more and more challenging to keep up with changing guidelines, especially with rare tumors or rapidly developing fields of therapeutic interest. Scientists, in turn, produce good-quality evidence and frequently fail to get their research converted into standard practice. Health-tech startups build potentially valuable AI solutions but do not have long-term exposure to actual clinical processes (Adami et al., 2018). Administrators are in need of consistency, safety, and professional autonomy. The individual cultures were outstanding. Together, they stalled.

Oncology as the Breaking Point

The driving change force became cancer care. Throughout the departments at IEO, oncologists expressed the same: it was now getting more difficult to make decisions, not necessarily due to uncertainty but due to information being spread across guidelines, publications, and registry and clinical trial databases. AI-based clinical decision support systems provided relief in theory—technologies that can combine the features of patients, evidence, and treatment options and present them in real time. However, previous efforts to bring in such technologies had been unsuccessful. Clinicians did not believe opaque recommendations. Scholars were concerned with simplifying. Administrators were reluctant to incorporate outside platforms into high-stakes decision-making. The technology existed. Alignment did not.

Creating Shared Ownership at the Foundation

IEE was shifting gears and revamping the way innovation is constructed. Instead of considering AI tools the finished product to be implemented in the hospital, the hospital presented them as co-developed clinical tools. Oncologists assisted in establishing the clinical questions which were worth answering. Researchers criticized information sources, assumptions, and constraints. Startup partners repackaged interfaces to align tumor board workflows with generic dashboards. The leadership of the hospital gave governance, legal, and long-term commitment. These partnerships were permanent, not ad hoc. Multidisciplinary meetings replaced single demonstrations. The loops of feedback were fixed and not periodic (Tzelves et al., 2022). None of the groups could claim ownership of the innovation—the partnership could. This common property changed opinions. AI was not brought in, but now it was built together in real and honest collaboration.

Translating Between Professional Languages

The other barrier that was underestimated was language. Researchers talked in odds and groups. Technologists were scalable and feature focused. Clinicians were also risk tolerance oriented, patient oriented, and responsibility oriented. Teams that excelled in their work took time in translation. The results of AI were reformulated clinically:

- Why is this option suggested?
- What evidence supports it?
- In what areas is there loss of understanding?

AI systems were integrated into multidisciplinary tumor boards at IEO as another point of view but not as an authority. Recommendations were connected openly to guidelines, studies, and specific factors to the patient. Such a position maintained clinical autonomy and increased understanding: intentional listening. AI entered into conversation instead of a decision.

Leadership as Cultural Glue

The role of institutional leadership was important. Leaders at IEO were cultural mediators instead of being solo sponsors. They took care of clinic time to co-develop clinicians. They justified collaboration with startups and academic organizations. They did not give in to the urge to scale at a very fast pace without building trust. Notably, they established standards under which success would be gauged on the quality of adoptions and clinical confidence, not the performance metrics. The importance of cross-disciplinary cooperation was announced by its leaders, which was a sign that integrating into culture was not only a strategic priority but also an operational one.

Initial Influence in Practice

With the maturing of AI-assisted tools, they started being valuable. There was higher access to updated evidence and increased adherence to guidelines in the tumor boards. Junior clinicians were empowered to deal effectively with complicated cases using recommendations that were clear and traceable. It is important to note that AI has even refuted some of the conventional ideas, which ensured further debate and not unconditional acceptance. These incidents emphasized the fact that the system was a learning trigger rather than a decision-maker. Improved, more timely, and consistent planning of the care benefited patients indirectly without sacrificing the human judgment that was at the heart of oncology.

Confronting Ethical and Cultural Tensions Together

Ethical issues were discussed at an early stage and openly. Matters of bias, explainability, and accountability were addressed as design concerns rather than as fixes once the implementation is made. The performance of models was evaluated among the demographics. Clinicians identified edge cases where suggestions were perceived to be wrong. The administrators provided adherence to the European standards of data protection and clinical governance. Trust was enhanced by jointly resolving ethical issues. Innovation became safer due to shared responsibility.

Unexpectedly Early Scaling Down Without Identity

The wider adoption became in both local partnerships and in IEO, the more difficult the issue of cultural balance became. There were variations in practice in the regions, but safety and quality had to be standardized. The solution was modularity. The basic AI capabilities were uniformized, and interfaces and workflows could be adjusted on the local level. This method was respectful of professional identity and consistent. Again, it was more a matter of cultural design and effective listening than technological architecture.

Teaching Through Blended Cultures

The experience of IEE shows that there is one major rule: innovation grows faster when cultures clash rather than being rivals. Knowledge in clinics without technical aid is stagnant. Without clinical trust, technology fails. Theoretical research is inapplicable. Without inclusion, leadership loses legitimacy. New ideas are born at the crossroads.

Conclusion: When Innovation Speaks Many Languages

The European Institute of Oncology did not apply AI to work in cancer care by favoring one culture over another. It was successful in providing room within the institution to allow academic rigor, clinical wisdom, entrepreneurial agility, and institutional leadership to co-exist. AI was made believable, practical, and viable by merging cultures deliberately. In medicine, technology is sometimes simpler to develop compared to knowledge. The experience of Italy teaches us that, once disciplines learn how to address each other, collaborate, and listen, innovation at last gets a voice and patients start to feel the difference.

References

Adami, H. O., Berns, A., Celis, J. E., de Vries, E., Eggermont, A., Harris, A., Zur Hausen, H., Pelicci, P. G., & Ringborg, U. (2018). European academy of cancer sciences—position paper. *Molecular Oncology, 12*(11), 1829–1837. https://doi.org/10.1002/1878-0261.12379

Tzelves, L., Manolitsis, I., Varkarakis, I., Ivanovic, M., Kokkonidis, M., Useros, C. S., Kosmidis, T., Muñoz, M., Grau, I., Athanatos, M., Vizitiu, A., Lampropoulos, K., Koutsouri, T., Stefanatou, D., Perrakis, K., Stratigaki, C., Autexier, S., Kosmidis, P., & Valachis, A. (2022). Artificial intelligence supporting cancer patients across Europe-The ASCAPE project. *PloS One, 17*(4), e0265127. https://doi.org/10.1371/journal.pone.0265127

Chapter 5

Communicate and Eliminate Barriers

Cross-communication is essential to promote innovation. By removing virtual or physical barriers to communication, ideas have a better chance of being realized.

Transparency is key to effective relationships, which are required for innovation to thrive. The depth and width you share will determine the size of your success. Look for every opportunity and platform to share while actively eliminating barriers to communication. Effective communication will make or break innovation. If active or passive resistance rises, so must your communication. While technology provides great tools to reach many, do not neglect the power of in-person eyeball-to-eyeball dialogue.

GEORGIA | BATUMI CENTRAL HOSPITAL MEDICAL TOURISM SUCCESS | EDWARD W. MARX

Batumi Central Hospital Innovation and Inclusivity in Georgia's Medical Tourism Revolution

The global rise of medical tourism represents a fundamental shift in how individuals access healthcare, driven by the powerful forces of globalization, cost disparity, and consumer choice. While nations like Thailand, India, and Mexico have long dominated this market, a small Black Sea nation has engineered a remarkable entry into this competitive field through strategic innovation and systemic reform. The country of Georgia has not merely joined the medical tourism industry; it has redefined its value proposition by eliminating the traditional barriers that deter potential patients. This transformative effort is not just a national policy but is exemplified at the institutional level by facilities like Batumi Central Hospital. By leveraging geographic advantage, technological integration, and a profound cultural shift towards patient-centricity, Batumi Central

DOI: 10.4324/9781003780175-5

Hospital has become a blueprint for how regional medical centers can successfully compete on the global stage, turning the challenges of a post-Soviet system into pillars of success.

Georgia's foray into medical tourism is built upon a foundational national innovation: the radical dismantling of its corrupt, Soviet-era healthcare system. Post-2003, the government implemented aggressive reforms, purging corrupt officials and encouraging massive private investment in healthcare infrastructure. This created a fertile environment for medical tourism to flourish, characterized by a core set of national advantages: cost savings of 50–70% compared to Western Europe and the United States, a liberal visa regime that facilitates easy travel, and a burgeoning reputation as a safe, culturally rich tourist destination. However, these national strengths alone are not enough to win the trust of international patients. They must be operationalized at the hospital level, where fears about quality, communication, and logistical complexity directly influence decision-making. Batumi Central Hospital, part of the larger EVEX medical network, recognized that success hinged on directly addressing these barriers through a multi-faceted strategy of access, quality, and experience.

We dive into three of the six communication challenges and barriers to success.

Trust and Perceived Quality Barriers

The first and most significant barrier Batumi Central Hospital eliminated is the barrier of trust and perceived quality. For a patient considering traveling abroad for a critical procedure, the single greatest concern is whether the care will be safe and effective. Mere claims of excellence are insufficient. Batumi Central Hospital, through the EVEX network, addressed this by securing Joint Commission International (JCI) accreditation. This was not a superficial achievement; it required a top-down overhaul of clinical protocols, patient safety measures, and administrative processes to meet the most rigorous international standards. This accreditation acts as a universal symbol of quality, immediately signaling to potential patients from Europe, the Middle East, and beyond that the care they will receive is commensurate with what they would find in their home countries.

Summary Table Barriers and Strategic Responses

Barrier to Medical Tourism	*Batumi Central Hospital's Strategic Response*
Quality & Trust	JCI Accreditation; association with the reputable EVEX network; showcasing Western-trained doctors.
Advanced Technology	Private investment in state-of-the-art medical equipment and modern facilities.
Logistical Complexity	Dedicated patient coordinators; end-to-end service managing travel, visas, and accommodation.
Communication & Language	English-speaking staff; seamless communication from first contact through follow-up.
Financial Uncertainty	Transparent, all-inclusive upfront pricing.
Location & Appeal	Leveraging Batumi's status as a holiday destination to promote "medication" (medical + vacation).

Furthermore, the hospital strategically showcases the profiles of its medical staff, emphasizing Western training and international experience. This proactive approach to building trust transforms the hospital from an unknown foreign entity into a verified, reliable partner in the patient's healthcare journey.

Logistical and Communication Barriers

Secondly, the hospital systematically dismantled the logistical and communicative barriers that make medical tourism daunting. The process involves immense complexity: navigating visas, arranging travel, coordinating appointments, and overcoming language differences. Batumi Central Hospital innovated by embracing a facilitator model. Rather than forcing the patient to manage these complexities, the hospital offers—either directly or through partnered agencies—a seamless, end-to-end service. This includes:

- Dedicated Patient Coordinators: English-speaking coordinators act as a single point of contact for the patient from the first email through their recovery, arranging consultations, providing cost estimates, and answering questions.
- Travel and Visa Logistics: Assistance with securing visas, booking flights, and arranging airport transfers removes a major source of anxiety.
- Accommodation and Concierge Services: Partnerships with local hotels and recovery facilities allow for the creation of all-inclusive packages. The hospital understands that the patient is also a tourist, and they facilitate exploration by helping plan cultural excursions and experiences.

This holistic approach to the patient journey reframes the narrative. It is no longer about a patient struggling to access care in a foreign country; it is about a guest arriving for a streamlined, managed experience where their only job is to heal and explore.

Transactional Patient Experience Barriers

Finally, Batumi Central Hospital brilliantly leveraged its geographic and cultural identity to eliminate the barrier of a purely transactional clinical experience. Located in the vibrant coastal city of Batumi, the hospital offers what few competitors can: a genuine "medication" experience. While a hospital in a dense urban capital might offer clinical excellence, Batumi provides a therapeutic environment. Patients can recover while breathing the fresh sea air, taking gentle walks along the Black Sea coast, and enjoying the region's renowned cuisine and hospitality. This unique value proposition is a powerful marketing tool and a genuine contributor to patient outcomes, as a positive and relaxing environment can aid significantly in recovery.

Furthermore, the hospital integrated technology to enhance both the clinical and administrative experience. The adoption of Georgia's national e-Health system ensures efficient management of electronic medical records and transparent billing, preventing the "sticker shock" of hidden fees that can plague medical travel. Telemedicine capabilities allow for seamless pre-procedure consultations and post-procedure follow-ups, maintaining the care continuum even after the patient has returned home. This tech-forward approach not only improves efficiency but also reinforces the message that the hospital is modern, transparent, and committed to long-term patient relationships.

The Outcomes

The quality of clinical care is equivalent to those of other large medical centers. In some specialties, specifically those most closely associated with international patients, it is modestly higher. Costs are 25% of what patients can expect from services performed in other highly developed nations.

Improving Communication and Overcoming Barriers

In conclusion, the story of Batumi Central Hospital is a masterclass in targeted innovation within the medical tourism sector. Its success is not an accident but the direct result of a deliberate strategy to dismantle the very barriers that define the industry's greatest challenges. By securing JCI accreditation, it demolished the barrier of trust. By implementing a concierge-style, end-to-end service model, it eradicated the barrier of logistical complexity. And by harnessing the unique restorative power of its location in Batumi, it transformed the barrier of foreign recovery into a selling point of unparalleled value. Batumi Central Hospital, and Georgia as a whole, demonstrate that the future of medical tourism lies not in being the cheapest option, but in being the most accessible, trustworthy, and holistically appealing one. They have proven that a world-class patient experience is the most powerful innovation of all.

Nothing here is magic or out of reach for any other hospital in the modern world. It is a matter of being serious about communication amongst all parties from operations to clinicians to technicians. It is about rigorously identifying barriers and being honest and transparent about them. No finger pointing. No blaming or shaming. It does require strong leaders who are willing to be humble and create a culture of safety.

Healthcare innovation is commonly approached as a technical issue. Algorithms must be accurate. Systems must integrate. Infrastructure must scale. However, many undertaking falter way before any of such limits are achieved. They do not pass the level of understanding. University Hospital Zurich (USZ), which is among the largest academic medical institutions in Switzerland, faced this fact when it tried to implement AI-assisted triage and imaging prioritization in its emergency department. The technology worked. The evidence was strong. Still, adoption stalled. Better communication turned out to be the key unlock to progress and not better AI (Demaidi, 2023).

A High-Performing System With Hidden Friction

USZ has been in a healthcare system that is characterized by precision, autonomy, and high professional standards. Clinicians expect rigor. Administrators want responsibility. Regulators expect clarity. AI-based triage and prioritization tools in imaging became potentially beneficial when the workload in emergency departments grew and was accompanied by a more complex level of diagnostics (Amann et al., 2020). The earlier pilots were able to identify cases of critical concern faster and better allocate their workload. However, there was uneven uptake on the frontline. There are those clinicians who adopted the tools. Others quietly ignored them. The obstacle was not technological. It was interpretive.

When Everyone Heard Something Different

The leadership of USZ started by listening. Clinicians raised the issue of accountability: Who answers the call in case AI identifies a case wrong? Administrators were interested in throughput and safety measures. IT teams talked in terms of probabilities and performance of the system. Risk and compliance became the focus of legal teams. Both parties were right—in their own frame. The thing was that these frames never coincided.

Reframing AI as a Shared Clinical Process

Instead of rushing deployment, USZ stopped implementation and gave attention to communication architecture. Artificial intelligence was not presented as a tool or system anymore. It was re-formulated as clinical process support, which is governed by the same principles as any other diagnostic aid. Language was consciously changed. The outputs of AI were evaluated on a clinical level rather than technical. The issue of responsibility was defined at the beginning and many times: clinical judgment was always sovereign. This reframing lowered the anxiety levels prior to every line of code being modified.

Making Assumptions Explicit

Surfacing unspoken assumptions was one of the most crucial actions that USZ performed. Clinicians thought that AI advice would take precedence over them. Administrators took resistance to cultural inertia. The IT teams presupposed that performance metrics were self-descriptive (Alanazi, 2023). Organized groups were formed in which these assumptions could be made publicly—and corrected. After naming misunderstandings, the power of misunderstandings was lost.

Defining Accountability Without Ambiguity

One of the greatest obstacles to adoption was that of blurred responsibility. USZ addressed this head-on. According to the governance documents, it was clearly stated:

- AI devices present prioritization and not decisions.
- Clinicians have the complete responsibility and accountability.
- Older conflict with AI catalyzes review but not override.

This clarity mattered. Clinicians were now able to communicate without jeopardizing professional identity and legal liability.

Aligning Communication Across Roles

USZ was able to make sure that there was consistency in messaging. What the leadership said in the public was strengthened locally by the department heads. What was focused on training was what was reflected in governance documents. What was described by IT teams reflected what clinicians had witnessed in practice. This orientation helped avoid ambivalent messages, one of the most frequent murderers of innovation.

Local Champions as Translators

As an alternative to the top-down communication approach, USZ established clinical champions among emergency medicine and radiology. These people became translators, explaining AI in a clinical language, discussing the concerns informally, and feeding the real-life feedback upwards. Their authority was more than any published memo.

Simplifying the Conversation, Not the System

Curiously, the technology did not change much. The difference was in the way it was discussed. Contextualization of performance measures was done. Edge cases were recognized freely. It was not called a secret but was limited. This sincerity brought on credibility. Perfection is not required of the clinicians. They need clarity.

Results That Followed Understanding

The more communication barriers were broken, the more they were adopted. Prioritization with the help of AI was employed with greater frequency. Emergency imaging cases were previously discovered. The ED teams were found to have better situational awareness during peak periods. Most indicatively, clinicians started to propose improvements, an element that reflects ownership, as opposed to compliance.

Leadership That Repeated the Message

USZ leaders also realized that communication cannot be a single occasion. Repeats, clarifications, and reinforcement of the messages were done throughout forums. Confusion again arose but was not rejected. The momentum of change continued since the knowledge was retained.

Lessons in Eliminating Invisible Barriers

The experience of USZ reveals a very important lesson: The majority of obstacles to innovation cannot be identified in project plans. They exist in words, suppositions, and silent fear. USZ made way for technology by taking communication as infrastructure.

Conclusion: When Understanding Unlocks Innovation

University Hospital Zurich failed in AI implementation since its algorithms were on the premium level. It was successful since it eradicated the stagnation that perverted cooperation. The hospital turned hesitation into participation by synchronizing the language, defining responsibility, and discussing issues, which were debated openly. The failure of innovation in the healthcare sector does not happen due to resistant people. It fails when individuals lack understanding of it. Technology can eventually do its job as communication is enhanced.

References

Alanazi, A. (2023). Clinicians' views on using artificial intelligence in healthcare: Opportunities, challenges, and beyond. *Cureus, 15*(9). https://doi.org/10.7759/cureus.45255

Amann, J., Blasimme, A., Vayena, E., Frey, D., & Madai, V. I. (2020). Explainability for artificial intelligence in healthcare: A multidisciplinary perspective. *BMC Medical Informatics and Decision Making, 20*(1).

Demaidi, M. N. (2023). Artificial intelligence national strategy in a developing country. *AI & Society, 40*. https://doi.org/10.1007/s00146-023-01779-x

*****

FRANCE | CLEARING THE STATIC: HOW HOSPITAL EUROPÉEN GEORGES-POMPIDOU LEARNED THAT COMMUNICATION WAS THE REAL INNOVATION BEHIND AI IN RADIOLOGY | SAKSHIKA DHINGRA, EDWARD W. MARX, ADITI U. JOSHI AND ALINE NOIZET

Barriers in the healthcare setting are seldom apparent. They conceal themselves in silos, presumptions, rules, and unarticulated fears. When innovation halts, most people point an accusing finger at technology, yet more commonly it is communication that is the real bottleneck. This lesson is made apparent in the first instance at Hospital Européen Georges-Pompidou (HEGP), which is one of the flagship academic hospitals in the AP-HP system in France, and where the initial use of artificial intelligence in the radiology department became apparent. The hospital did not find it difficult due to the immaturity of the algorithms or the absence of infrastructure. The sluggishness occurred due to the different languages used by the stakeholders. Autonomy was of concern to radiologists. Risk and returns oriented administrators. The focus on regulators was on safety and accountability. Vendors were talking in terms of performance. It is only then that innovation started to be scaled: when HEGP viewed communication itself as the impediment to overcome.

Meeting Hospital Reality and National Ambition

France has led on the national level in digital health strategy in Europe, and AI in medical imaging has been identified as a priority area. AI-radiology was anticipated to be faster in reporting, provide better triage, and enhance quality intra-regionally. In this national drive, HEGP was in a good position to dominate, with high-level volumes of imaging, scholarly education, and electronic infrastructure. Pioneer pilots were introduced especially in emergency and chest imaging. The tools technically worked as expected. Yet adoption was uneven. Radiologists adopted AI support to some degree and disengaged or bypassed it to others. The same technology brought about very diverse results within departments. It was not performance but alignment that was the problem.

Surfacing Invisible Barriers

Early concerns that were raised by the frontline radiologists at HEGP were not taken seriously at first. They raised questions on how AI suggestions can make inroads into professional judgment, how responsibility would be allocated when computers are in disagreement with clinicians, and whether the use of AI in the long term would undermine diagnostic autonomy. The hospital leadership, on the other hand, saw AI through systems lens standardization, efficiency, and throughput. In that regard, reluctance appeared as opposition. Another complication came in as regulatory complexity with regional interpretations of validation, procurement, and data protection requirements bringing about uncertainty. Every group was operating reasonably in its context. The matter was that all these frames never were properly aligned (Amann et al., 2020).

Reframing the Conversation

The turning point was that the development of AI as an initiative of change to clinical assistance, with shared responsibility, was reframed by HEGP leadership in collaboration with AP-HP digital health leadership. Instead of supporting performance improvement, leadership provided organized platforms to discuss. Radiologists, hospital administrators, legal teams, IT leaders, and AI vendors were in moderated discussions, which were aimed at unearthing concerns, not solving them at once. Notably, the skeptical mind was not kept down. The issues of professional identity, bias, and trust were explicitly accepted. By approving doubt, resistance has come into view—and thus could be dealt with.

Creating a Shared Language

Linguistics was one of the most effective interventions. Technical language was replaced with clinical language. The metrics of sensitivity, specificity, false positives, and workflow effects, which radiologists already rely upon, were discussed as the AI outputs. On the same note, systems of governance were represented as protective systems rather than compliance costs. Validation protocol policies were placed as protective measures to protect both patients and clinicians, as AI was not an authority but an assistance tool. This common language minimized misunderstanding and achieved credibility.

Removing Structural Barriers

It was not possible to communicate. HEGP collaborated with AP-HP management to eliminate structural friction points that enhanced the mistrust. Accountability rules were put in place: AI systems were decision-support systems, but ultimate clinical responsibility always fell on the physician. The procurement processes were also made leaner whereby departments could embrace the approved tools without duplicating their validation processes. The data-sharing agreements were standardized, which minimized the legal uncertainty and time delays. Every barrier taken down supported the message that the system was not compelling clinicians to struggle to innovate.

Local Conversations, Scalable Consistency

Although there was a national standard to offer structure, implementation was local. The HEGP departments were advised to implement AI tools to their workflows instead of aligning workflow with technology. Critical roles were taken by clinical champions. These radiologists enabled peer consultations, exchanged initial outcomes, including limitations, and resolved issues between teams. This reciprocal dialogue helped to avoid the impression of being imposed on top and increased trust. Innovation started to be collaborative and not dictated.

Results Driven by Alignment

With the increase in communication, better outcomes ensued. There was better priority in emergency cases as reported by emergency radiology teams. In high-volume environments, reporting turnaround times got better. Radiologists were more confident in AI-aided triage after governance and accountability were evident. It is noteworthy that the adoption did not change significantly without significant modifications to the underlying tools. It was trust rather than technology that won the day (Demaidi, 2023). AI stopped being viewed as an external force and instead became seen as an extension of radiologists' professional capabilities.

Leadership That Communicated Relentlessly

HEGP leadership realized that communication is not an innovation process but a base of it. The messages were posted multiple times in different forums, explained and supported by doing. The issue of resistance was dealt with at an early stage instead of being redefined as failure. The leaders knew that silence could largely conceal underlying issues and would make every effort to bring them out. This continuation carried on and kept things together.

Conclusion: When Communication Becomes the Catalyst

The experience of AI in radiology in France was not a scale that could be based on better algorithms. At Hôpital Europa Georges-Pompidou, this was achieved through the elimination of stasis that prevented cooperation. The hospital overcame skepticism by breaking communication barriers, which were organizational, linguistic, and cultural barriers. Acceleration to innovation did not happen when machines started to be more intelligent but when the people could understand each other. Innovation is not supported by communication in the health sector. It enables it.

References

Amann, J., Blasimme, A., Vayena, E., Frey, D., & Madai, V. I. (2020). Explainability for artificial intelligence in healthcare: A multidisciplinary perspective. *BMC Medical Informatics and Decision Making, 20*(1).

Demaidi, M. N. (2023). Artificial intelligence national strategy in a developing country. *AI & Society, 40.* https://doi.org/10.1007/s00146-023-01779-x

*****

FINLAND | HOW HELSINKI UNIVERSITY HOSPITAL CO-CREATED PREDICTIVE HOSPITAL FLOW TO MAKE INNOVATION EVERYONE'S WORK | SAKSHIKA DHINGRA, EDWARD W. MARX, ADITI U. JOSHI AND ALINE NOIZET

Healthcare innovation has a certain hierarchy. The problems are defined by strategy teams, solutions are developed by technologists, funding is approved by leadership, and adopting the outcome is expected to be undertaken by clinicians. Resistance arises when this sequence is failing, as regularly occurs. In Helsinki University Hospital (HUS), the largest academic health system in Finland, executives made another decision: the reason innovation does not work is not that clinicians are resistant to change but rather that they are frequently not included in the process of developing it . There is a lack of communication and active interest in eliminating discovered barriers. This understanding redefined the approach to one of the most enduring problems at HUS, hospital flow. Through communication and co-creation of predictive analytics with clinicians, operational personnel, technologists, and patients, HUS has turned capacity management into a collective organizational capacity building in lieu of a technical project.

A Recognizable Strain Within a High-Performing System

HUS has more than 1.6 million clients and operates in several hospitals and specialties. Though it is known that Finland has an efficient, equitable healthcare, inpatient capacity at HUS experienced mounting pressure in the late 2010s. Emergency departments were sometimes congested, there were delays in elective procedures during periods of demand, and the staff were frequently subjected to a last-minute shift in bed space. The paradox was obvious: HUS had plenty of data. Admission histories over years, diagnosis-related groups, trends by seasons, and patterns of discharges were readily available. Previous efforts to implement capacity dashboards and forecasting instruments had been pushed under the carpet. Theories were produced but not believed (Schein, 2010). There were dashboards, which were not used frequently in day-to-day operations. Employees felt management had constructed these tools around them rather than involving them.

Reframing Hospital Flow as a Shared Experience

The turning point came when leaders at HUS reframed the problem. Instead of asking, "How do we optimize hospital flow?" they asked, "Who experiences hospital flow, and how?" This question changed the prism of efficiency in the system to lived experience. Flow mentioned by nurses referred to interruptions and bed changes that were constant. It was perceived by physicians as postponed operations and clinical prioritization disagreements. It was traversed by operations teams using spreadsheets, phone calls, and escalation meetings. It was a form of uncertainty, waiting, and abrupt transfers to patients. The leadership provided room in which the solution could be collectively owned by acknowledging that there was no group that could be said to be the owner of hospital flow.

Opening the Design Process

Instead of acquiring a predictive analytics platform in secret and secluding the implementation process, HUS actively opened up the design process. Interdisciplinary workshops were conducted between the clinicians, ward managers, IT personnel, data scientists, and patient representatives. The respondents were requested to explain frustrations and then come up with solutions. They discussed barriers and how to overcome them. These arguments showed important insights. Nurses noted that predictions out of context in terms of staffing were useless. Doctors said that discharge forecasts that do not incorporate clinical ambiguity would never be relied on. Patient advocates emphasized the emotional impact of transfers against expected and delayed communication. These attitudes influenced the design requirements. The goal was not to predict the situation exactly but to have collective situational awareness.

Technology as a Common Language, Not a Command System

This system involved a combination of historical data, real-time data, and machine learning models to predict admissions, discharges, and bed occupancy among sites. However, it was not technical sophistication that made it distinctive; it was accessibility. Outputs were created in a collaborative style, with plain language and graphics instead of technical indicators. Problems were solved with predictive responses to issues that were teams' real problems:

- Where is the pressure going to manifest tomorrow?
- Which of the wards will it feel first?
- What options do we have today?

There was no encouragement to blindly follow predictions because clinicians were requested to question them. The feedback loops enabled the teams to indicate the differences between the forecasts and reality that were utilized by data scientists to maintain the models. Trust was built over time, but not due to an ideal predictive power but because users aided in the development.

Patients as Partners in Flow Design

The representatives of patients were visible during the process. They focused on the idea that flow decisions influenced dignity to the same extent that logistics did. Waiting without information added to anxiety. Transfer of care on wards was interrupted. HUS responded by combining predictive insights in the form of proactive communication protocols. In the cases where the predictions of potential delays and transfers were made, patients received the information in the earlier stages, even when the information was not pleasant. Silence was replaced by transparency, and compassion was integrated into operational planning. Innovation was not limited to efficiency but also experience (Schein, 2010).

Governance in the Absence of Gatekeeping

Diffusion of accountability will lead to failure in co-creation. HUS has prevented this by creating explicit forms of governance that facilitated working together without centralizing authority. There were no changes in the autonomy of clinical teams to make care decisions. Response to the anticipated pressure was organized by the operations teams. Leadership observed with no micromanagement. The maintenance and upgrading of the system were moved around various departments, which supported the notion that predictive flow was an organization asset rather than an IT asset. There was no one group of owners of the innovation—and that was the goal.

Change at a Systematic Level

With the maturity of the system, better outcomes ensued. The HUS had fewer last-minute cancellations due to elective procedures, better coordination of admissions and discharges, and a more streamlined process of wards transfers. Crowding occurred less in the emergency department during peak periods, not due to a decrease in demand but more due to better-coordinated response. Probably the most indicative sign was adoption. Predictive insights were included in daily huddles and planning meetings (Berwick, 2016). Staff used the system due to the fact that it helped them to work as opposed to the fact that policy demanded they do so.

Cultural Change That Lasted Longer Than the Tool

The collaborative approach transformed over time and was no longer limited to hospital flow. Staffing models, outpatient scheduling, and digital triage initiatives were staffed in a similar way in teams. The innovation became more of a practice rather than a project. This transformation of the culture came particularly in handy in times of discontinuity, when predictive accuracy was low and collaboration habits were high. The use of teams in solving problems and eliminating barriers was more efficient as teams got used to solving problems.

Conclusion: When Innovation Belongs to Everyone

Helsinki University Hospital was not able to resolve hospital flow through construction of the smartest algorithm. It did it through construction of the widest ownership. It is through co-creation of predictive analytics with the daily sufferers of the issue that HUS transformed innovation into a collective task as opposed to a delegated change. The system was sustained because people believed in it—and people believed in it because they were its creators. Innovation can not be part of a small group in healthcare. It must belong to many. The experience of Finland demonstrates that a solution developed in collaboration endures, and when innovating turns into a work of everybody, it works.

References

Berwick, D. M. (2016). Era 3 for medicine and health care. *JAMA*, *315*(13), 1329. https://doi.org/10.1001/jama.2016.1509

Schein, E. H. (2010). *Organizational Culture and Leadership* (5th ed.). Hoboken, New Jersey Wiley.

Chapter 6

Stress Simplicity

Do not overcomplicate a solution to a problem; keep the following principle in mind: "When you have two competing theories that make exactly the same predictions, the simpler one" is better to implement.

It seems counterintuitive, but the majority of innovations are rather simple. The temptation to take a problem and create a complex solution exists in most of us. We tend to overthink an opportunity and therefore overengineer a fix. Innovation is often as basic as developing an elegant yet simple solution to a complex issue or opportunity, not the opposite way around. If the innovation can't be easily explained, start again.

SWEDEN | FROM PERSON TO PATIENT AND BACK AGAIN | NICOLAS WAERN

Why the Future of Health Starts With Us and Must Echo Beyond the Hospital

When a close relative of mine was diagnosed with breast cancer, I didn't first see a medical failure. I saw a system and a design failure. Everything that mattered about her life *before* she became a patient was effectively invisible. Important events had happened years earlier. Signals existed. Context existed. Data existed. But it lived in disconnected systems, local databases, personal memory, and paperwork such that no one ever looked at together.

Some of it wasn't connected to the national health system at all. It was stuck in systems that handled her previous challenges with her heart. Her medicine wasn't accounted for, and this spelled disaster. Some of it was never considered "medical," so it didn't count. Some of it simply disappeared.

When she finally entered the hospital, the system suddenly came alive.

But it woke up without memory. Everything before her first visit was hidden in plain sight, but she lacked the tools and systems to convey what her life was all about. Everything during care was

DOI: 10.4324/9781003780175-6

fragmented across specialists and departments, and everything after treatment was barely taken into account. They failed to understand the medicines she was taking for her heart, and everything was completely fragmented.

And to be honest, the healthcare system is not really meant to truly care about individuals. In Sweden it's called "sick-care" and "sick-house" for hospitals. This is where we go when we are sick. But where should we go when we are not sick? And should we even go anywhere, or should experts come to us? The longevity moment is gaining momentum, rightfully so. But numbers everywhere are pointing in the wrong direction. And why is that? For my close relative, she was never really treated as a whole person. For a while, she was a patient. But there were no real goals tied to her stay, and the past and future were painfully irrelevant. Quality of life metrics were non-existent. Her reality was reduced to snapshots—most often accurate, but clinical, documented snapshots—detached from the life that gave them meaning.

What she needed was not someone else's averages, pathways, or generalized protocols that were built up based on decades of fragmented ways of seeking insight.

She needed her own reality, understood over time. Her daughter was amazed with what LLMs could provide at the time. Every piece of recommendation, comment, and expert-driven jargon she could get, she fed to ChatGPT. She didn't know if it was 100% accurate, but it quickly got her to understand what the doctors were talking about. The memory and interactions she gained quickly became a life saver for her and for her mother. But she was always conscientious about the hallucination factor, and that's what led to the creation of Life Atlas.

Seeing the Pattern With Buildings and Bodies: Why This Was Familiar

At the time, I had spent years working with smart buildings, smart heating systems, real estate assets, broken construction life-cycles, and so-called "intelligent buildings." For the most part, there were usually a lot of intelligent people and not-so-smart buildings. Interoperability and the different nuances of it has been something I have been interested in for decades—technical interoperability; semantic interoperability; syntactic, legal, social, and security aspects; and contextual and goal-based interoperability, to mention a few. My professor in IT management was obsessed with healthcare, so healthcare fragmentation and professional bureaucracies by Mintzberg were not news to me. Quite the opposite.

I had been taught about the "five model." Where systems are in the middle, and where roles, hierarchy at the top, processes to the left, culture and goals to the right and people below. What was missing from this model was always data, knowledge, context, and a spatial understanding over time. Systems at the center are too technocratic, and what should be in focus is always the reality we have, in this case the person themselves. So, the moment I saw first hand what was happening to my relative, I recognized the pattern immediately.

In real estate, asset owners often do not know:

- where their data is
- who controls it
- how fragmented it is
- what value it could unlock if understood longitudinally

Real estate owners constantly try to improve buildings by adding more systems—more sensors, more dashboards, more software—without ever fixing the underlying problem: the absence of a shared model of reality and the importance of knowledge as well as wisdom. Data-driven is the norm, and that's completely ridiculous. There's more data than ever, but if we don't understand what it means and how to contextualize it and create impact over time, what's the use?

The relationship between DNA, epigenetics, and lifestyle information is similar to trying to determine what repairs a building needs by relying only on floor plans drawn forty years ago. It's only when we understand the past and the present and can simulate what decisions today lead to a better impact with the goals of the user in mind that we can finally get somewhere. But real-estate owners are plagued by conflicting goals, cultural ways of working that are hard to change, and business models that sometimes do more harm than good. Healthcare is doing the same thing. We are adding layers of technology to systems that are broken by design, and we fail to take into account the most important factor of them all: You. Us. We. My relative.

The First-Principles Failure

From first principles, healthcare today has a paradox at its core. It is one of the most advanced systems humanity has ever built, yet it only meaningfully "sees" people during a narrow window of crisis. Front door, at the hospital, and back-door experiences are fragmented across time. Static labels have a hard time finding meaning if it hasn't happened before. Doctors do not necessarily work together nor understand each other, and past performance dictates how reality should be observed. Before illness, life happens, but the system is blind. During care, the system acts, but without full context. After care, learning stops, and continuity fades, most of the time forever, or trapped within the confines of memories soon to be lost by physicians, care-givers, patients, and their families.

We End Up With a Recurring Loop

Person → Invisible → Patient → Fragmented Data → Discharge → Invisible Again

This is not a tooling problem. It is not an AI problem. It is not a data problem. It is a conceptual mistake, thinking that systems matter more than people. We keep trying to make fragmented systems better when many of those systems should not exist at all. They exist only because we never built something more fundamental.

The Missing Foundation: Digital Twins Done Properly

The future of health cannot be built by optimizing hospitals alone. It requires a new foundation: personal digital twins. Not (just) institutional twins. Not vendor-owned profiles. Not surveillance replicas. But person-owned, longitudinal digital twins that represent a human being across time. A Life Atlas digital twin is not a copy of a person; it is a living model of understanding—connecting past, present, and future in ways that people, systems, and AI can all reason about.

Two Principles Are Absolute

1. Personal data should never be shared. Ever.
2. Every test, trial, and recommendation should be tested virtually first.

What moves outward are anonymized insights, communicated through boundary-spanning objects that allow collaboration without compromising identity or ownership. Data won't go to experts. Data won't be shared with large language models (LLMs) or even small language models (SLMs). Experts will go to where anonymized data resides in the confidential twin. Insight will be generated and shared, but data will always stay with the user. People can innovate and share dynamic insights at the speed of latency with others globally in a quantum safe, and soon to be quantum augmented, continuous fact-finding missions guided by experts, AI agents, and people all working together.

This is how we blend:

- the past, present, and future of an individual
- the trajectories of generations
- human experience and machine intelligence

Preserving Human Meaning in a Data-Driven System

Why Fragmented, Generalized, Static Cold Data Never Worked

Healthcare has tried to capture data for decades, assuming understanding would follow. It never did, because data without people is meaningless. Data without life is a failure to understand context. Trying to improve health using only lab values and codes is like renovating a building using only floor plans—without ever talking to the people who live inside or taking real-time data and future simulations seriously. You can optimize airflow and energy use, but you will fail to create a space that actually works. This is why Life Atlas works even without AI: because the person is the center. Our past, present, and future are visualized in ways that humans can understand first. AI comes later, as a collaborator—not as the authority, making it easier for experts, AI, and real-time data to create foundational AI models for life.

Life Atlas does not just collect data. It has been developed to transform data, context, meaning, expert annotation, and observed personal impact into human-specific foundational life models. These models blend:

- lived experience and self-reported feedback
- lifestyle patterns and goals
- wearable signals
- blood work and biomarkers
- DNA and epigenetic insights
- environmental and social context

not as isolated streams, but as one coherent life. Large and small language models, experts and AI agents help interpret, simulate, and reason—but only on top of this grounded foundation. This is how health literacy improves naturally. People do not only receive instructions from their past. They gain understanding from simulations made from a global pool of futures, including their own.

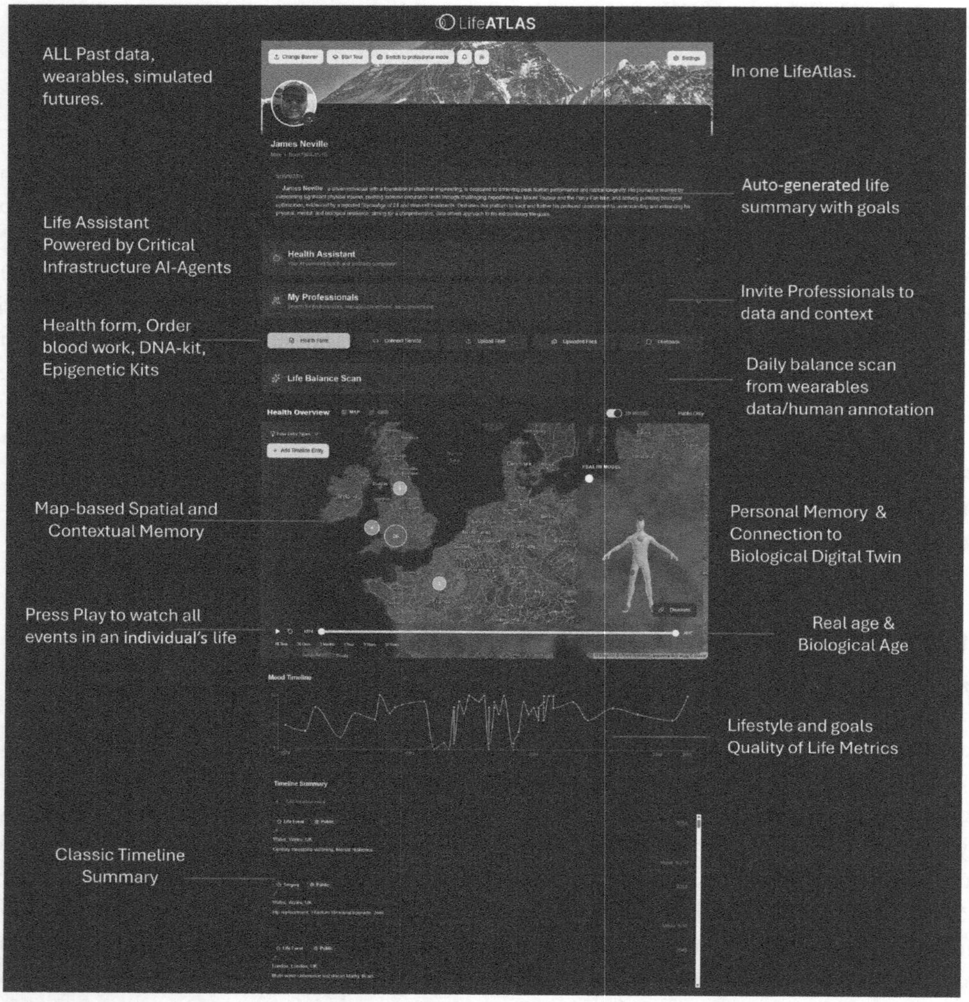

Figure 6.1 Life Atlas interface, spring 2026, depicting digital twins in action with humans and the planet as boundary-spanning objects to accelerate meaningful knowledge transfer between sociotechnological actors in spatially aware multi-agentic ecosystems. From Data to Foundational Life Models.

Humans Are Assets Too, Just More Valuable

In critical infrastructure, we accept that assets need:

- preventive maintenance
- performance optimization
- reduced downtime
- context-aware operation

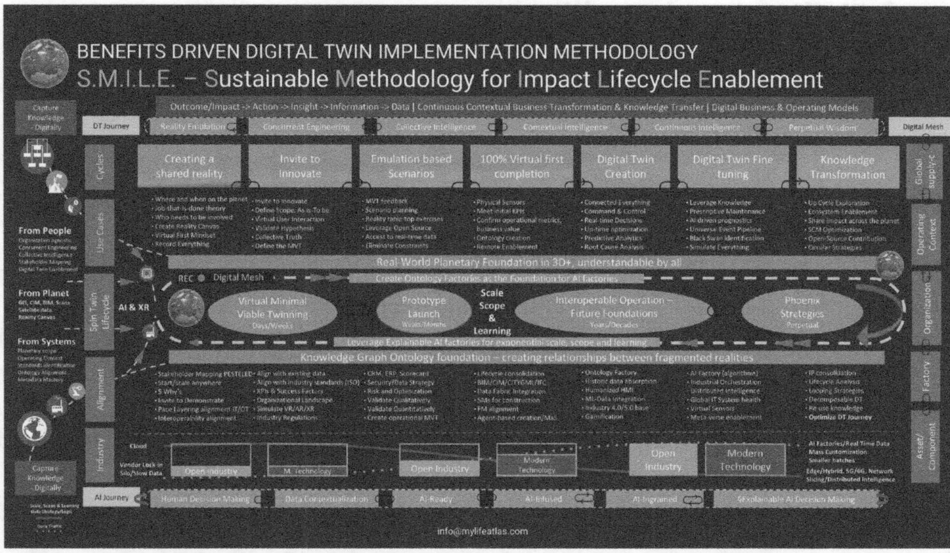

Figure 6.2 Digital twin methodology from Industry 5.0 applications. From reality emulation to perpetual knowledge based on creating shared realities, virtual first implementation, and knowledge transformation based on decentralized and confidential compute and HPC + quantum safe/augmented acceleration.

Downtime is expensive. Reactive fixes are inefficient. Human beings are no different. We are not factories of steel and concrete but systems of flesh and blood that move intelligence, creativity, and meaning forward. Life Atlas treats humans with the same seriousness we apply to critical infrastructure—while keeping agency, dignity, and ownership intact. The same methodology for Industry 5.0 is equally applicable here.

A Living Ally

For my close relative, her Life Atlas has become an ally: a way to understand where she has been, where she is, and where she is heading, and even more importantly, a visually understandable way for others to understand the same. A way to negotiate continuously with her surroundings—systems, professionals, and eventually machines—through her Life Programmable Interface (LPI). Sometimes this is done through numbers, sometimes through visualizations. Soon, it will be through experiences when the spatial web is here for real. It's always been here—the planet, I mean. It's just that we have forgotten about it for a while, staring at the systems we have made instead of the life we are meant to cherish. Our lives do not need to be re-explained. They already have places to store the memories we have created over time. Capturing all of this precious and personal knowledge and keeping it decentralized and secure will have major benefits in the robotics era. This is how future robots and AI companions will truly know us: not through surveillance but through continuity of memory that is ours to share, or to keep, but still leverage for our own benefit.

Toward Civilizational Intelligence

When individuals have digital twins, those twins can:

- connect to past and future trajectories
- share anonymized insight across generations
- learn continuously without exposing identity

We aim to exemplify and to create something larger than healthcare. ChatGPT usually agrees with this, but it is a way to truly create civilizational intelligence. Research will shift from studying fragmented snapshots of sick people to working with living, continuously updated synthetic cohorts grounded in real life trajectories. "First-in-human" studies will increasingly happen first in simulation—safe enough to explore, real enough to matter. Drugs to market will be no more; it will be drugs from generated insights from people, and drugs to people, in record times. Precision recommendations will usher in a new era of precision medicine.

Ending Where It Must Not End—Back to Life and Back to Reality

Life is more than being a patient. And the future of health will not begin at the hospital door—nor end there. Hospitals will of course have digital twins of "themselves," and they too will be actors in a global network that works more dynamically to share insight, not just fragmented data. Individuals will capture what we already generate, understand what we already live, and share wisdom without giving up ourselves. For my relative, this means that she will be able to continuously train her own foundational AI models in the confines of her home, realizing that data centers will be in everyone's home. The data dark ages are slowly but surely going away, and we will all step into an impact renaissance where we share longevity recipes and patterns at the speed of latency, where each individual twin is orchestrated by AI agents that help us seamlessly navigate through life, updating and refreshing constantly.

By stressing simplicity and using the only dashboard that truly works—reality itself, and ourselves—we build systems that learn, endure, and echo forward, not just into healthcare but something that can live forever and accelerate knowledge into the long memory of humanity itself. The ultimate form of simplicity to create a shared reality is when we are using the planet and the human body as the visual anchors we all can relate to. This is how we can be the same but different across different stages of life—from person to patient and back again, spanning generations.

*****

PORTUGAL | A PERSONAL DIGITAL TWIN TO UNDERSTAND VENTRICULAR EXTRASYSTOLES AND REDUCE FRICTION IN LONGITUDINAL CARE | BRUNO CAMPOS

I can tell you the health of my smartphone battery with more confidence than I can explain the health of my heart on an average Tuesday.

My phone reports battery cycles, temperature, background drain, and performance bottlenecks, and it offers clear actions: close this, update that, optimize here. My health signals are scattered: a wearable app, a clinical portal, PDFs, calendar stress, training logs, and, too often, my memory.

That fragmentation became more than an inconvenience when I started focusing on a very real question: how do my premature ventricular extrasystoles (PVCs) behave in real life, across weeks and months, and what can I change in my lifestyle and stress patterns to reduce them?

Setting the Context

Europe is moving fast in digital health: EHR modernization, interoperability programs, patient portals, analytics platforms, and an accelerating wave of AI pilots. Yet at the moments when decisions matter most, daily life and clinical follow-up, many of us still operate in an episodic snapshot model.

We measure. We store. We document. But we struggle to connect clinical measurement (Holter outputs, labs, clinician notes) with real-world context (sleep, stress, caffeine, training load, travel, routine disruption). Clinicians are asked to interpret partial timelines with limited context. Patients are asked to remember triggers across months. Health systems absorb the cost through repeated assessments, inefficiency, and missed prevention opportunities.

This is why the Innovation Pathway theme "Stress Simplicity" resonates with me: innovation is not always about adding a new layer; sometimes it is about removing friction so the right decision becomes easier.

Define the Innovation

My innovation is a personal digital twin, designed explicitly around stress simplicity.

Not a perfect physiological simulation. Not a medical device. Not an academic model. A pragmatic, evolving representation of my health that has one job: turn fragmented signals plus real-world context into longitudinal understanding and conservative next steps, without adding burden.

In practice, my digital twin does three things:

- Unify: aggregate personal health data into a coherent timeline (wearables, habits, clinical outputs).
- Contextualize: attach the "why" around the "what" (sleep, stress, caffeine, alcohol, hydration, training intensity, routine changes, symptoms).
- Support action: produce a small number of low-risk prompts and questions to guide behavior change and improve the quality of clinical conversations while preventing overinterpretation.

My design rule is simple: if I cannot explain it in five minutes, it is too complex. If it increases anxiety or friction, it is the wrong design.

Case Study/Illustrate the Example

I experience ventricular extrasystoles. Like many people, it is easy to get stuck between two unhelpful extremes: ignore them because they feel inconsistent or obsess over them because they feel unpredictable.

What helps is longitudinal clarity.

My objective is to understand whether my PVC burden changes with:

- daily stress and sustained workload
- sleep quantity and quality
- caffeine and alcohol patterns
- hydration and nutrition routines
- training intensity, recovery, and fatigue
- routine disruption (travel, late nights, long meetings, deadlines)

Instead of treating PVCs as isolated snapshots ("that Holter on that day"), I want a repeatable learning loop: under which conditions do PVCs increase, under which conditions do they decrease, and what lifestyle adjustments reduce their frequency or burden?

Monitoring approach: repeated 72-hour Holter + daily context

Over several months, I am running repeated 72-hour Holter monitoring and cross-referencing each Holter period with the contextual timeline captured in my digital twin.

The digital twin acts as an integrator:

- Holter windows define measurement periods
- daily context explains what was happening during those windows
- comparisons across multiple Holters allow pattern discovery
- "what I changed" is tracked between cycles, so learning becomes cumulative

To maintain adoption, I limit inputs to what I can capture consistently:

Holter/Clinical

- start/end of each 72-hour Holter
- key outputs (PVC burden, notable patterns/events) captured as structured fields
- a short summary of clinician feedback when available

Physiological Signals

- resting HR trend
- sleep duration + a simple perceived sleep quality score
- training load with a flag for high-intensity days
- baseline activity

Lifestyle and Stress Context

- daily stress score (30 seconds)
- caffeine intake (simple count)
- alcohol (yes/no + simple amount)
- hydration flag (good/poor)
- disruption flag (travel/deadlines/late nights)
- brief symptom notes when relevant

Decisions (Small Experiments)

- caffeine cut-off time (e.g., none after 12:00)
- strict sleep window for seven days
- training deload week
- hydration protocol
- short daily stress-reduction practice

Outputs (two things only)

To avoid dashboard overload, the twin produces:

1. A one-page summary per Holter period (context, changes vs prior, trends, three conservative clinician questions, two to three low-risk actions)
2. A comparison view across Holter periods (context differences vs outcome differences + a clearly labeled "hypothesis list")

That is stress simplicity: less noise, more usable learning.

Barriers and Lessons Learned

Barrier 1: Data access is still too hard. Even when data is "mine," it is often locked in ecosystems or exported as PDFs. Manual transcription increases errors and reduces adoption.

Lesson: start with what is reliably capturable today; prioritize repeatability over perfection.

Barrier 2: Semantics and comparability. "Stress" can mean physiological strain, psychological load, or both. Units and reference ranges vary.

Lesson: build a tiny personal "data dictionary" early (definition, source, units, interpretation as trend vs absolute).

Barrier 3: Overinterpretation risk (especially with arrhythmias). Tracking PVCs can increase anxiety, and AI can unintentionally amplify false certainty.

Lesson: guard rails are non-negotiable: questions, not diagnoses; trend-first; conservative language; clinical review when needed; soft alerts.

Barrier 4: The human factor. A tool that requires constant effort is not innovation; it is a hobby.

Lesson: design for minimal burden: few inputs, consistent routine, clear outputs, obvious next actions.

The Human Aspect

The biggest impact was not technical, it was behavioral.

The twin reduced:

- Cognitive load: less guessing ("Is this worse?", "What changed?") because the timeline is structured.
- Emotional noise: a calm, trend-based view reduces the oscillation between denial and catastrophizing.

It also improves clinical conversations. Instead of vague impressions, I can bring a concise one-pager:

- "Here is the Holter window."
- "Here is what life looked like during that window."
- "Here is what I changed since last time."
- "Here are three questions I want to validate with you."

This does not replace clinicians. It helps me become a better participant in longitudinal care.

Vision for the Future/Repeatability for Readers

My personal digital twin is small, but the pattern scales. It mirrors what European health systems are trying to achieve: integrate timelines, reduce fragmentation, and support better decisions with less burden.

Future plan: using ChatGPT Health (January 2026) once available in the EU.

With ChatGPT Health launched in January 2026, my next step is to adopt it when it becomes available in the EU/EEA. My aim is not "more AI." It has less friction.

I plan to use ChatGPT Health as the conversation and synthesis layer for my digital twin workflow to:

- produce consistent, clinician-ready one-pagers per Holter window
- translate raw logs into a clear narrative: what changed, what might explain it, what to try next
- preserve guard rails by design (questions not diagnoses, conservative language, trend-first reasoning)
- reduce manual work so the system remains sustainable over months

Three repeatable lessons for European innovation leaders

1. Longitudinal care needs longitudinal artifacts (not episodic snapshots).
2. Interoperability must reduce cognitive load (not add screens).
3. Guard rails must ship with innovation (safety, uncertainty, escalation boundaries, human oversight).

Simple starter template

- pick one outcome (arrhythmia follow-up, hypertension, recovery, diabetes, post-op rehab)
- select five to ten signals maximum
- add two to three context fields (sleep quality, stress score, one trigger)
- produce one output (weekly or period-based one-pager)
- define guard rails (trend-based; no diagnosis; clinician review rules)
- measure success by friction: time-to-capture, time-to-understand, time-to-act

Conclusion: From Data to Decisions

This essay does not claim that a personal digital twin solves arrhythmias. It claims something more realistic and more useful: a simple, contextual, longitudinal model can reduce friction, improve decisions, and improve the quality of clinical conversations.

For me, the purpose is clear: understand how ventricular extrasystoles behave in my real life over months and identify which lifestyle and stress-related adjustments may reduce their frequency or burden, supported by repeated 72-hour Holter monitoring and structured context.

That is "Stress Simplicity" in practice: not more complexity, not more dashboards, just a clearer path from data to decisions.

****

NETHERLANDS | LESS, NOT MORE: HOW ERASMUS MC USED SIMPLICITY TO MAKE DIGITAL INNOVATION STICK | SAKSHIKA DHINGRA, EDWARD W. MARX, ADITI U. JOSHI AND ALINE NOIZET

It is hardly ever true that healthcare fails due to lack of ideas. In more instances, it breaks due to accumulation. Obsolete workflows are not eliminated, and new tools are introduced. Alerts stack on top of alerts. The paperwork grows as time to do it diminishes. Clinicians are not just slowed down with one system; they are overwhelmed with dozens in many hospitals. This fact could not be overlooked in the inpatient departments of Erasmus University Medical Center (Erasmus MC), which is among the biggest academic hospitals in the Netherlands. Nurses also claimed that they spent more time on screens than on patients. Leadership talked of digital maturity, but frontline staff were in pieces. Artificial intelligence or sophisticated analytics was not the starting point of the next innovation project at Erasmus MC. It started with a much more challenging question: What can we take away?

When Digital Maturity Turns Into Digital Friction

Erasmus MC is considered digitally advanced in many ways. Computerized physician order entry, electronic health records, medication administration systems, and clinical dashboards were already in place. The surveys of the internal staff, however, showed that dissatisfaction remained constant, especially within nursing teams. Hospital leaders contracted a time-motion study in a number of inpatient wards in order to determine the problem. The findings were striking. The number of times per hour that nurses had to switch systems was in the dozens. Activities that were supposed to take a natural flow were broken down into various platforms which required autonomous logins, confirmation, and documentation procedures. No single system was broken. The two were overpowering. Lack of innovation was not the problem. This was inappropriate innovation.

Reframing the Innovation Question

Instead of inquiring about which new technology to implement, clinical and digital leaders at Erasmus MC redefined the issue. The guiding question was changed into: Where does technology generate friction rather than value? They had innovation teams on the wards, not to redesign everything but to see where care was stalling. They followed nurses on medication rounds, admissions, and changing of shifts. Every pointless click, redundant entry, and manual workaround was recorded. Crucially, leaders fought the impulse to seek a thorough redesign. This was not an overhaul-based transformation project. It was a subtraction exercise.

Designing for Flow, Not Features

The resultant solution was intentionally small. Erasmus MC did not switch its EHR or bring another dashboard in place. Rather, the hospital introduced a lightweight workflow automation layer, which is meant to coordinate the existing systems silently. Relevant flowsheets automatically updated when vital sign values were typed in. Any abnormal values that were triggered prompted follow-up work without the need for any individual documentation. The administration of medication also updated the inventory and compliance checks in the background (Boonstra et al., 2020). During handovers, the most important information was consolidated into a single, simplified view. There was no introduction of new screens unless it was necessary. Whenever a process could be automated without disrupting the user's workflow, it was. The principle was quite easy to work with: in cases when the innovation could not be described in a single sentence, it was too complicated.

Nurses as Architects of Simplicity

This project was successful due to the fact that nurses were not consulted retrospectively, they were consulted at the start. The workshops were organized in the form of practical questions:

- Is this step really a value addition?
- Do we need this alarm, or is this noise?
- Is this decision automatable, deferable, or removable?

Dozens of small adjustments were made instead of one overall change. Individual changes were small in themselves. The combination of them radically transformed the everyday working process. Simplicity was not imposed. It was co-designed.

Case Study Outcomes at Erasmus MC

Measurable improvements were implemented in pilot wards within months. Time of documentation per shift was reduced. The efficiency of completing tasks was increased. Interruptions decreased. Nurses stated that they felt more in control of their process of work. More importantly, there was no worsening of safety indicators. There were no increments of medication mistakes. The adherence was constant or better. Automation also minimized memory and multitasking—two recognized causes of clinical error in a number of instances. The strongest of them, however, was qualitative. Nurses reported their shifts as less disorganized. Not easier—but calmer. This difference was relevant in an environment where cognitive overload is frequently a cause of burnout (Downing et al., 2018).

Leadership That Protected Simplicity

Leadership restraint was important. Hospital executives did not give in to the urge to increase the scope of the solution. When vendors offered additional features, leaders returned to the same question: Does this make work simpler? This disciplined approach reflects broader findings that successful digital transformation requires governance structures that prioritize human-centered implementation rather than unchecked technological expansion (Demaidi, 2023). In case of uncertainty of the answer, the feature was delayed or rejected. Leaders also made time to go through refinements over and over again, as simplicity is seldom developed on the initial design cycle. It involves constant testing, removal, and modification. Through this, simplicity was not viewed as an absence of ambition but rather a discipline.

Technology That Knows When to Disappear

The technology that was used in this initiative was not new. Rule engines, integrations, and basic analytics were established. Humility made the innovation successful. The system was most effective when clinicians did not pay much attention to it. The indicator of success was not the use of the dashboard but the decrease in the demand of attention. This was the opposite of the common story of innovation—where publicity is a probable indicator of worth. At Erasmus MC, one of the criteria of success was invisibility (Downing et al., 2018).

Lessons in Stressing Simplicity

The Erasmus MC experience supports one of the key lessons of the Voices of Innovation, namely that simplicity is not the lack of innovation but rather a deliberate design. Healthcare organizations tend to think of progress as addition, more tools, more information, more functionality. This was proven wrong in this case. The progress was by diminution, harmony, and simplicity. Erasmus MC minimized the cognitive load by not making solvable issues complex, thus maintaining quality and safety.

Conclusion: Doing Less, Better

With the speed of the digital transformation of the European health systems, attraction to addition will only increase. Novel technologies will guarantee insight, efficiency, and compliance. Some will deliver. Many will not. Erasmus MC is not anti-technology. It is pro-discipline. Innovation does not thrive in unbridled concentration but is improved by intentional elimination of resistance. In emphasizing simplicity, Erasmus MC brought sanity to clinical practice and reminded us that not only are the greatest innovations the ones that do less and better but that there are times when the latter are all but identical to the former.

References

Boonstra, A., Versluis, A., & Vos, J. F. J. (2020). Implementing electronic health records in hospitals: A systematic literature review. *BMC Health Services Research, 14*(1). https://doi.org/10.1186/1472-6963-14-370

Demaidi, M. N. (2023). Artificial intelligence national strategy in a developing country. *AI & Society, 40*. https://doi.org/10.1007/s00146-023-01779-x

Downing, N. L., Bates, D. W., & Longhurst, C. A. (2018). Physician burnout in the electronic health record era: Are we ignoring the real cause? *Annals of Internal Medicine, 169*(1), 50. https://doi.org/10.7326/m18-0139

******

SWEDEN | SUBTRACT TO CARE: HOW KAROLINSKA UNIVERSITY HOSPITAL REDUCED CLINICAL STRESS BY DESIGNING FOR SIMPLICITY | EDWARD W. MARX, ADITI U. JOSHI AND ALINE NOIZET

Complexity in the healthcare sector usually disguises itself as sophistication. A number of dashboards, alerts, and protocols are introduced under the best intentions—but more often than not, clinicians will find themselves being given the reverse of the desired result. Stress rises. Attention fragments. Involuntary care is more difficult, not safer. This paradox was directly experienced in Karolinska University Hospital. One of the largest and most advanced academic hospitals in Europe had noticed that the increasing level of digital maturity was silently straining its cognitive capacity. It was not a different system or a clever algorithm. It was subtraction.

When Excellence Became Overwhelming

Karolinska is a global entity and leader in terms of research, tertiary care, and innovation. Over the years, it had piled up layers of electronic infrastructure: electronic health records, decision support systems, quality registries, reporting needs, and compliance audits. Each system worked. Together, they were overwhelmed. Clinicians said that they devoted more mental resources to workflow than to patients. Alerts were vying against each other. Paperwork grew and time diminished. Stress was not accidental anymore; it was structural. To the leadership, an important realization was that workload was not the cause of burnout but rather unwanted complexity in everyday work.

Asking a Radical Question

Instead of asking the question "What should we do better?", Karolinska was asking something more uncommon: "What can we remove?" This inquiry redefined innovation as not addition but as elimination. Simplicity was a strategic aim rather than an aesthetic inclination. The hospital initiated a multidisciplinary initiative based on the cognitive load rather than the productivity indicators. The focus was to detect friction, which is something that disrupts clinical flow without evident value.

Mapping Stress, Not Just Tasks

The initial step was observation. Instead of observing efficiency, teams followed clinicians around the wards, clinics, and operating theaters with the purpose of learning about stress. They tracked:

- Interruptions per hour
- Intersystem switching

- Redundant documentation
- Distracters disregarded instinctively instead of intuitively

It was eye-opening to them. A large number of stressors were minor and could be individually handled, but when combined were inexorable. It was not a single bad system. It was an accumulation.

Designing for Fewer Decisions

Karolinska developed a rule: any extraneous decision comes at the expense of attention. In collaboration with clinicians, design teams sought those decisions that did not necessitate active judgment:

- Repetitive confirmations
- Duplicate data entry
- Low-value alerts
- Fields that are used infrequently and that are mandatory

These were automated, filled in, or removed where possible. Notably, this was not a centrally done thing. Every specialty was involved in the determination of what constituted necessary in their setting. It was the simplicity of one who was doing the work.

Reducing Alerts Without Reducing Safety

Among the most effective changes that were made was on alert management. Instead of incorporating smarter alerts, Karolinska also minimized the number of alerts. Clinical teams conducted a line-by-line review of existing alerts. Alerts that had seldom been followed through on or that had been already covered by other safeguards were eliminated. What was left were less ambiguous signs relating to significant risk (Babanataj et al., 2019). The outcome was quite unexpected by skeptics: safety indicators did not deteriorate. In some areas, they improved. Clinicians listened once more—because they were no longer tired of attention.

Documentation That Followed Care

Another significant cause of stress was documentation. In the course of time, notes were becoming longer but less useful. Karolinska restructured documentation templates to represent clinical reasoning and not billing logic and historical habits. Unnecessary sections were eliminated. The space of narrative was safeguarded. It was not to make the notes shorter but more understandable. Clinicians said that they spent less time on paperwork and more time on thoughts. The mood of work changed from anxious to oriented (Yi-Frazier et al., 2022).

Technology That Disappeared

One of the success factors was holding back. The only tools that were introduced were ones that cut down steps and did not introduce new steps. However, in other instances, the improvements to users were not visible: imperceptibly orchestrated systems, data flow without prompts, and work done automatically where there were upstream activities. The new leadership approach used a strange measure of success: when clinicians did not pay attention to the technology, it was likely successful.

Leadership That Protected Simplicity

Defense needed to be simple. New features were still being proposed by vendors. New requirements were brought about by regulatory constraints. Internal departments pushed for more data gathering. Discipline was the leadership's response. One question had to be addressed by each suggested addition: Does this lessen or increase cognitive load? The change was postponed if the response was ambiguous. By taking this position, scope creep was avoided and clinicians were informed that simplicity was safeguarded.

The Emotional Impact of Less

The most vivid results were not direct numerical. Clinicians described:

- Fewer interruptions
- More predictable days
- Reduced mental fatigue
- Greater sense of control

Stress did not disappear. Healthcare is a stressful field. But chaos diminished. The talk on burnout was no longer about helplessness. Work had become manageable again in teams.

Simplicity as a Continuous Practice

Karolinska got to know that simplicity is not a one time thing. It must be maintained. Periodical complexity auditing was implemented. Friction points could be marked by clinicians. Little increments added to substantial relief. Innovation was made less noisy—but more efficient.

Lessons in Stress Reduction

The experience of Karolinska points to the non-intuitive lesson that safety and simplicity do not go hand in hand. Too much complexity is a way of hiding risk by anesthetizing the attention. Sanity brings back alertness. Redundancy is another method of resilience that healthcare organizations tend to pursue. Karolinska was able to attain resilience by being clear.

Conclusion: When Less Becomes a Clinical Advantage

Karolinska University Hospital was not able to minimize stress by requesting clinicians to become tougher and faster. It alleviated stress through the consideration of human boundaries. The hospital purposefully removed complexity to make a place where judgment, presence, and care can exist. Karolinska is an alternative: a model of innovation that gives less weight to the load in a healthcare system that is in a race to add features. Sometimes the greatest addition is the one that you do not make; the greatest addition you make boldly is the one that you remove.

References

Babanataj, R., Mazdarani, S., Hesamzadeh, A., Gorji, M. H., & Cherati, J. Y. (2019). Resilience training: Effects on occupational stress and resilience of critical care nurses. *International Journal of Nursing Practice*, *25*(1), e12697. https://doi.org/10.1111/ijn.12697

Yi-Frazier, J. P., O'Donnell, M. B., Adhikari, E. A., Zhou, C., Bradford, M. C., Garcia-Perez, S., Shipman, K. J., Hurtado, S. E., Junkins, C. C., O'Daffer, A., & Rosenberg, A. R. (2022). Assessment of resilience training for hospital employees in the era of COVID-19. *JAMA Network Open*, *5*(7), e2220677. https://doi.org/10.1001/jamanetworkopen.2022.20677

*****

NETHERLANDS | DESIGNING CALM INTO CARE: HOW ERASMUS MC REDUCED COGNITIVE STRESS THROUGH SIMPLICITY | SAKSHIKA DHINGRA, EDWARD W. MARX, ADITI U. JOSHI AND ALINE NOIZET

Healthcare systems tend to react to stress through resilience training, changes of staffing, or performance bonuses. Leaders at Erasmus University Medical Center (Erasmus MC) in Rotterdam reached a different conclusion. Much of the stress that clinicians become involved with is not an issue of personal failure or a workload situation—it is a design problem. It is made as a result of fragmented journeys, over-variation, and cognitive overload incorporated into ordinary work. Instead of asking clinicians to deal with their patients with more skill, Erasmus MC posed an even simpler question: how can care environments be specifically designed to be more relaxed, transparent, and humane? The outcome was a long-term initiative to eliminate friction in everyday clinical practice and showed that simplicity was not the antithesis of sophistication but one of the most potent facilitators.

A High-Performance Academic Center Under Strain

Erasmus MC is one of the largest academic medical centers in Europe, with highly specialized tertiary care and a large teaching and research center. Its size, sophistication, and ambition are some of its strong points. But the same qualities were slowly straining themselves. There was a proliferation of clinical pathways. Documentation requirements increased. Digital tools over time tended to be accumulated and not integrated. Clinicians did not find it challenging because they lacked competence or commitment but because routine care meant that they had to negotiate systems, screens, and competing priorities all the time. It was not a dramatic stress, but it was a consistent one.

Recognizing Complexity as a Clinical Risk

One of the most important lessons in Erasmus MC was the realization that the issue of complexity had become one of patient safety. Systems were taking up cognitive bandwidth instead of care. The essential indications were lost in too much information. Developments needed a reconstruction of context rather than continuity. Notably, stress was not only born in the cases of an emergency. It was integrated into a normal day-to-day routine, admissions, and handovers, daily decision-making. This re-framing moved the efforts to improve towards the addition of tools instead of deliberate subtraction (Aspland et al., 2019).

Designing for the Real Clinical Day

At Erasmus MC, work was initially studied in reality rather than in written form. Multidisciplinary teams observed ward rounds, admissions, discharges, and pathways of escalation. They found duplication, unwarranted decision points, and variation which did not contribute to clinical value. Workarounds were viewed as design indicators as opposed to staff failures. In case clinicians habitually ignored steps, the issue was supposed to be with the system. The simplicity of the design became a discipline that was based on the frontline care realities.

Simplifying Information at the Point of Care

Among the changes that had the most significant effect was the redesign of the information presentation. There was a harmonization of the clinical dashboards. Interfaces were designed to exhibit what was important and not all that might be important. The common clinical cases were taken as the defaults as opposed to infrequent edge cases. Alerts were justified in such a way that only the ones that needed the urgent attention broke the working process. The rest were clustered to be reviewed at optimum times. This minimized cognitive noise and helped clinicians to be focused when doing crucial tasks.

Standardizing Without Undermining Judgment

Standardization was well scoped. Individuals at Erasmus MC differentiated between clinically significant and merely habitual areas of variation. The documentation formats, handover structure, and escalation criteria were standardized in order to minimize mental work that was not needed. This had no restrictions on professional judgment. Quite the contrary; it was guarded. Clinicians no longer wasted power in the determination of either where to write the information or where to locate the information (Aspland et al., 2019). They would be able to concentrate on the interpretation of data, risk weighing, and work with patients. It did not make work any easier—but made it clearer.

Reducing Stress at Transitions of Care

One of the key points of stress was found to be transitions. There was a tendency toward ambiguity in ownership and responsibility in regard to admissions, handovers, and discharges. Erasmus MC dealt with this by defining accountability, standardizing elements of data, and making sure that information followed the patient and not the department. The continuity was supported by a digital system rather than repetition. Last-minute scurries were reduced. The escalation of miscommunications reduced (Yi-Frazier et al., 2022). The system was made purposely to stand still even at the time of pressure.

Leadership That Valued Cognitive Health

Most importantly, cognitive load was seen as a viable organizational issue by Erasmus MC leadership. The time spent on redesign was safeguarded. Priorities were influenced by frontline feedback. Leaders did not give in to the temptation of overloading the already busy environments. Ease was advanced to a strategic virtue rather than an operation preference. This was an indicator of respect—towards clinicians and their interests, skills, and boundaries. The staff was not just identified as professionals but as human beings who worked within their limited cognitive ability (Aiello et al., 2011).

Outcomes That Changed Everyday Experience

The outcomes did not resemble dramatic announcements but consisted of real daily improvements. Clinicians said that there were fewer interruptions and clearer priorities, and they were more aware of the situation. Documents were made more regular and unloadable. There was reduced time spent by teams explaining the processes and coordinating care. More to the point, safety and rigor were not involved. In many cases, they improved. Clarity reduced error. Focus improved execution.

A Cultural Shift Toward Thoughtful Design

Gradually Erasmus MC became skeptical about needless complexity. New initiatives were considered not only in terms of clinical value but also in terms of cognitive effect. Executives habitually posed the question: What will replace this? This culture also did not limit technology to meetings, policies, and reporting structures. Nobility was adopted as a collective duty and not an ideal.

Lessons in Stress and Simplicity

Erasmus MC proves that it is not a heroic task or a decrease of expectations to reduce the level of stress. It involves being humble, that is, being ready to accept that the problem is usually created by systems and not individuals. The hospital has enhanced clinician experience, and it has reinforced care quality by considering simplicity a design principle instead of a constraint. Complex care does not imply complex systems. It entails the need to have systems that take into consideration human limits.

Conclusion: Calm Is Designed, Not Discovered

It was not accidental that calm was created at Erasmus MC. It was deliberately built. The hospital demonstrated that stress in healthcare is more often than not built up and can thus be destroyed by alleviating the cognitive burden and removing unneeded friction in day-to-day tasks. With the increased complexity of healthcare systems, Erasmus MC provides a potent example: simplicity should be deliberate, as in such a case, care, clinicians, and patients will be safer, and the systems can think clearly when it is most needed.

References

Aiello, A., Khayeri, M. Y.-E., Raja, S., Peladeau, N., Romano, D., Leszcz, M., Maunder, R. G., Rose, M., Adam, M. A., Pain, C., Moore, A., Savage, D., & Schulman, R. B. (2011). Resilience training for hospital workers in anticipation of an influenza pandemic. *Journal of Continuing Education in the Health Professions*, *31*(1), 15–20. https://doi.org/10.1002/chp.20096

Aspland, E., Gartner, D., & Harper, P. (2019). Clinical pathway modelling: A literature review. *Health Systems*, *10*(1), 1–23. https://doi.org/10.1080/20476965.2019.1652547

Yi-Frazier, J. P., O'Donnell, M. B., Adhikari, E. A., Zhou, C., Bradford, M. C., Garcia-Perez, S., Shipman, K. J., Hurtado, S. E., Junkins, C. C., O'Daffer, A., & Rosenberg, A. R. (2022). Assessment of resilience training for hospital employees in the era of COVID-19. *JAMA Network Open*, *5*(7), e2220677. https://doi.org/10.1001/jamanetworkopen.2022.20677

*****

SWEDEN | REMOVING THE NOISE: HOW KAROLINSKA UNIVERSITY HOSPITAL SIMPLIFIED CLINICAL PATHWAYS TO REDUCE SYSTEM STRESS | DHINGRA, MARX, JOSHI, NOIZET

The topic of stress in healthcare has been frequently addressed as a personal phenomenon, such as burnout, emotional exhaustion, and moral distress. Leaders arrived at a different conclusion at Karolinska University Hospital in Sweden. A lot of the pressure that clinicians act under is not individual. It is structural. It is incorporated in the jagged trails, overabundance of variation, redundancy of steps, and systems where interpretation is required. This complexity over time is directly corrosive to attention and care and quietly exacerbates stress. Instead of asking clinicians to get tougher, Karolinska decided to restructure the space that they operated in. The hospital demonstrated that simplicity is not a trade-off by intentionally simplifying clinical processes, limiting unnecessary variation, and explicitly defining the logic underlying decisions. It is a performance, safety, and sustainability strategy.

Excellence Strained by Complexity

One of the most developed academic hospitals in Europe is Karolinska University Hospital, which integrates tertiary care, research, and education in several campuses. Complexity came along with this excellence. The growth in medical knowledge led to the growth in clinical guidelines, subspecialty protocols, documentation standards, and digital tools: optimization of different departments locally. With time, variability grew, not necessarily due to patient need but because the systems tolerated it. Clinicians used to follow through several sets of orders between similar cases, with inconsistency in handovers and concurrent documentation processes. Monotonous decisions made demanded repeat cognition. It was not an acute load; it was an unremitting one. Complications were accepted as a fact and along with them an unrelenting background of stress.

Recognizing Variation as a Source of Stress

Karolinska repackaged the issue. Rather than the variation being considered a quality problem, leaders started to consider it a stress amplifier. Mental energy is exhausted when clinicians make decision after decision with equally acceptable alternatives available. In cases where there is no need to diverge in pathways, coordination is lost. During the case of implicit but not explicit expectations, there are more mistakes and frustration. Notably, this stress was not an emergency in the first place. It built up in the course of daily care. The hospital realized that cognitive noise reduction was a force that could be as effective as the addition of new capabilities.

Choosing Thoughtful Standardization

It was not aimed at eliminating clinical judgment but to eliminate unwarranted judgment. Multidisciplinary teams named high-volume, high-impact situations where evidence was robust and unwarranted variation was prevalent, including sepsis management, elective surgical courses, and chronic disease severity inpatient flows. Karolinska produced default pathways as opposed to strict protocols. These gave the best evidence-based clear starting points, even though they retained the option of deviating in the case of clinical justification. It was focused on clarity and not control. Standardization was not presented as a restriction but support.

Making the Right Path the Easy Path

One principle came to mind: the most evidence-based and safest option is also supposed to be the easiest one to follow. Order sets were restructured such that suggested actions were brought to the forefront. Unnecessary options were eliminated. Clinical workflows were associated with documentation templates, as opposed to administrative logic. Clinicians did not need to look around trying to find the right approach anymore—it was in sight (Babanataj et al., 2019). This minimized decision fatigue, sped up routine care, and provided time to shift attention to the more complex clinical reasoning and patient interaction.

Simplifying Multidisciplinary Collaboration

Karolinska is a big academic hospital, which relies on multidisciplinary cooperation. However, collaboration in itself was a complicated matter. There was a difference in expectations of rounds, consults, and handovers between units. Much of the knowledge was tacit, which was disadvantageous to trainees and rotating employees. Its response to this situation was to standardize communication structures without professional roles flattening. Common language replaced specialized lingo. Clear structures were used to determine what was required, when, and by whom when it came to information. Predictability increased. Coordination improved. Stress among junior clinicians reduced (Kwok et al., 2021).

Technology Used to Reduce Noise

Digital systems were viewed as simplifiers and not creators of more complexity. Dashboards were reduced to show only clinically actionable information. Alerts were investigated and harshly cut down. The implementation of decision support was done only at those points where it was truly valuable. It is interesting to note that Karolinska was not seduced into digitizing all processes. Certain complexity was eliminated instead of being automated. Technology was tacit—and more productive.

Leadership That Defended Simplicity

To keep it simple, there had to be discipline. The hospital leadership considered new initiatives, metrics, and tools considering only one aspect. What will this replace? Suggestions which would increase the workload but not decrease any other workload were questioned or postponed. More importantly, simplification was initiated by clinicians. Frontline teams found areas of friction, experimented with changes, and formulated solutions. Leadership offered immunity against initiative overload and indicated that simplicity is an organizational virtue rather than a short-lived project.

Stress Reduction Without Lowering Standards

The consequences were not dramatic but significant. Clinicians stated that the expectations were better understood, interruptions were reduced, and routine decisions were more confident. Procrastination in time on navigating systems was reduced. The time spent with patients also increased. Diversity decreased without compromising personal treatment. Stress was not eliminated, but it was more closely associated with real clinical complexity as opposed to administrative clutter. The quality, safety, and experience were enhanced jointly (Yi-Frazier et al., 2022).

A Shift in Organizational Mindset

Gradually, a common principle was established in Karolinska: complexity will have to prove its worth. In cases where a process was complex, it had to provide clear clinical good. Otherwise, it was automatically simplified. This attitude was not limited to the clinical pathways but also to meetings, reporting structure, and internal communication. Respect turned into simplicity—respect towards clinician attention and patient trust.

Lessons in Stress and Simplicity

Karolinska's experience supports a crucial point of view: stress is not always experienced by people, but it is designed into systems much earlier. It does not involve the reduction of stress by reducing standards. It involves the alignment of systems with the way of thinking, decision making, and teamwork among people. Uncomplicatedness is no enemy of excellence. It enables it.

Conclusion: When Less Becomes More

Asking clinicians to do less did not alleviate stress at Karolinska University Hospital. It helped to lessen stress with the creation of mechanisms that required less unwarranted effort. The hospital maintained its autonomy by eliminating unnecessary variation and defining clinical pathways, which also helped to get back on track. Karolinska provides a potent counterargument in a healthcare setting where complexity is frequently confused with sophistication: the most cutting-edge systems are those that eliminate unnecessary components rather than those that add more. Attention returns when there is less noise. Additionally, care gets better.

References

Babanataj, R., Mazdarani, S., Hesamzadeh, A., Gorji, M. H., & Cherati, J. Y. (2019). Resilience training: Effects on occupational stress and resilience of critical care nurses. *International Journal of Nursing Practice*, *25*(1), e12697. https://doi.org/10.1111/ijn.12697

Kwok, C. S., Muntean, E.-A., & Mallen, C. D. (2021). The patient pathway review: A new method of evaluating clinical practices to understand the complexities of real-world care. *Critical Pathways in Cardiology: A Journal of Evidence-Based Medicine, 20*(4), 213–219. https://doi.org/10.1097/hpc.0000000000000267

Yi-Frazier, J. P., O'Donnell, M. B., Adhikari, E. A., Zhou, C., Bradford, M. C., Garcia-Perez, S., Shipman, K. J., Hurtado, S. E., Junkins, C. C., O'Daffer, A., & Rosenberg, A. R. (2022). Assessment of resilience training for hospital employees in the era of COVID-19. *JAMA Network Open, 5*(7), e2220677. https://doi.org/10.1001/jamanetworkopen.2022.20677

*****

SWEDEN | SLOW IS SMOOTH: HOW KAROLINSKA UNIVERSITY HOSPITAL REDUCED CLINICAL STRESS BY SIMPLIFYING INFORMATION FLOW | DHINGRA, MARX, JOSHI

Speed has been confused with efficiency in the modern healthcare setting. A speedy documentation process, faster handovers, and quick decision making are considered milestones of improvement. However, speed in the absence of clarity overwhelms thinking and risks and corrosively undermines clinician wellbeing. This was not the conclusion of Karolinska University Hospital in Stockholm but the result of reflection. Karolinska is one of the most developed academic medical centers in Europe and was highly digital and protocol driven with clinical rigor that was of high esteem internationally. Nothing in the system had failed—but the system was showing signs of strain. Karolinska did not require clinicians to work faster and become more resilient but instead made some processes slower by simplifying. By doing this, it was able to show a contrapuntal fact: once information flow is free, care will naturally advance.

When Precision Turned Into Pressure

Karolinska is built on the foundation of the reputation of precision medicine, research excellence, and patient safety. With time, such strengths became congested with information. Clinical pathways proliferated. Alerts increased. Guidelines expanded. All the additions were justifiable in themselves. Cognitive congestion was formed by them together. Clinicians reported days of micro-decision-making: which alert had to be addressed at this moment, which pathway to use, which data point was urgent at this point. These decisions were not crushing ones. Their constant presence was. The cause of stress was not ignorance but rather an overload of signals to pay attention to.

Reframing the Goal: From Speed to Smoothness

Karolinska re-packaged the problem instead of asking how to make work go faster: Where does information interrupt care and not support it? Based on high-reliability sectors, executives adopted a leadership philosophy: slow is smooth, smooth is fast. When information would come in the proper order, at the proper time, speed would become a natural occurrence. Stress alleviation was made a design goal that did not serve as a wellness initiative. This reframing moved the focus of the improvement efforts to flow rather than acceleration (Yi-Frazier et al., 2022).

Untangling the Information Stream

The initial intervention was concerned with sequencing. Missing data were not a problem to clinicians but simultaneous data. There was no hierarchy in receiving lab results, alerts, messages, and documentation prompts. Karolinska redesigned clinical interfaces in such a way that the information was in rhythm with care. Dangerous indicators were early manifestations. Details of the context were only used where necessary. The non-urgent prompts were postponed. Things were not taken down without any reason; things were not kept without a purpose. The system started talking in a more intimate manner—distinctly.

Reducing Cognitive Switching

Context switching was one of the most important causes of stress: switching screens, mental models, and priorities many times. Karolinska took care of this by grouping similar duties in sequential lines. The entire process of ordering, documentation and review was synchronized in such a way that the clinicians were able to complete meaningful units of work without being interrupted. Notably, the hospital did not give in to the urge to introduce new dashboards. It instead retired existing ones. The idea was not to have fewer clicks but fewer mind changes. Switching in cognition was reduced and continuity of thought was restored.

Protocols That Guided, Not Governed

The Scandinavian medical model relies on protocols, which in Karolinska had over time evolved to being prescriptive instead of supportive. Multidisciplinary teams revisited protocols from a different perspective: Does this lessen the uncertainty—or apply pressure? Flexibility was reinstated where rigidity was caused without clinical advantage. Decision support tools became redefined as advice as opposed to directives (Bernardi et al., 2019). When clinically appropriate, deviations from protocols were explicitly permitted. This restored professional autonomy and reduced anxiety associated with potential non-compliance.

Silence as a Deliberate Design Choice

Intentional silence was among the most visible developments. Karolinska lowered the number of alerts and unnecessary messages significantly. Silence was also considered a resource and not a lack. Clinicians stated that they could think better. Conversation with patients decreased. Wards were less anxious and more concentrated. The constant background noise of alerts and notifications was significantly reduced. Concentration was once again possible.

Leadership That Resisted Acceleration

There was a need for effective leadership during these changes. In an organization that values efficiency and accuracy, slowness can seem retrogressive. The leaders at Karolinska never stressed simplifying as a withdrawal against excellence but a restoration of it. New projects were introduced slowly. Change was sequenced. The leaders cushioned the teams against constant optimization processes and upheld the importance of doing fewer things better. Advancement was no longer ruthless.

Emotional Safety Through Predictability

With the simplification of work flows, there was more predictability. Clinicians had less to be surprised by, fewer last-minute escalations, and more definite expectations. Such predictability minimized emotional load (Aspland et al, 2019). Stress never disappeared—but it became not constant but a series of events. Discussion on burnout went beyond being an issue of survival to one of sustainability. Peace was no longer incidental; it was organizational.

Measuring What Actually Matters

Karolinska went beyond throughput in its metrics. Teams kept an eye on metrics like:

- Time to clinical decision confidence;
- Alert relevance and actionability; and
- Interruptions per shift.

Instead of focusing on speed, these metrics measured cognitive quality. The findings demonstrated improved clinician satisfaction and fewer oversight-related errors without sacrificing results.

Simplicity as a Form of Respect

In essence, the Karolinska methodology regarded simplicity as respect, respect towards attention, respect towards judgment, and respect towards human cognitive limitations. People were supposed to adjust to technology rather than the opposite. The concept of minimalism was not doing less of something; rather, it was eliminating what distracted people.

Lessons in Stress Reduction

The example of Karolinska University Hospital shows that work is not a source of stress in itself. Stress usually comes about due to the way work is structured and delivery of information. Healthcare systems can preserve the health of clinicians and patients by eliminating the extra features that require resilience instead of necessitating it. Smooth systems protect individuals.

Conclusion: Calm as a Clinical Asset

Karolinska did not relieve the stress through pushing clinicians or automation. It minimized stress through creating less stressful care. The hospital simplified the flow of information, restored judgment, and reduced cognitive noise, thus enabling people to think clearly again. In healthcare, composure is not complacency. Safety is a precursor to it. And even the most advanced innovation is also knowing when to go slowly and how to do it.

References

Aspland, E., Gartner, D., & Harper, P. (2019). Clinical pathway modelling: A literature review. *Health Systems, 10*(1), 1–23. https://doi.org/10.1080/20476965.2019.1652547

Bernardi, S., Mahulea, C., & Albareda, J. (2019). Toward a decision support system for the clinical pathways assessment. *Discrete Event Dynamic Systems, 29*(1), 91–125. https://doi.org/10.1007/s10626-019-00279-9

Yi-Frazier, J. P., O'Donnell, M. B., Adhikari, E. A., Zhou, C., Bradford, M. C., Garcia-Perez, S., Shipman, K. J., Hurtado, S. E., Junkins, C. C., O'Daffer, A., & Rosenberg, A. R. (2022). Assessment of resilience training for hospital employees in the era of COVID-19. *JAMA Network Open, 5*(7), e2220677. https://doi.org/10.1001/jamanetworkopen.2022.20677

Chapter 7

Recognize and Reward

Recognize or reward the efforts of stakeholders to innovate even at the smallest levels.

To maximize innovation potential, we must not forget the power of motivation in human behavior. People will largely do what they are primarily rewarded and recognized for. For innovation to thrive, consider launching multiple reward and recognition programs to reinforce culture, enhance engagement, and encourage collaboration. Programs should reward not only those who generate ideas but also all the support teams enabling success. That which is rewarded and recognized is repeated. Innovation will multiply commensurate with affirmation given.

KOSOVO | HACKATHON ON DIGITAL HEALTH AND AI | EDWARD W. MARX

Hackathons are a great way to combine creativity, technology, and teamwork into an extensive workshop format. For participants, it offers a unique platform to expand skills, develop innovative solutions, and network with peers and industry experts. Teams work under time pressure to solve real-world problems, aided by mentors and experts, leading to practical, creative, and implementable solutions. Finally, hackathons are a great tool to recognize and reward participants by funding winning ideas into viable solutions.

Pristina Innovate Healthcare

The Hackathon on Digital Health and AI took place in April 2025 in the Kosovo capital of Pristina. The ICR Lab is the primary organizer and supported by the Ministry of Education and Research of the Federal Republic of Germany in collaboration with Martin Luther University of Halle-Wittenberg. Kolegji Heimerer and other partners are reimaging the "innovate.healthcare" hackathon model of Healthcare Futurists Gmbh into "pristina.innovate.healthcare" to bring to southeast Europe future "healthpreneurs," an opportunity to innovate healthcare under great mentoring and expertise for a 48-hour hacking marathon.

With the overall theme of "Pristina Pulse: Care, Creativity, Collaboration and Change," invitations were extended throughout southeast Europe, and hundreds responded.

DOI: 10.4324/9781003780175-7

Hackathon Recruitment Messaging

The future of healthcare needs bold ideas and collaborative minds to tackle its growing challenges. From rising demands on healthcare systems to the need for more accessible and patient-centered solutions, there's never been a more crucial time to step up. Whether it's creating smarter health tools or rethinking how we approach wellbeing, your skills and creativity can make a real difference.

In addition to digital and social media recruitment campaigns, traditional outreach methods such as billboards were also used. One of the campaign's most visible slogans was "Better Artificially Intelligent than Naturally Ignorant" (Figure 7.1).

The recruitment strategy aimed to attract a broad and interdisciplinary group of participants, including technology enthusiasts, healthcare professionals, designers, and entrepreneurs. Participants were encouraged to contribute their ideas, energy, and creativity to help shape future healthcare solutions, while the organizers provided the platform, mentoring, and logistical support required to develop new concepts.

The hackathon was designed as an intensive forty-eight-hour innovation event focused on developing practical ideas for healthcare challenges. In addition to networking opportunities and the collaborative atmosphere typical of startup environments, participants worked closely with coaches and mentors who were experts in healthcare, artificial intelligence, digital health, remote monitoring, and related fields.

The goal of the event was to enable interdisciplinary teams to develop and present early-stage solution concepts within a short timeframe, demonstrating how collaborative innovation could generate new approaches to complex healthcare problems.

We believe that innovation is magic that happens when people with no blinders on and from different backgrounds meet in a stimulating environment to dedicate time to a specific field of interest. For us, this is healthcare. This is why we are trying to create the perfect ecosystem where

Figure 7.1 Welcoming Entrepreneurs for Hackathon on Digital Health and AI

we think we will see innovation happen right in front of us. Our goal is to provide you with the best minds and tangible challenges to really make a difference in healthcare and patient care.

Hackathon Process

"innovate.healthcare" is a hackathon and a networking venue. Our goal is to bring bright minds and great ideas together in a stimulating environment. We want people to interact and interchange ideas, thoughts, wishes, and beliefs, for this is the cradle of new entrepreneurial endeavors. We want you to interact with each other on eye level, and we want the participants to be able to go out after this event and start founding their own companies in healthcare.

First, you must become interested in the event and purchase a ticket for participation. After a reverse pitch by the challenge owners Saturday morning, you will select your team. The teams will break into their team rooms and work there until Sunday noon. The reverse pitch means the challenge owner must present the challenge and themselves to the audience. This helps spread the content of the individual challenges among the participants and is the first exercise in pitching.

Participants decide which challenge they want to work on. However, we have mechanisms to ensure that each team has a good mix of different profiles, such as a (bio-)medical, design, developer, or business profile. Diversity is what we believe to be the keystone for successful innovation. Get your blinders off and go ahead.

Participants were provided all basic necessities during the event and could sleep at the venue as well.

Hackathon Sample Reverse Pitches

Airguard. Air Pollution and Health.

Background: Air pollution contributes to over 7 million deaths annually, with significant impacts on respiratory, cardiovascular, and mental health. Despite growing awareness, many people are unaware of how air quality directly affects their day-to-day health or what they can do to mitigate its impact.

Advances in digital health and technology provide opportunities to better understand, monitor, and combat air pollution's effects, empowering individuals and communities to make healthier choices.

Problem: The problem isn't just the pollution—it's the lack of accessible tools to interpret air quality data and provide actionable guidance. Many citizens are unaware of what the numbers mean, how pollution impacts their health, or what steps they can take when air quality is poor.

Actual challenge: We want to reclaim the outdoors as a space for health while addressing the challenges of air pollution. Using the possibilities of digital transformation in the health sector, how can we create solutions that:

- Bridge the gap between air quality data and actionable insights for individuals and families;
- Empower users to make informed decisions about outdoor activities, commuting, or protecting their health during periods of high pollution;
- Provide real-time guidance on practical actions, such as wearing masks, using air purifiers, or choosing safer outdoor locations;
- And create solutions that are accessible, engaging, and tailored to urban communities like Pristina?

CoNurse. Enhancing Nursing Education With AI

Background. Arta, a first-year nursing student, excels in the classroom but freezes during her first clinical rotation. The theory she learned feels distant as she faces real patients. She hesitates before starting a procedure, unsure if she's doing it right. Her supervisor is busy, and she struggles to find clear, structured guidance when she needs it most. Like many students, Arta wishes she had a reliable way to reinforce her skills, track her progress, and build confidence in real-world scenarios.

Problem. For nursing students like Arta, the transition from theory to practice can be overwhelming. Performing procedures under pressure, remembering key clinical guidelines, and gaining confidence all require continuous support. Yet feedback is often limited, learning resources are scattered, and students have no real-time way to track their skill development. Without structured guidance, they risk feeling unprepared for patient care.

The Challenge. How can AI bridge the gap between classroom learning and hands-on practice? Your task is to develop a digital tool that provides nursing students with step-by-step guidance on procedures, personalized study recommendations, and real-time skill tracking. Could AI-powered quizzes, interactive feedback, or structured access to essential resources make clinical training more effective? Design a solution that helps students like Arta gain confidence, improve their skills, and feel prepared for their future in healthcare.

SpeakTx. AI-Powered Speech Therapy Support for Patients

Background. Leona, a 52-year-old teacher, suffered a stroke six months ago. While her recovery has been steady, she struggles with speaking clearly, making everyday conversations frustrating. She attends speech therapy, but with limited sessions and generic exercises, progress feels slow. Meanwhile, 10-year-old Arian, who has a speech delay, finds traditional speech therapy dull and difficult to follow. For both, practicing at home is a challenge—motivation fades, feedback is scarce, and tracking improvements is complicated.

Problem. Speech therapy is essential for millions of people like Leona and Arian, yet accessibility remains a major barrier. Not everyone can attend frequent in-person sessions, and existing digital solutions often lack personalized feedback, leaving patients uncertain about their progress. Many lose motivation, making consistent practice difficult. Therapists, too, struggle to monitor improvements remotely.

The Challenge. Your task is to design an AI-powered tool that transforms speech therapy into a more engaging and effective experience. How can AI provide real-time feedback on pronunciation and articulation? Can it personalize exercises based on individual progress? Could gamified or interactive elements make practice more enjoyable? And how might patients and therapists easily track improvements over time?

Create a solution that helps Leona, Arian, and countless others gain confidence in their speech—one word at a time.

Recognition

After the final pitches were completed, a jury of distinguished judges convened and discussed the merits of each innovation. Judges came from government, universities, industry, and healthcare. They considered all of the great concepts focused around:

- Streamlining patient data management.
- Enhancing diagnostic accuracy.

- Improving access to healthcare in underserved regions.
- Collaborative problem-solving.
- Reducing healthcare system burdens.
- Addressing workforce shortages via technology.
- Promoting preventive care through AI-driven insights.

Key Innovation—AI-Powered Health Fact-Checking Tool

A team from the Technical University of Munich (TUM) Heilbronn developed a tool designed to detect health-related misinformation in seconds. This solution aimed to improve health literacy by quickly verifying the accuracy of medical claims online. Given the rapid rise of consumer driven AI in healthcare, the judges felt that this kind of tool could help protect both the public and healthcare providers. Given the speed and the human centric design of the tool, ease of use would minimize any burden to utilization. Therefore swift adoption is expected. The team was rewarded with a partnership from one of the sponsors, Healthcare Futurists. The tool is expected to be released in 2026.

Outcomes

Recognition and reward are powerful motivators. Leveraging a hackathon model can accelerate innovation. As the Pristina Innovate Healthcare demonstrates, when you combine recognition and reward with an accelerator like a hackathon, you can indeed change the world.

*****

ENGLAND | WHAT GETS VALUED GETS SUSTAINED: HOW GUY'S AND ST THOMAS' USED RECOGNITION TO MAKE INNOVATION STICK | EDWARD W. MARX, ADITI U. JOSHI AND ALINE NOIZET

Health Care systems are rife with pilots which do not scale. New tools are released, initial excitement dies away, and innovation softens and fades in the background due to the pressure of operations. The absent factor is not technology or talent. In more cases, it is reinforcement. The leaders of Guy and St Thomas NHS Foundation Trust (GSTT) came to the realization that innovation cannot prevail due to its clinical soundness or strategic alignment. It continues to survive since individuals perceive themselves as having done the difficult job of change. By integrating recognition and reward into the dynamic of innovation, not as an add-on but as a part of innovation, GSTT made digital advancement a habitual and recurrent trend, as opposed to a one-time achievement.

A High-Performing System Under Constant Pressure

Guy and St Thomas is an extensive and intricate NHS Trust based in the United Kingdom and covering a wide variety of hospital locations and with a very diverse target population. The company is known all over the world to excel in its clinical services through cancer, cardiovascular medicine, and transplantation. Similar to the majority of NHS organizations, though, GSTT is placed under unremitting pressure. The increased need, lack of people to carry out the task, and economic limits restrict the time and energy to be used in experimentation. Innovation is in competition with delivery—and delivery always wins. The digital transformation initiatives would not be an exception (Alanazi, 2023). As the Trust spent a lot of money on electronic health records, analytics, and clinical decision tools, leaders recognized that there was a common pattern: the adoption was uneven. There were teams which were inclined and those which lost interest with the termination of initial support. The issue was not resistance. It was sustainability.

Seeing Innovation as Labor

The leadership at GSTT had an ultimately important observation, which is that when it comes to innovation, one has to work hard, and in order to work hard, one has to be reinforced. Redesigned workflows, introduced digital tools, or attended improvements initiatives were placing additional work on top of already challenging jobs, and this work was often hidden work. At the time when that work was not appreciated, it became optional. At the time it became optional, it vanished. The Trust redefined innovation as a type of clinical work that is worthy of recognition, position, and advancement.

Redesigning Recognition, Not Just Incentives

Innovation contributions started to show up in:

- Performance reviews;
- Promotion and leadership pathways;
- Internal communications and town halls;
- Awards and Trust-wide showcases;
- Teams that improved patient flow using digital tools were highlighted alongside clinical excellence awards;
- Nurses who redesigned documentation workflows received the same visibility as research leads; data analysts and operational staff were named, not anonymized;
- Recognition became public, consistent, and meaningful.

Making Teams the Unit of Reward

The decision to acknowledge teams and not individuals is one of the most conscious decisions made by GSTT. Innovation in healthcare is hardly seen as the outcome of one hero. It is a product of cooperation among clinicians, IT, managers, and support personnel. Rewarding teams at the Trust precluded competition and strengthened joint ownership (Berwick, 2016). Technological improvements in multidisciplinary groups resulted in invitations to present their work internally. Their solutions were used as references to other departments. Innovation ceased being a matter of individual risk, and it began to be a source of collective pride.

Linking Recognition to Patient Impact

At GSTT, recognition was never abstract. It was directly linked to the benefit of the patient. Outcomes like shorter wait times, increased safety, better patient experiences, and less work for staff are highlighted by awards and showcases. This framing was important. Physicians believed they were being compensated for providing better care rather than for "digital adoption." Technology is now a tool rather than a message.

Technology That Enabled Measurement Without Punishment

Digital devices were of significant supporting importance. Improvements in flow, safety, and productivity were tracked using analytics platforms. But information was employed to point out success, not failure. Dashboards were put into contexts (Demaidi, 2023). Diversity raised questions, not accusations. Teams were motivated to explore and experiment. GSTT also made participation safer by removing measurement and punishment. Employees were not afraid to try, learn, and change since mistakes were not seen as failures but rather as a part of the process.

Leadership That Modeled the Behavior

The need to recognize was established by senior leaders at GSTT. Board meetings were used to discuss innovations that were successful. Executives visited showcases and mentioned the contributions of frontline staff in communications. Leaders took to stages to celebrate teams that were at work. This exposure was a strong message: this was a place where innovation was important, and the individuals driving it were important as well. There was no delegation of recognition. It was modeled.

Cultural Shifts That Followed Reinforcement

Over time, behavior changed. Teams started coming up with ideas and not orders. Clinicians requested information to test hypotheses. It was not analog resistance to digital tools. Probably the most significant thing was that innovation ceased to be perceived as an additional effort. It was incorporated in professional identity. Employees said they felt proud to have done their part to improve the system, not only in one-on-one encounters with a patient.

Tangible Results Beyond Morale

The impact was measurable. GSTT had more favorable reports of the use of digital tools and more stable use of standardized pathways, as well as positive engagement among professional groups. The projects which stalled before due to pilots being sustained and scaled were resurrected. The rates of turnover in teams that were digitally engaged decreased. Mutual work between technical and clinical staff enhanced. Recognition never superseded governance or strategy—but it increased both.

Avoiding the Trap of Tokenism

GSTT was keen not to be superficially recognized. Prizes were not given out haphazardly. The criteria were clear. Acknowledgement was gained by influence and hard work. This ensured credibility, and cynicism was avoided. To leaders, what was given was also given. The failure to learn through the initiatives that did not work was not denied, which strengthened psychological safety. Innovation was perceived as development, not excellence.

Lessons in Recognizing and Rewarding Innovation

The experience of Guy and St Thomas highlights a very simple yet frequently ignored fact; people imitate things that are reinforced. Goodwill is not sufficient in healthcare systems. Innovation is time consuming, emotionally demanding, and professionally risky. Once such investments are recognized, they are multiplied. Awareness is not a tender strategy. It is infrastructure.

Conclusion: Making Innovation Worth Repeating

Guy and St Thomas have not unlocked innovation through giving orders or purchasing superior technology. It opened innovation by appreciating those that enabled change. The Trust incorporated recognition into career trajectories, culture, and leadership actions and thus made innovation something that clinicians sought to maintain rather than something they suffered. Recognition is not a luxury in the field of healthcare where the need is infinite and the attention is limited. It is how progress survives. What is valued is repeated. Innovation was repeated at GSTT.

References

Alanazi, A. (2023). Clinicians' Views on Using Artificial Intelligence in Healthcare: Opportunities, Challenges, and Beyond. *Cureus, 15*(9). https://doi.org/10.7759/cureus.45255

Berwick, D. M. (2016). Era 3 for Medicine and Health Care. *JAMA, 315*(13), 1329. https://doi.org/10.1001/jama.2016.1509

Demaidi, M. N. (2023). Artificial Intelligence National Strategy in a Developing Country. *AI & Society, 40.* https://doi.org/10.1007/s00146-023-01779-x

****

SPAIN | WHAT GETS RECOGNIZED GETS REPEATED: HOW HOSPITAL CLÍNIC DE BARCELONA USED INCENTIVES TO TURN POPULATION HEALTH DATA INTO ACTION | SAKSHIKA DHINGRA, EDWARD W. MARX, ADITI U. JOSHI AND ALINE NOIZET

Healthcare innovation tends to be a silent killer. Dashboards are constructed, pilots are introduced, and population health plans are proclaimed; however, nothing changes frontline practice. The issue is seldom unavailability of data and will. In more cases, it is a lack of motivation. During learning in Hospital Clinic de Barcelona, which is one of the top academic Spanish medical centers, leaders discovered that the adoption of population health analytics did not make a difference in care until teams were identified and rewarded for using them. By aligning incentives with clinically relevant outcomes, the hospital shifted population health analytics from a reporting burden to a resource for everyday clinical decision-making.

A Data-Rich, Action-Poor Hospital

Hospital Clínic, like much of the publicly funded health system in Spain, was able to access a wide range of population-level data. By integrating with the shared health record (HC3) of Catalonia, clinicians would be able to see longitudinal data about admissions, chronic disease indications, medication adherence, and socioeconomic risk factors. Even after that, population health insights were seldom touched on in everyday clinical practice. Reporting was delayed, dashboards were not close to the patient interactions, and clinicians focused on urgent clinical requirements and not abstract measures, whereas the leadership focused on prevention and chronic disease management. Frontline teams could not understand how analytics would translate to any meaningful action. The hospital lacked engagement rather than analytical ability.

Population Health as Clinical Work: Reframing

The breakthrough occurred after the Hospital Clínic leadership redefined population health as the fundamental clinical work and not a managerial activity. Multidisciplinary clinical teams were also invited to assist in defining the actual population indicators that really mattered as opposed to forcing them to deliver on performance targets. Primary care-hospital integrated teams reduced their priorities to a few:

- Heart failure preventable readmissions.
- The management of glycemic control of complex diabetes patients.
- Polymorphic medication compliance in older patients.

The decrease in the metrics allowed improvement to be seen and practiced. Population health was no longer the work of everyone but something done on a daily basis.

Incentives That Reinforced the Right Behaviors

The only aspect that stood out in the Hospital Clinic approach was the reinforcement of participation. The hospital also integrated the recognition and small incentives into population health programs, as opposed to using mandates only. Other care teams that minimized unnecessary admissions among high-risk patients were acknowledged publicly during departmental meetings. Internal communications and annual performance reviews focused on highlighting multidisciplinary units that increased the rate of preventive screening. Some of the events also associated with successes included the growth prospects or group-based monetary rewards. More importantly, it was not only physicians who were recognized (Berwick, 2016). Data analysts, care coordinators, pharmacists, and nurses were recognized as equals. This strengthened the notion that population health improvement was not an individual accomplishment but a community effort.

Technology Made to Empower, Not to Evaluate

Advanced analytics and risk stratification applications were referred to as support personnel. The usage of predictive models helped to identify those patients likely to deteriorate so that intervention would take place earlier. Dashboards focused on trends with time and not the point-to-point comparisons (Porter & Lee, 2015). Notably, data was presented as a learning resource, as opposed to a grading mechanism. The comparisons between performances were put in perspective and performance improvement discussions were made and based on improvement but not blame. The leadership style minimized defensiveness by not being punitive, which promoted experimentation. Engagement was enhanced when clinicians did not feel evaluated but supported.

Leadership That Made Recognition Visible

The management of the hospital had a crucial role to play in the visibility of success. The accomplishments in population health were mentioned in the executive briefs, internal newsletters, and innovation displays. Teams were invited to introduce their approaches and discuss lessons learnt, including failures. Leadership was an indicator of the importance of doing what was desired, as it was reinforced continuously. In the course of time, teams started to actively demand data and consultational support and develop their improvement projects. What came to be understood became the norm.

Measurable Outcomes, Cultural Shifts

The results were tangible. The results of Hospital Clínic included the increased effectiveness of communication between the specialists of the hospital and the primary care, the decline in preventable admissions to the hospital with specific chronic diseases, and a more regular follow-up of the high-risk group. The cultural change was also significant. Population health was no longer considered an administrative burden by clinicians. Rather, it has been integrated into professional identity—a field where teams could show impact, innovation, and leadership.

Avoiding the Incentive Trap

Leadership was also careful not to overfinance participation. Incentives were deliberately small so that they would complement intrinsic motivation and not replace it. Learning and mutual progress, not competition, were prioritized. Successful and struggling teams were recognized to have insight and efforts. This balance maintained trust and prevented gaming of measurements.

Conclusion: How to Make Innovation Worth the Effort

Population health innovation requires clinicians to put in some effort today to gain returns in the future that may not be seen. This made Hospital Clinic de Barcelona successful due to its tangible efforts that were realized in terms of recognition, shared achievement, and aligned incentives. The hospital made data action and will into impact by recognizing innovation as work and that work should be given a reward. The message is simple: healthcare systems which want population health strategies to survive have to reward not only results but the individuals who help to implement them.

References

Berwick, D. M. (2016). Era 3 for Medicine and Health Care. *JAMA*, *315*(13), 1329. https://doi.org/10.1001/jama.2016.1509

Porter, M., & Lee, T. (2015). *The Strategy That Will Fix Health Care*. https://www.aerodigestive.us/wp-content/uploads/2020/11/Porter-Lee-2013-The-strategy-that-will-fix-health-care-annotated.pdf

******

IRELAND | MAKING IMPROVEMENT VISIBLE: HOW ST. JAMES'S HOSPITAL USED RECOGNITION TO TURN DATA INTO DAILY PRACTICE | SAKSHIKA DHINGRA, EDWARD W. MARX, ADITI U. JOSHI AND ALINE NOIZET

Healthcare systems spend a lot of money on data. Dashboards are constructed, indicators are made, and reports are distributed. Nevertheless, the process of improvement is stopped so frequently not because the information is incorrect but because the people who are supposed to use it feel invisible and unrewarded or they do not see the point. This is a reality that was experienced by St. James Hospital in Dublin. St. James, as the largest teaching hospital in Ireland, did not lack analytics ability. What it lacked was traction. There were metrics, and conduct was not altered. Innovation projects were initiated enthusiastically and gradually died out. It was not the improved data but rather the change in what the hospital decided to see that eventually changed the hospital.

When Insight Failed to Motivate Action

The population that St. James serves is complex, and it is at the center of the academic and tertiary care in Ireland. With time, it established good performance measurement in the aspects of quality, safety, and patient flow. However, leaders saw a trend. Although the use of metrics was also talked about at the top levels, the frontline use was disproportionate. Clinicians were aware of the objectives, yet quality improvement efforts were in conflict with clinical demand. Data felt abstract. Effort felt invisible. It was not an issue of resistance. It was hesitation driven by a lack of recognition.

Reframing Improvement as Professional Contribution

The St. James leadership intentionally changed the paradigm: the improvement work would be addressed as clinical contribution but not as an additional work. Rather than requiring teams to meet targets, the leaders posed an alternative question: What do we want to publicly appreciate at work? The solution transformed the way the hospital was recognized.

From Dashboards to Stories

The hospital no longer used impersonal reporting of performance and started using narrative recognition. Instead of releasing lists of measures, St. James started celebrating groups that delivered better results in the conditions of reality. The process was viewed as problem solving, as opposed to compliance. In the case of a surgical ward that decreased delays in discharge due to an improved interdisciplinary coordination, the narration was on how the nurses, therapists, and junior doctors restructured handovers, not the percentage of the change. Data validated success (Alanazi, 2023). Recognition explained it.

Recognizing Teams, Not Individuals

One of the key design decisions that were made in a critical manner was to promote teams and not individuals. The issue of improving healthcare is not easily accomplished by one individual. This reality was reflected in St. James's approach, which emphasized recognition of teams rather than individuals. Multidisciplinary teams were recognized in key clinical governance forums, including governance meetings, departmental reviews, and internal publications (Berwick, 2016). This strengthened the ownership by the collective and prevented competition. Appreciation was not separatist but integrative.

Linking Analytics to Meaningful Wins

There was no discarding of analytics. They were repositioned. Data analysts assisted in converting metrics into actionable insights, hence supporting the teams. More importantly, when teams acted based on such insights, the work became apparent. No longer was betterment a secret requirement. It turned into a triumphant success. Clinicians started relating data to agencies instead of surveillance.

Leadership That Modeled Appreciation

Top management became involved. In their communications, frontline improvement work became a regular reference on the part of executives, not as a slogan but as a practical example. This exposure was an indication that the leadership embraced improvement achieved in the face of adversity. Notably, praise was not only given to flawless results. Those teams that tried and got things wrong or changed direction were not ignored. This ensured psychological safety.

Avoiding the Trap of Token Rewards

St. James did not over-financialize recognition. Though there were certain programs involving small incentives, professional pride, visibility, and learning opportunities were targeted. Career development, attendance of conferences, and leadership exposure were associated with improvement. It was not fake recognition.

Cultural Shift Over Time

When recognition was made habitual, behavior changed. Data support was actively requested by teams. Ideas of improvement appeared naturally. Meetings on analytics became inquisitive. Clinicians were no longer asking: "Why we should do this?" They said, "Can we be the second team to make it better?" There was intrinsic motivation, which was, however, maintained by recognition.

Measuring What Gets Repeated

The hospital not only followed up on outcomes but on interaction:

- Clinician-led improvement initiatives.
- Interdisciplinary involvement.
- Constant profits after pilot stages.

Findings indicated increased sustainability of change. Programs worked due to the sense of ownership—and value—by people.

Recognition as Infrastructure

At St. James, recognition was not a supplement but a matter of course. It was embedded in governance cycles and learning forums as well as leadership routines. The enhancement ceased to be occasional and instead became constant. To be innovative, new tools were not needed. It required acknowledgement.

Lessons in Motivation

The experience of St. James highlights one simple fact: People imitate what they perceive to be of value. Numbers do not encourage change. Data are meaningful when they are recognized. With effort being rewarded, not only results, by healthcare systems, then innovation becomes sustainable.

Conclusion: When Visibility Fuels Progress

St. James Hospital failed to open the door to improvement because it was too demanding of clinicians. It opened up by seeing them. The hospital made analytics a living practice rather than static reports by acknowledging teams that were the ones that turned insight into action. Work is improving in the healthcare sector. Work deserves recognition. And when that work is recognized, progress naturally follows.

References

Alanazi, A. (2023). Clinicians' Views on Using Artificial Intelligence in Healthcare: Opportunities, Challenges, and Beyond. *Cureus*, *15*(9). https://doi.org/10.7759/cureus.45255

Berwick, D. M. (2016). Era 3 for Medicine and Health Care. *JAMA*, *315*(13), 1329. https://doi.org/10.1001/jama.2016.1509

Chapter 8

Co-Create Solutions

Appreciate the complexity of attention that innovation requires and expose the organization to demands from all stakeholders.

Innovation does not happen by innovators alone. We must be careful not to fall into a belief that innovation is reserved for one person or a special team whose primary function is to develop solutions to problems or invention to opportunities. Innovation is primarily cultural and thrives in team-based organizations. Avoid the trap that innovation is for a select few and all others are discounted. Innovation happens best when it becomes the culture of the entire organization and everyone has the opportunity to engage.

POLAND | ACCELERATING ADOPTION OF INNOVATIVE SOLUTIONS IN HOSPITALS AND HEALTHCARE SYSTEMS BY COLLABORATING WITH INNOVATORS | ALINE NOIZET

Introduction

Imagine a hospital struggling with a diagnostic process that takes weeks, while early detection could save lives. Picture a municipality unable to monitor water quality in real time, risking public health and environmental degradation. Consider the frustration of a tech startup with a breakthrough solution but no pathway to real implementation. These are not isolated problems; they are complex challenges that demand innovative responses that can't be solved alone. Real innovation requires co-creation: people with different perspectives, experiences, and expertise working together, sharing knowledge, and iterating toward solutions that are not only technically sound but adoptable, implementable, sustainable, and valuable for all stakeholders.

This is the heartbeat of modern innovation. Innovation rarely originates fully formed inside a single mind; it emerges where diverse minds intersect and collaborate. The InnoBuyer project,

DOI: 10.4324/9781003780175-8

supported by the European Union under Horizon Europe, exemplifies this mindset by bringing public and private organizations to develop solutions to concrete unmet needs.

Setting the Context

Organizations like hospitals or healthcare systems often encounter unmet innovation needs: problems that are recognized but cannot be solved with existing solutions. These needs reflect gaps between current capabilities and evolving societal demands.

The InnoBuyer initiative was created to address exactly this challenge: How can large organizations with unmet innovation needs and small, agile innovators come together to co-create solutions that bring an answer to a concrete problem and are ready for implementation?

InnoBuyer tested and validated a methodology aimed at accelerating sustainable adoption of innovation—from identifying a problem to piloting a solution and preparing the groundwork for adoption in real markets. It encourages shared ownership of outcomes between the healthcare institutions and the innovators.

This approach highlights a critical insight: innovation is primarily cultural—not simply about generating ideas but about engaging people across roles, departments, and contexts in shaping solutions together.

Define Your Innovation

In InnoBuyer's framework, innovation emerges through dialogue, shared exploration, and mutual shaping between the problem holders and solution creators.

Rather than commissioning solutions in the traditional way where an organization defines a need, posts a specification, and waits for vendors, InnoBuyer fosters a demand-driven process:

1. **Identification of unmet needs**—Challengers articulate their current unmet needs and explain why it matters for their institution and the expected outcomes.
2. **Open market consultation and solver matching**—Innovators engage with the problem holders, asking questions and testing assumptions together. At the end of the process, they select one innovator to work with.
3. **Co-creation of solutions**—the paired teams work collaboratively over several months to design, build, pilot, test, and assess interventions tailored to the need, in real settings.

Through such a program, innovation is not a "deliverable" from one party to another. It is a shared journey where both sides contribute and learn at every stage of the process with tangible lessons learnt that could be replicated in the future with other partners.

Case Study/Illustrative Examples

The InnoBuyer program has been deployed across different European countries and in different industries. Some examples from the healthcare sector follow.

PREPLEX—Predictive Appointment Planning at Hospital Universitario del Sureste (Madrid, Spain)

Hospital Universitario del Sureste faced lengthy waits and inefficiencies in clinical scheduling that strained staff and resources and delayed available appointments. The hospital partnered with Graphenus to co-create PREPLEX, a predictive analytics system designed to optimize appointment planning and resource use.

Earlydel—Delirium Detection System at Hospital General Universitario Gregorio Marañón (Madrid, Spain)

Delirium in hospitalized patients is often misidentified or detected too late, compromising outcomes. Hospital General Universitario Gregorio Marañón worked with eB2 to design Earlydel, an automated system that identifies early signs of agitation and confusion to enable preventive actions and early intervention.

Safe-Stay—Mobility Support at Wojewódzki Szpital Specjalistyczny(Olsztyn, Poland)

At Wojewódzki Szpital Specjalistyczny in Olsztyn, outpatient mobility within the hospital posed safety and logistical challenges. The hospital teamed up with Sterna to develop Safe-Stay, an intelligent mobility system combining foldable smart wheelchairs, real-time tracking, usage monitoring, and incident detection.

FHARMAVERSO—Interactive Digital Environment for Pediatric Growth Hormone Therapy at Hospital Universitario de Getafe (Madrid, Spain)

FHARMAVERSO supports children self-administering hormone therapies at home. In collaboration with MetaMedicsVR and hospital pharmacy teams, the co-created digital solution gamifies learning through interactive 3D simulations, games, and avatars to build confidence, improve adherence, and empower young patients in their treatment journey.

EndoPath—Early Detection of Endometriosis Catalan Primary Care Centers (Barcelona, Spain)

Endometriosis is a condition that impacts millions of women worldwide, yet diagnosis today can be slow, subjective, and costly and often missed in primary care. The challenge proposer, IdiapJGol, partnered with Mimark to develop a diagnostic tool that is objective, cost-effective, and suitable for primary care settings.

Barriers & Lessons Learned

Co-creation sounds promising, but it is not without challenges. In practice, teams encounter barriers that reveal deeper truths about innovation culture.

Bridging Communication and Cultural Gaps

Healthcare institutions and innovators often speak different "languages": one oriented toward regulatory compliance and public benefit, the other toward commercial viability and scalability. They also operate at different rhythms and timelines, with healthcare systems often moving more slowly and innovators working more agilely. Bridging these gaps requires regular communication, patience, and openness. Co-creation can also involve innovators from different countries and cultures, making clear communication even more critical to ensure alignment and success.

Lesson: Structured communication channels and regular check-ins are essential to avoid misunderstandings and foster trust.

Aligning Expectations

Current challenges and expected outcomes should be clearly defined and communicated from day one to ensure that all stakeholders are aligned from the beginning. Questions such as "What does success mean?" should be addressed early, with established milestones and agreed-upon KPIs to assess progress throughout the project.

Lesson: A clear scope of work and KPIs should be defined from day one.

Managing Uncertainty

Co-creation is an interactive process where teams often learn and build as they go, using continuous feedback loops. Teams must be flexible, comfortable with uncertainty, and willing to refine their understanding of the problem over time while also adapting to constraints posed by healthcare systems.

Lesson: Processes that embrace learning and experimentation—even when outcomes are not immediately predictable—open the door to deeper insights and stronger solutions.

Balancing Vision With Practicality

Innovators may propose ambitious technical solutions, but if these cannot be integrated into the daily operations of a hospital, the impact will be limited. Sometimes starting with a simpler solution is more effective for testing and gaining stakeholder buy-in before iterating toward a more complex version that may involve deeper integration with healthcare systems.

Lesson: Co-creation must involve not just ideation but applied implementation thinking—and this means testing and validating assumptions early.

Cultural and Structural Resistance

In some organizations, collaborative innovation can be seen as disruptive or risky. Staff may be hesitant to engage fully or to relinquish control. This is why it is important to involve the different stakeholders early in the co-creation process, gather their input, and ensure they understand the benefits of the co-created solution for both themselves and their patients.

Lesson: Building an innovation culture requires leadership endorsement, transparent incentives, and recognition of iterative design as a legitimate way of working.

The InnoBuyer experience demonstrates that these barriers are not blockers but learning opportunities. Through structured support, coaching, and shared methodology, participants can navigate them and emerge with stronger partnerships.

The Human Aspect

At the core of co-creation is a deeply human process. It is not about algorithms or workflows alone; it is about *people working with people.* The human dimension of co-creation makes it rich—and sometimes messy.

Empathy as a Design Foundation

Co-creation demands empathy: innovators must understand the lived experiences of the stakeholders and cultural context they design for, and organizations must listen with humility to external partners and be ready to be challenged.

Trust as a Currency of Innovation

Building trust between teams with different priorities is fundamental. Trust grows when communication is in place, when risks are shared, when feedback flows freely, and when both successes *and failures* are acknowledged as part of the journey.

Empowerment Through Participation

When people from diverse roles—from frontline workers to C-levels—participate in shaping a solution, they feel *ownership.* This increases the likelihood that solutions will be embraced, adopted, sustained, and scaled.

Co-creation humanizes innovation: it transforms it from a checklist of tasks into a shared adventure of discovery.

Vision for the Future & Repeatability

What can other organizations learn from the InnoBuyer model? And how can they apply co-creation in their own contexts?

Make Innovation Demand-Driven

Start by grounding innovation work in *real unmet needs* rather than abstract challenges. Use tools like open market consultations and stakeholder workshops to gather insights and challenge your needs and expectations before solution design.

Build Cross-Functional Teams

Ensure that teams include a diversity of expertise from different departments—users, domain experts, designers, IT teams, decision markers—so that solutions are holistic, not siloed.

Institutionalize Co-Creation

Beyond isolated projects, embed co-creative processes into organizational practices. This means training staff, adapting procurement rules, and aligning incentives with collaboration.

Support With Governance and Funding

Secure resources—both financial and time—to sustain co-creative innovation. The success of InnoBuyer was enabled in part by the structure and funding support from Horizon Europe. Similar initiatives can adapt elements of this model at regional, national, or organizational levels.

These steps create a *repeatable blueprint* for innovation that is participatory, ecosystem-driven, and oriented toward impact.

Conclusion: Co-Creation as a Driver of Healthcare Innovation

Innovation does not happen in isolation. It does not thrive in echo rooms or hierarchy-only decision making. It flourishes where diverse individuals come together, listen deeply, challenge assumptions respectfully, and commit to co-creating solutions that matter.

The InnoBuyer project exemplifies this truth. By bringing healthcare systems and innovators together, it makes innovation *inclusive*, *cultural*, and *team-based*. It demonstrates that when organizations open themselves to the demands and insights of multiple stakeholders, they unlock not only better solutions but stronger innovation ecosystems.

In essence, co-creation is not just a method—it is a mindset. It invites us to move beyond innovation as output toward innovation as shared learning and growth. If organizations embrace this mindset, they will not only solve today's challenges but become more resilient, adaptive, and ready for the challenges of tomorrow.

References

https://innobuyer.eu/

*****

FRANCE | DIGITAL INNOVATION AND CHANGE MANAGEMENT TO IMPROVE PATIENT PATHWAYS AND PATIENT EXPERIENCE | CELINE ORHOND

Digital Innovation, Change Management, and Patient Experience, A Winning Trio!

Digital innovations are often underused not because the technology is weak but because culture, relationships, and patient pathways are not taken into account.

Innovation in hospitals is only truly effective when associated with organizational transformation. Furthermore, healthcare organizations need to focus on patient experience to create value and to implement sustainable innovation.

Having worked on patient pathway, patient flow, and patient experience, as a medical doctor, a hospital director, or a provider director, with different public and private hospitals, it became clear to me that digital innovation is, above all, a human change-management challenge.

This essay shares three different innovative digital projects dedicated to patient pathways that I've led or been involved in and the lessons they offer to hospitals seeking to improve their efficiency and to co-create their own solutions:

- digitalization of the patient pathway
- development of a command center
- commercialization of a hospital hotel platform

Since COVID-19, many hospitals continue to struggle to improve their efficiency and to respond to patient and professional needs, especially in surgery and emergency care. Staff resources and bed capacity remain under pressure, and financial constraints are becoming stronger and stronger.

The real question is: how do patients move through the healthcare system, and how easily can professionals do their work? Patient and healthcare professional experience are central. Two things are necessary to answer these expectations: deep change management and digital innovation to transform hospitals. Both must go together.

Instead of starting from digital tools and then wondering how to implement them, we need to start from patient and professional experience. So how can we work on those two aspects to develop digital innovation faster? What are the main friction points?

Co-Create to Improve Patient Pathways

When I was director of patient experience and patient relations in a large private hospital in France, my mission was to improve the patient pathway and to digitalize it. Rather than starting from tools, I decided to start from patient and staff experience. I wanted to answer a simple question: how can we create value for the people who benefit from the hospital?

We decided to create a department dedicated to patient relations and patient experience, which I led and which had a seat at the executive committee. In private companies out of care, customers benefit from dedicated departments. But in hospitals, it's usually not the case. And that's a problem!

The core innovation wasn't a single product but a way of working: starting from patient experience. The first step was to map the patient experience all along the pathway. Then we decided to focus first on the worst part. We started by improving very concrete problems: the telephone switchboard, then hospital admission, patient transportation, patient discharge, and follow-up.

We first listened to patients: what did they say about each part of their pathway; what were their expectations? At the same time, we listened to the staff, looking for pain points and needs.

We then co-designed a new pathway, answering one simple question: how can we improve patient experience? This led us to work both on human and process reorganization and on tools that could help us. We needed indicators to measure our results in real time. For instance:

- How much delay do we have in operating rooms right now?
- How many patients aren't ready to undergo surgery on time?
- How long are patients waiting in the lobby?
- How many patients can go directly to their room without waiting?
- How long do patients currently wait to get an answer on the phone, and how many calls are abandoned?

Using this approach, we created a contact center, a discharge lounge, a new lobby, and a patient lounge.

Each time we worked simultaneously on improving organization to facilitate communication and on implementing digital tools dedicated to our needs. The hospital developed a patient portal, which later led to the creation of a separate spin-off dedicated to patient pathways. The portal was a major tool to improve patient pathways. It helped us to anticipate patients journeys: preparing all required documents before admission, providing identity and administrative details, qualifying patient identity for EHR, uploading and accessing results and documents, allowing the patient to read personalized instructions in advance, completing questionnaires and signing consent forms electronically, and chatting with patients to answer questions and prepare the journey.

Clinicians and administrative teams could review patients' files ahead of admission, identify missing elements, check the biological results, and communicate with patients.

The portal also allowed us to measure PROMs and PREMs when patients were discharged and to communicate better with patients and their families before, during, and after the stay.

We also implemented other digital innovations like a transport platform, a digital telephone system, and a virtual patient pathway with virtual reality. And perhaps more importantly: interoperability between all the software applications. This allowed each professional to access the information they needed at each moment: the right information for the right person at the right time. This is a key point: real-time information shared at the right moment for professionals and for patients plus constant feedback on results.

The other key point is anticipation of every part of the patient pathway. Again, digital tools are the only realistic way to achieve this in a hospital.

The impact was visible and measurable: patients with anticipated admission increased to 97%, and only 3% still needed to go to the admission office; patients arrived more often on time in operating rooms and were less anxious; ambulatory care and J0 admissions were developed; delays at reception were reduced; bed management became more efficient; delays in patient transportation reduced by 30%; patient satisfaction for welcoming rose to 93%; and overall activity increased by 10%, even with 15% fewer beds following COVID, while patient experience improved.

To allow it, the hospital had a strong culture of innovation, of integrating start-ups' solutions and developing digital tools closely with private companies. To go further we decided to create a digital third place for health with other hospitals, aiming to work closely with private companies at an early stage.

We started all this transformation from our own needs and focused on the results: improving patient and professional experience. It wasn't just an IT project; it was a strategic project for the hospital which wanted to improve its efficiency. Focusing on the patient pathway, and following patient experience, was a way to conduct a successful project for the hospital. This project was shared with clinical, administrative leaders, patients, and their representatives. When everyone works together, digital innovation can serve all the interests and become powerful and sustainable.

Co-Creating a Command Center With Professionals

Command centers are still rare in France. They are designed to share real-time information and to provide a global view of the hospital. I'm currently working with a technology company on the implementation of one of the first command centers in a large university hospital.

Starting again from the professional needs at each part of the patient pathway, we aim to orchestrate patient flows and share data from the emergency department, wards, operating theatres, and other key areas. Aggregating data coming from different software and using AI-based prediction, healthcare professionals will be able to see bottlenecks in the organization and anticipate them.

A typical scenario is to predict bed occupancy exceeded or an influx of patients in a recovering room and to provide specific information to the team to help them decide how to solve the problem without impacting activity and therefore patient experience.

As in the previous experience, the crucial work is organizational: reorganising care process, procure useful indicators to the staff, building dashboards co-designed with clinicians, defining rules for actions in response to alerts, and above all completing and sharing data in real time. Co-construction is essential, and workshops with healthcare teams are necessary to ensure that we provide real answers to staff needs, organise governance and roles, and turn information into action.

Working on digital innovations helps hospitals to transform themselves, but transformation is not just a consequence of innovation; it's the trigger that makes innovation truly integrated.

Co-Creating Hybrid Care With a Patient Hotels Platform

Of course, the patient pathway is not limited to the hospital building. To keep acute beds for those who truly need them and to support new models of care, patient hotel concepts have been developed in several countries.

Considering the lack of beds and the cost of hospitalisation, solutions like patient hotels emerged in France a few years ago. They offer an alternative to hospitalization for patients who live far from the hospital and have to be admitted to the hospital early in the morning or for patients who come repeatedly for ambulatory care such as chemotherapy or radiotherapy. These stays are reimbursed by national insurance, and the cost is around 80€ instead of around 1000€ or more for a night at hospital.

These models also help to improve patient experience as hotels are usually more comfortable than hospital rooms. However, the system, unlike in some countries like Denmark or Sweden, is still underused in France.

To develop it, digitalization is a major lever. I've been working with a private company that provides a platform to digitalize the whole process from engaging patients to prescription and billing. The digital platform works as a connector between hospitals, patients, and hotels. It helps with booking and coordination.

Working with hospitals, we notice again that it's not enough simply to acquire the solution. The important point is to work at the same time on pathway reorganization and on change management: how can healthcare professionals change their organization to improve bed management and patient experience while respecting their own experience and constraints? How can an hospital clarify its strategy of improving efficiency and therefore patient pathway and patient experience?

It's not enough to have the platform. Hospitals have to work on their culture, habits, and expectations to change the way they work and to improve patient experience. We therefore decided to develop a combined offer: hospitals that want to use the platform are supported to assess their current patient pathway organization and to identify the levers to develop the use of patient hotel.

As always, the work begins with a diagnosis of existing flows, the financial impact on the hospital, staff needs, and patient needs. The digital solution and the organizational changes have to be built together.

Lessons Learned: Making the Trio Digital Innovation, Change Management, and Patient Experience Work Together

Across these initiatives, the same barriers to digital innovation always appear. How to overcome them:

- **Start with experience, not technology**
  Cultural resistance is strong when digital tools are perceived as something imposed "from above," even when some staff were involved in the choice. Some professionals worry that digital tools will depersonalize care or increase workload. Inviting them to co-design and to focus on patient experience helps bring them together around a common goal: the patient, the reason we are all here, the one we've been or will be one day! It gives meaning to work and to change.
- **Focus on sharing real-time data and on communication**
  Fragmented information and lack of shared communication are problems for all healthcare professionals. Building shared answers helps develop innovative digital tools. Focusing on the daily indicators teams really need encourages them to complete systems in real time and to share data: data from patients (PREMs, PROMs, information collected via a portal), data from the hospital as a whole, and data from its different departments. Involve all the staff to enhance data quality and work on interoperability and integrated systems. Furthermore, these data help you to show concrete results from your innovation.
- **Be user friendly**
  Don't complicate day-to-day work. Be sure not to create an overload on professionals. Some innovations seem simple and seem to add value, but we need to be sure that they don't take more time than they save, so measure it. And if we want patients to accept innovations dedicated to their pathway, we must also ensure that tools are simple and easy to use for them.
- **Always pair digital innovation with organizational change**
  It's not enough to buy (or to sell) a solution. Nobody's happy when a tool is rarely used. We must always combine organizational diagnosis, change management, and digital innovation. This includes, governance, clear roles, training, and supporting new ways of working.
- **Concentrate on value-based health care**
  The key question is: what value do we create for patients? Digital projects and organizational changes should be assessed on their impact on outcomes that matter to patients, on their experience, and on the efficient use of resources, not only on technical performance or budget.
- **Give meaning and recognize teams**
  Lack of time makes it difficult to focus on new tools and new organizations, even when they seem simple and when they will probably improve work. Bringing meaning and hope through patient experience, clear indicators directly linked to quality of care, and visible improvements helps to support change. All healthcare professionals want to do good work. Communicating about the hospitals they work in, when things go well, and when they innovate is very important. The feeling of belonging matters, and recognition of teams is a powerful lever for successful digital and organizational transformation.

Considering all stakeholders co-responsible for projects helps simultaneously improve patient experience, professional experience, and healthcare system efficiency. By co-creating organizational and digital innovation at the same time, we make innovation real and sustainable.

And it all starts with one simple step: mapping the patient journey and listening carefully to everyone!

*****

SPAIN | CO-CREATING THE FUTURE OF HOSPITALS AND THE MULTIPLE PS: P8 HEALTH | JORDI SERRANO PONS

Part I: The Present and Future of Hospitals

During 2025, I had the privilege of writing a book entitled *Hacia el Futuro de los Hospitales* (*Towards the Future of Hospitals*) (1), published by LID Editorial as part of the HealthTech collection. The book aims to imagine what hospitals of the future will look like, starting from today's reality, its challenges, and the opportunities that innovation and emerging technologies offer to enable the paradigm shift we urgently need. This transformation must be driven by the implementation of value-based care and by a renewed humanism that places both patients and healthcare professionals at the very center.

In summary, these future hospitals are defined as wall-less and decentralized hospitals, integrated with primary care and with multiple preventive pathways. Technology enables patients to actively participate in these future health plans, while the hospital itself becomes a system that preserves ecosystems: a truly green hospital.

This first part of the chapter summarizes the key ideas of *Hacia el Futuro de los Hospitales* (*Towards the Future of Hospitals*) (1), currently available in Spanish, with the ambition of producing an English edition and other language versions in the near future.

Hospitals in the Year 2055 (1)

Imagine that we are living in the year 2055. Prevention has finally become queen.

After many years of structural crisis across multiple sectors, including healthcare, most European countries—following unprecedented integration and acceleration—adopt a new constitution. This constitution guarantees a minimum level of universal health coverage for all European citizens and residents, one of the issues with the strongest social consensus. The main goal is clear: no one should become impoverished because of poor health.

Many national and regional governments implement value-based care systems, allowing the coordination of interventions across public and private sectors. Technology has finally made it possible for lifelong exposures to be considered in every healthcare intervention. The exposome—the totality of environmental, lifestyle, and socioeconomic exposures—has become the foundation of electronic health records across Europe.

Amanda, a 30-year-old intensive care physician who also manages an accelerator called TheFutureIsNow within her hospital, is leaving an intense shift. She smiles. She is lucky. Her hospital receives significant resources for prevention and research because it has done its homework.

It is somewhat paradoxical: she enjoys the adrenaline of intensive care, the flow state it creates, yet she also loves working in an institution with strong resources for preventive innovation, because her hospital has excellent strategic planning capacity and has secured most of the government funding linked to integrated value-based care implementation.

Healthcare models have shifted in recent years toward proactive and preventive medicine. Most hospital funding is channeled into five major prevention programs: cardiovascular prevention, brain prevention, liver prevention, oncology prevention, and personalized medicine. Funding for treating specific diseases can still be used routinely but only if the hospital has first established a preventive program with the patient, which represents a large part of the expenditure.

In cases where preventive programs have not been properly implemented within the population, the hospital must provide justification. If the percentage of patients without appropriate and personalized preventive pathways exceeds 15%, the hospital and its associated wall-less primary care network—forming an integrated hospital–primary care center–wall-less healthcare (HPCWW) system—lose their research staff recruitment bonus.

Hospital leadership positions are now typically occupied by experts in preventive and personalized medicine. The role of the chief patient officer has become central. The wall-less hospital and its digital ecosystem have become proactive patient seekers within the community, identifying biomarkers that guide interventions and improve prevention. There are as many biomarkers as grains of sand on a white beach.

Challenges and Solutions for Hospitals in 2025 (1)

Hospitals in 2025 face multiple challenges. In *Towards the Future of Hospitals*, we selected ten key challenges along with existing innovative strategies and solutions:

1. From workforce shortages to intelligent mitigation of human resource scarcity
2. From staff burnout to active prevention and caregiver support
3. From economic restrictions to diversified funding
4. From patient underrepresentation to full inclusion as a key actor in decision-making
5. From long waiting lists to reduction through efficiency and technology
6. From limited inter-hospital collaboration to integrated and synergistic networks
7. From disconnection with primary care and prevention to true system integration through value-based care
8. From population aging to effective chronic disease management
9. From increasing antimicrobial resistance to responsible prescription
10. The combinations of AI with robotics, biotechnology, personalized medicine, advanced biomarkers, and innovative therapies are immense. From unsustainable environmental impact toward comprehensive hospital sustainability

In most of these challenges, HIMSS approaches are essential: blend cultures, use people with IT, create road maps, collaborate and listen, communicate and eliminate barriers, stress simplicity, recognize and reward, and co-create solutions. Among these, co-creation is fundamental to guarantee healthcare transformation, particularly in value-based care initiatives.

Hospitals of the Future: Wall-Less, Intelligent, and Sustainable

We have imagined a hospital in 2055 and described today's challenges. Considering current limitations and the potential of technology, *Towards the Future of Hospitals* (1) advocates for highly decentralized environments that fully leverage digitalization and artificial intelligence. Healthcare becomes accessible anytime and anywhere while ensuring economic sustainability and equitable access.

- Wall-less hospitals: decentralization enables treatments and consultations outside hospital buildings through strengthened primary care, advanced telemedicine, wearable devices, and continuous remote monitoring.
- Intelligent hospitals: AI integration and automation improve operational efficiency, reduce costs, and optimize patient experience.
- Sustainable hospitals: infrastructure is designed ecologically, minimizing environmental impact through renewable energy, efficient waste management, and green architecture.

Part II: Co-Creating the Multiple Ps of Health and Medicine—P8 Health

P8 Health

In the first part of this chapter, we saw how AI and other disruptive technologies can transform hospitals and healthcare institutions.

Preventive programs in both public and private systems reinforce this necessary trend. For instance, Gustave Roussy Hospital in Paris (2) created Interception, a cancer prevention and screening program for high-risk populations. Sanitas, through Mi Salud Genómica (3), sequences part of the genome with genetic counseling and specialized medical coordination to develop personalized health plans. In Spain, the PAPPS program (4), promoted by semFYC, provides systematic guidelines for preventive activities in primary care.

In Singapore, the Ministry of Health (MOH) (5) launched Healthier SG in July 2023 as a major transformation of its healthcare system to strengthen preventive care. To date, more than 1.3 million residents have enrolled, and over 1,000 general practitioners participate.

Finally, NEKO Health (6), co-founded by Daniel Ek, has made prevention and check-ups "glamorous," offering non-invasive full-body health scans that detect early abnormalities in skin, cardiovascular parameters, and other biomarkers. It is excellent news that prevention is becoming attractive.

Healthcare transformation requires anticipating disease and personalizing care. The so-called 5Ps of medicine describe this paradigm shift. Two key Ps are prevention, essential to preserving healthcare sustainability, and prediction, supported by AI and emerging biomarker technologies.

In the literature, two main approaches exist: one considers precision the fifth P, emphasizing biomedical personalized medicine (7), while another adopts population-based as the fifth P, highlighting community health (8).

The addition of new Ps is constant. In the population-oriented article we selected, persistence is introduced as a sixth P (8). Many more Ps may be added.

In this context, we created P8 Health: a personalized health initiative where the "8" initially represents the five Ps plus three additional Ps: primary care, planetary health, and purpose-driven health.

Feedback and co-creation with colleagues confirmed the relevance of many other Ps (patient, proactivity, persistence). Ultimately, we chose to define the "8" as an inverted infinity symbol, reflecting the endless potential Ps that contribute to proactive health.

P8 Health aims to personalize health plans to help individuals maintain wellbeing in a biosphere that is also healthy.

Active Listening

The multiple Ps require a symphony and a score—a personalized plan guiding toward wellbeing. This symphony must be listened to and co-created by patients and healthcare professionals. Without listening and meaningful dialogue, healthcare cannot truly be personalized.

Are patients listened to in today's reactive health systems? Unfortunately, in most cases, the answer is no. Healthcare professionals rarely have enough time.

How can this be solved? Imagine arriving at a medical consultation where you can exchange information for two hours and learn self-care through a "slow medicine" experience supported by new technologies. This consultation may take place in a beautiful building, a community neighborhood center, or even in a forest setting.

The foundation is simple: two sofas facing each other, deep listening, and progressive technology.

Voice Recognition

In P8 Health, clinicians do not use computers in the traditional way. Instead, they wear a microphone and use voice-recognition software to avoid losing time writing clinical notes. In short: two sofas, listening, and technology.

The Exposome

The goal of P8 Health is to obtain the most complete medical history possible to understand the patient's exposome: lifelong exposures shaping health.

This deep anamnesis explores habits such as nutrition, sleep, harmful substances, physical activity, psychological stress; medical history factors such as metabolism, inflammation, immune response; environmental determinants such as air pollution and workplace toxins; and socioeconomic context.

Diagnostics and Education Through Biomarker Technologies

In P8 Health consultations, various technologies are used to measure and educate patients about daily health monitoring. Clinicians spend part of the two-hour visit teaching patients the meaning of these biomarkers.

Technologies such as portable ultrasound and remote videoplethysmography are used to perform screenings and assess early cardiovascular risk markers.

Progressively, a small drop of blood is analyzed through new spectrophotometry technology measuring twelve key parameters, opening the door to more advanced multi-omics biomarkers.

After these tests and thirty minutes of health education, patients receive a personalized intervention plan for the following twelve months. In recent months, genetic, transcriptomic, and metabolomic testing has been incorporated to deepen personalized prevention

Thoughtful and Intelligent Use of Technology to Promote Slow Medicine

The combination of these technologies with a two-hour human-centered consultation creates a unique experience that P8 Health aims to disseminate widely, regardless of socioeconomic status.

Different progressive levels of testing are proposed, but health education is central, as habits remain the main driver of effective prevention.

The consultation of the future is not a screen-driven visit but a slow, deeply human encounter—eye to eye—supported by progressive digital biomarkers, portable imaging, and planet-friendly prevention.

References

1. Hacia los Hospitales del Futuro. (2025). *Jordi Serrano Pons*. Editorial LID.
2. Gustave Roussy. *Cancer Prevention*. https://www.gustaveroussy.fr/en/interception
3. Sanitas. *Programa pionero en salud genómica*. https://corporativo.sanitas.es/mi-salud-genomica/
4. Programa de Actividades Preventivas y de Promoción de la Salud (PAPPS). *semFYC Madrid: Sociedad Española de Medicina de Familia y Comunitaria*. https://papps.es/
5. Ministry of Health Singapore. (2023). *Enhancing Preventive Health and Aged Care*. https://www.moh.gov.sg/newsroom/enhancing-preventive-health-and-aged-care/
6. Neko Health. *Neko Health: Preventive Health Scanning*. Stockholm: Neko Health. https://www.neko-health.com/gb/en
7. Longo, U. G., De Salvatore, S., Candela, V., Berton, A., Schena, E., Nazarian, A., & Denaro, V. (2021). Personalized, predictive, participatory, precision, and preventive (P5) medicine in rotator cuff tears. *Journal of Personalized Medicine*, *11*(4), 255. https://doi.org/10.3390/jpm11040255.
8. Borrás-Blasco, J., & Navarro-Ruiz, A. (2024). Integration of Persistence in the 5P-Medicine Approach for Age-Related Disorders: From 5P to 6P Medicine. *International Journal of Health Care Quality Assurance*, *36*(2), mzae026. https://doi.org/10.1093/intqhc/mzae026.

*****

DENMARK | THE QUIET REVOLUTION: HOW AARHUS UNIVERSITY HOSPITAL CO-CREATED AMBIENT VOICE TECHNOLOGY THAT HELPED CLINICIANS LISTEN | SAKSHIKA DHINGRA, EDWARD W. MARX, ADITI U. JOSHI AND ALINE NOIZET

The examination room is a place where there has always been attention. A patient speaks. A clinician listens, observes, and acts. However, in the last ten years, a new entity has occupied that space: the computer. Screens required attention, keyboards were time consuming, and documentation kept on taking clinicians outside the individuals they were intended to serve. This tension broke at Aarhus University Hospital, one of the largest academic medical centers in Denmark. The clinicians were not averse to digital technologies; they were annoyed that the technologies transformed the very nature of the clinical interaction. Paperwork had to be made, but the manner in which it was done was in conflict with the human essence of medicine. Speech recognition algorithms were not the starting point of the next innovation. It began with listening.

Hearing the Problem Clearly

Teamwork in hospitals is a rather flat structure and has high participation of clinicians in decision-making, which is typical in Denmark. As the issue of documentation load became an issue of repetition at Aarhus University Hospital, the leadership was tempted to sell a solution to the problem. They instead developed structured forums in which the clinicians were able to narrate their findings. Doctors were free to talk about typing and their patients. Nurses have narrated how they were able to reconstruct some conversations hours later when they remembered them. The shift was also observed by patients, who would stop in the middle of a sentence when the clinicians would look at screens. It was not just a time-management problem. It was an attention problem. By posing a matter not as a technical problem but making it experiential, leaders made sure that the definition of the problem was right first before considering a solution.

An Invitation to Co-Create

Instead of buying off-the-shelf dictation products, Aarhus University Hospital collaborated with clinicians, linguists, and technologists to investigate ambient clinical voice technology systems, which are able to record and organize clinical dialogue automatically. Clinicians were at the very beginning placed as co-designers rather than end users. Preliminary models were subjected to actual examination rooms. Doctors and nurses were urged to break demonstrations, criticize production, and abandon features that were considered intrusive and unnatural. Certain early versions were unsuccessful. Recording was interfered with by background noise. The medical setting was misinterpreted. These failures were not swept under the carpet. They turned out to be common learning experiences that fostered trust between the technical and clinical teams. Co-creation made the process go more slowly—but more firmly committed.

Designing for Presence, Not Perfection

The decision that had the biggest impact on the design was not a technical one but a philosophical one. This was not aimed at producing ideal documentation. The aim was to bring back presence in the clinical encounter. The system created draft documentation instead of fully automated notes which were reviewed, edited, and finalized by the clinicians. This distinction mattered. Designers minimized anxiety and over engineering by setting lower expectations of automation. The technology was positioned as a helper rather than a writer. A medical record was still under the responsibility of clinicians. Attention was restored to them by the system.

Listening Across Disciplines

The implementation required careful attention to the intersections between ambient voice technology and privacy, governance, IT infrastructure, and patient trust. Aarhus University hospital involved these stakeholders at an early stage. Consent models were made by privacy officers. IT departments made sure that EHR integration was smooth. The leaders of clinical governance explained accountability. Patients were made aware of how conversational recordings were made, processed, and secured. Their feedback was used to affect both procedural and technical design. This participatory strategy increased implementation time periods but enhanced sustainability. Most of the serious concerns had already been taken care of by the time wider implementations were reached.

Case Study: What Changed in the Examination Room

The reported modifications as perceived by clinicians were subtle yet strong. Eye contact increased. There was a more natural flow of conversations. There was shorter time taken in typing during visits. The documentation was done closer to the point of care, and this minimized the after-hours and cognitive carry-over. Clinicians reported that they felt less stressed mentally when coming to busy clinic days (Alanazi, 2023). The technology was not able to remove documentation—but it brought back equilibrium between listening and recording (Downing et al., 2018). Patients noticed as well. Most of them said that they felt more involved and less distracted (Demaidi, 2023).

Measurable Outcomes, Human Gains

The pilot tests at Aarhus University Hospital indicated the decrease in documentation time per encounter, as well as a positive shift in the clinician satisfaction scores (Blease et al., 2023). Qualitative outcomes, however, were equally considered by the leadership. Clinicians stated that they felt more like clinicians. Patients felt heard. These cues supported a main point: the key to the success of the innovation was not the level of its technical refinement but its very origin.

Leadership That Made Space for Collaboration

The enabling role of hospital leadership was very important, as it created psychological safety. Clinicians were also advised to express their dissatisfaction without the fear of being termed resistant. When one mentioned that something did not work, it was considered progress. Premature scaling was also something the leaders did not like. Adoption was on a voluntary basis at early stages. Adoption was achieved naturally through word of mouth by clinicians who posted positive reviews. Innovation is transmitted by trust and not dictated.

Lessons in Co-Creation

The Aarhus experience reminds us of one truth which many people forget when it comes to healthcare innovation, which is that listening is a strategic skill. The hospital did not want to solve the wrong problem by listening to clinicians, patients, and partners. Co-creation changed ambient voice technology into a helpful feature instead of it being a disruptive one. The innovation survived not due to its impressive nature but because it was created jointly.

Conclusion: Innovation That Knows When to Be Quiet

With the trends of ambient technologies spreading across the globe, the Danish strategy provides a model that can be replicated. Start by listening. Invite collaboration. Accept imperfection. Protect presence. Aarhus University Hospital has proved that innovation does not have to take over the clinical domain in order to work. The strongest technologies in some cases are the ones which step back to enable clinicians to do what they do best and listen.

References

Alanazi, A. (2023). Clinicians' Views on Using Artificial Intelligence in Healthcare: Opportunities, Challenges, and Beyond. *Cureus, 15*(9). https://doi.org/10.7759/cureus.45255

Demaidi, M. N. (2023). Artificial Intelligence National Strategy in a Developing Country. *AI & Society, 40*. https://doi.org/10.1007/s00146-023-01779-x

Downing, N. L., Bates, D. W., & Longhurst, C. A. (2018). Physician Burnout in the Electronic Health Record Era: Are We Ignoring the Real Cause? *Annals of Internal Medicine, 169*(1), 50. https://doi.org/10.7326/m18-0139

*****

SPAIN | HUMAN INTELLIGENCE FIRST: HOW HOSPITAL CLINIC DE BARCELONA DESIGNED AI AROUND CLINICAL REALITY | SAKSHIKA DHINGRA, EDWARD W. MARX, ADITI U. JOSHI AND ALINE NOIZET

Digital health projects tend to commence with a technical inquiry: What can technology do? In Hospital Clinic de Barcelona, which is one of the leading public academic hospitals in Europe, the starting point was different. Leaders put a more challenging and more significant question: What do clinicians require assistance with—and what should stay human? Such a difference influenced the introduction of artificial intelligence into clinical activity at Clínic. The hospital developed AI as a continuation of clinical intelligence instead of seeking automation or algorithmic authority. Technology was designed to serve human beings and not to control them. It led to the creation of a model of digital adoption, which was based on trust, realism, and professional respect.

A High-Pressure Clinical Environment

Hospital Clínic de Barcelona is located in the middle of the Catalonian public health system. It is a tertiary referral center that takes care of complex cases in the area of hepatology, oncology, transplant medicine, and infectious diseases and is also located in a densely populated urban area. Clinicians have high workloads. There is an increased patient complexity. Clinical recommendations change fast. The amount of research is massive, but it is difficult to transform the research into practical decisions. Data was stored in multiple systems, such as in labs, imaging, genomics, and registries, and frequently clinicians were forced to combine it mentally under time pressure (Demaidi, 2023). There was already technology in place. What was missing was support.

Early Digital Friction

The clinic was highly digitized, like most large hospitals. There were electronic records, order entry systems, and data repositories. However, clinicians reported a paradox, increased data and less clarity. This tension was expressed in early AI pilots. Certain tools generated scores or predictions of risks out of context. Others caused alerts that were competing with clinical priorities. Doctors were concerned with fatigue related to alerts, false reassurance, and medico-legal ambiguity. It was not a problem of being resistant to innovation. It was opposition to false responsibility. Clinicians had their way: they would take assistance but not substitution.

Defining a Boundary Between Human and Machine

In response, the clinic's leadership set clear limits. Instead of dictating behavior, AI would be used to enhance perception. Its function was to draw attention to signals that people might overlook, particularly in fields with a lot of data, while firmly delegating interpretation and decision-making to clinicians (Downing et al., 2018). Instead of being a catchphrase, this idea became a design constraint. Three questions had to be addressed by any AI tool that was introduced:

1. Does it lessen mental strain?

2. Does it protect the autonomy of clinicians?
3. Is it possible to explain its logic at the patient's bedside?

The tool was either rejected or revised if the response to any of the questions was negative.

Clinicians as Designers, Not Users

The cultural change in the clinic was one of the most crucial changes. Clinicians were not invited as validators in the development of AI but rather as co-designers. A collaboration between multidisciplinary teams of physicians, nurses, data scientists, and IT staff took place to figure out actual painful clinical areas. Instead of beginning with available data, they began with workflow: at what decision points there were uncertainties and how information was then being processed. This strategy altered results. Interfaces became simpler (Boonstra et al., 2020). Outputs were put in clinical language. The results of AI were not shown in different dashboards but together with known data. It is people that adapt to technology, rather than the other way around.

Practical Applications That Respected Judgment

The applications of AI were implemented in the spheres, where pattern recognition was most important, including early detection of deterioration, chronic conditions, and transplant follow-up. As an illustration, predictive models were used to identify liver disease patients who were at risk of decompensation. The system did not give orders but emphasized trends, situational issues, and levels of confidence. The information was discussed on rounds and was discussed by clinicians with colleagues and action determined. Notably, clinicians would not be penalized for ignoring the system. Overrides were expected. This legitimized conflict and maintained accountability. AI was not a second opinion but a second set of eyes, offering additional perspective without replacing clinical judgment.

Training That Built Confidence, Not Dependency

The clinic made direct investment in the education of clinicians. Doctors were educated on the process of model training, the constraints of the data and the emergence of bias. This transparency mattered. By approaching the model with critical engagement rather than defensiveness, clinicians were able to collaborate with it once they understood the reasons behind its successes and limitations. Clinical reasoning was not threatened by AI outputs, but it became an ingredient of its reasoning. Skepticism was later overtaken by confidence. This was not due to the perfection of AI, but its flaws were obvious and could be handled.

Governance That Reinforced Human Control

Great governance systems supported the people-first policy. Each AI system was allocated a clinical owner. Performance was checked on a regular basis, with a focus on unintended consequences. More importantly, the responsibility did not change. Clinical responsibility was also human, and that was recorded in documentation. The recommendations of AI were taken as inputs, not a decision. This honesty helped to put the minds of clinicians and regulating bodies at ease. The advancement of innovation did not undermine professional standards.

Benefits That Felt Real

The influence of this strategy was not significant but effective. The clinicians stated that they had better situational awareness and reduced information search time. Multidisciplinary consultations were narrowed down. Junior physicians were more supported in complicated cases. Probably most significantly, the use of AI did not produce any cultural backlash: no story of deskilling or control loss. Technology found its legitimacy in remaining on its course. The indirect benefit was more regular monitoring, earlier intervention, and visual clinical communication in patients.

Leadership That Protected the Philosophy

A very important but silent role was played by hospital leadership. They opposed the urge of vendors to scale too soon or narratives of market transformation. Rather, they focused on the aspects of fit, trust, and sustainability. The extension of pilots was done when necessary. When there was uncertainty of value, tools froze. Clinician feedback was not empty words. The respect which was foreshadowed by this restraint was reciprocated. The reason innovation was propelled forward was that it was desired by the people and not dictated.

Lessons From Clínic

Effective digital health transformation is more about role clarity than it is about technological ambition, as demonstrated by Hospital Clínic de Barcelona. AI functions best when it:

- Supports judgment rather than replacing it,
- Reduces noise rather than adding it, and
- Operates transparently rather than opaquely.

Clínic avoided the typical problems of overautomation and underutilization by building technology around human expertise.

Conclusion: Technology That Knows Who Is in Charge

In Hospital Clinic de Barcelona, artificial intelligence failed to transform care delivery. It strengthened it. By making the demand that human beings stay in control, and by making technology to acknowledge that fact, the hospital developed a prototype of AI implementation that clinicians will trust, leaders can regulate, and patients will gain. With more and more healthcare systems adopting digital tools, with claims of using them to build complexity, Clínic provides a reminder of the wisest systems: those that make humans more human.

References

Boonstra, A., Versluis, A., & Vos, J. F. J. (2020). Implementing Electronic Health Records in Hospitals: A Systematic Literature Review. *BMC Health Services Research*, *14*(1). https://doi.org/10.1186/1472-6963-14-370

Demaidi, M. N. (2023). Artificial Intelligence National Strategy in a Developing Country. *AI & Society*, *40*. https://doi.org/10.1007/s00146-023-01779-x

Downing, N. L., Bates, D. W., & Longhurst, C. A. (2018). Physician Burnout in the Electronic Health Record Era: Are We Ignoring the Real Cause? *Annals of Internal Medicine*, *169*(1), 50. https://doi.org/10.7326/m18-0139

*****

SPAIN | AI-DRIVEN ADAPTIVE INTERVENTIONS TRANSFORMING SUPPORT FOR CHILDREN WITH DYSLEXIA AND/OR ADHD | MANUEL HERNÁNDEZ

Introduction

Every day, millions of children across Europe struggle to sustain attention, regulate their behavior, or understand what they read. This is not a matter of ability or motivation; it is the result of systems that cannot personalize support at the pace at which each child's brain develops.

At the intersection of health and education, this mismatch leads to frustration, low self-esteem, and widening gaps in learning and well-being.

ATENXIA Was Created to Reduce That Gap

- To offer a tool that combines science, technology, and empathy in the service of child neurodevelopment.
- To demonstrate that cognitive intervention can be effective, adaptive, and—perhaps unexpectedly—enjoyable.
- And above all, to prove that when a solution is designed properly, children want to return to it . . . even after completing the intervention.

Setting the Context: The Challenge in Health and Education

Attentional and literacy-related difficulties, such as those associated with ADHD and dyslexia, are highly prevalent, affecting between 15% and 20% of the child population. These conditions have direct consequences for academic performance, mental health, social integration, and future opportunities.

The structural challenge is twofold.

Shortage of Professionals

Health and education systems across Europe—and globally—do not have enough psychologists, therapists, counselors, and specialists to support all the children who need help.

The result:

- long waiting lists,
- lack of early intervention,
- fragmented or discontinued treatments,
- and profound inequalities depending on territory or available resources.

Interventions That Are Difficult to Scale

Most current interventions rely on face-to-face, highly individualized work, making it nearly impossible to reach all cases.

This is where innovation can break barriers by creating *evidence-based digital solutions* that expand professional capacity without compromising clinical or educational quality.

It is within this context that ATENXIA was born: as a digital health and education platform designed to deliver personalized, scientifically validated interventions—anywhere.

Defining the Innovation: 100% In-House AI Developed With the University of Granada

ATENXIA does *not* use ChatGPT, Gemini, or any other generic market models.

Its AI engine is developed entirely in house, purpose-built to:

- adapt attentional profiles,
- personalize cognitive interventions,
- adjust difficulty between sessions,
- generate unique intervention pathways for each learner,
- and integrate indicators of progress, motivation, reaction times, and improvement patterns.

All of this is grounded in scientifically validated protocols and developed in close collaboration with the University of Granada through the Mind, Brain and Behavior Research Center (CIMCYC) of the University of Granada (UGR)—the only research center in psychology in Spain accredited as a Maria de Maeztu Unit of Excellence by the State Research Agency of the Ministry of Science, Innovation and Universities.

The platform integrates child neuropsychology, cognitive science, data analytics, and motivational experience design. The result is a system that understands and adapts to each child's learning pace.

ATENXIA also operates under the highest ethical standards:

- protection of children's data,
- strict GDPR compliance,
- no use of personal data to train external models,
- and full transparency in adaptive mechanisms.

In essence, ATENXIA is a tool that extends the capacity of health and education professionals.

Case Study: A Pilot Across Fifty Schools That Transformed an Entire System

In 2024, ATENXIA launched one of the most ambitious neurocognitive intervention pilots in Spain: fifty public and publicly funded schools in the province of Granada, in collaboration with the Territorial Delegation for Educational Development and Vocational Training, and for Universities, Research and Innovation.

This pilot represented a model convergence of health and education:

- over 100 teachers trained,
- coordinated educational guidance teams,
- scientific supervision by the University of Granada,
- hundreds of students with attentional or literacy difficulties,
- standardized implementation,
- and early, measurable outcomes.

Early Impact: Changes From Sessions 3–4

One of the most striking findings—consistent with the average across our pilots—was that teachers observed visible changes from the third or fourth session onward:

- greater ability to initiate tasks,
- improved emotional regulation,
- longer sustained attention,
- reduced frustration and avoidance,
- and increased participation and enthusiasm.

This pattern was repeated across most schools, particularly among students with pronounced attentional and learning difficulties.

A Human Story

One school counselor shared that a student who had been unable to complete a reading task independently for years managed to finish several exercises on their own after only a few sessions with ATENXIA: "We saw him smile while working—something that had never happened in this area before."

Barriers and Lessons Learned

The Professional Gap

Europe faces a structural shortage of specialists to address the growing number of cases.

This pilot showed that a scalable digital solution can:

- reduce waiting lists,
- reach rural or hard-to-access schools,
- complement in-person clinical and educational work,
- and allow specialists to support more students without burnout.

Teacher Workload

Teachers reported that ATENXIA reduced their cognitive load and improved classroom management. Students who previously required intensive one-to-one attention were able to work more autonomously under effective supervision.

Unlimited Scalability

Being fully online, ATENXIA scales without physical limits: a single professional can supervise multiple students in parallel through automated monitoring dashboards.

Intervention Without Pressure

After completing their programs, many children asked to continue "playing" with ATENXIA.

This reveals something crucial: The intervention is experienced as positive, increasing adherence and reducing the stigma associated with learning difficulties and ADHD.

The Human Factor: When Therapy Becomes Play

Professionals working with ATENXIA consistently highlight that one of the system's greatest achievements is that children feel they are "playing," not "being treated."

Several professionals wrote to us after the programs ended to say, "My patients ask when they can play with ATENXIA again, even though they've already completed the intervention." This shift in perception is profound:

- intrinsic motivation becomes the driver of improvement,
- intervention changes from "something difficult" to "something I enjoy."

Alignment With Public Policy and the Sustainable Development Goals

ATENXIA sits at the core of European strategies for educational digitalization and digital transformation in child health.

The pilot aligns with:

- digital learning agendas,
- inclusive education strategies,
- Horizon Europe priorities in neurodevelopment and edtech,
- and plans for integrating evidence-based digital tools.

Contribution to SDGs: 3, 4, and 10

- **SDG 3—Good Health and Well-Being:** early access to high-quality, scalable, evidence-based neurocognitive interventions.
- **SDG 4—Quality Education:** inclusive, personalized education and large-scale support for learning diversity.
- **SDG 10—Reduced Inequalities:** accessible tools from any location, reduced waiting lists, and equal opportunities.

Vision for the Future: An Integrated Health and Education Ecosystem

ATENXIA does not aim merely to improve attention exercises or literacy skills; it seeks to transform how health and education collaborate to support child neurodevelopment.

In the coming years, our vision includes:

- research studies with the University of Granada to identify risk trajectories,
- integration with educational systems across other European regions and MENA,
- predictive models enabling intervention before severe difficulties emerge,
- and professional platforms that unify data, progress, and personalization.

What we aim to build is a real ecosystem where teachers, psychologists, speech therapists, and families share information and work within a single scientific and digital framework.

Wrap-Up: Connecting with the HIMSS "Create Solutions" Process

ATENXIA proves that when a solution is designed from science, powered by proprietary technology, and focused on the holistic well-being of the child, entire health and education systems can be transformed.

Creating solutions is not just about building technology. It is about understanding real needs, listening to professionals, families, and—most importantly—children.

ATENXIA demonstrates that cognitive intervention:

- can be scalable,
- can be integrated into classrooms,
- can support professionals,
- can reduce inequalities,
- can align with global agendas,
- and can become an experience children want to continue—even after it ends.

When that happens, we are not just creating solutions: we are creating future opportunities for an entire generation.

Reference

Blease, C., Bernstein, M. H., Gaab, J., Kaptchuk, T. J., Krumholz, H. M., & Mandl, K. D. (2023). Computerization and the future of the patient–clinician relationship: Opportunities and risks of AI-enabled documentation. *Journal of Medical Internet Research, 25*, e45512. https://doi.org/10.2196/45512.

Conclusion

Europe is quietly redefining the future of healthcare. Unlike the siloed approaches seen elsewhere, the European models blend cutting-edge technology with a fundamental commitment to accessibility and equity. This unique convergence is generating some of the world's most pragmatic and human-centric health tech solutions. The innovations are not just about flashy gadgets; they are about building a more resilient, efficient, and patient-empowered system.

Another key differentiator driving innovation amongst the diverse European countries is payment models. European healthcare payment models are primarily aiming to ensure access regardless of income. This overall dynamic creates both head winds and tail winds not experienced elsewhere. These forces combined create a culture where innovation becomes a force multiplier, both motivational and, frankly, a matter of survival.

Voices of Innovation—Europe contains stories from over twenty countries representing hundreds of health systems and hospitals. Sprinkled throughout are examples of cross-border innovations improving patient and family experiences. The key areas primarily coalesce around:

The Data-Driven Diagnosis Revolution: At the heart of the European advance is the strategic use of data. Stringent privacy regulations like GDPR have not stifled innovation but have instead fostered a culture of "secure-by-design" data utilization. Cross-border initiatives, such as the expansion of Estonia's e-Health Record, are enabling seamless and secure sharing of patient information between member states. Furthermore, AI-powered diagnostic tools are moving from labs into clinics. These systems are being trained on diverse European population data to help clinicians detect diseases like cancer and neurological disorders earlier and with greater accuracy, reducing wait times and improving outcomes.

Telehealth and Remote Patient Monitoring (RPM) Become Mainstream: The shift from hospital to home is accelerating across the continent. Europe is leveraging its strong primary care foundations to integrate telehealth, making routine consultations more efficient and accessible, especially in rural areas. Beyond video calls, innovation shines in RPM. Wearable sensors and smart home devices allow for continuous monitoring of patients with chronic conditions like diabetes, cardiac diseases, and COPD. This real-time data flow empowers patients in their own care and enables clinicians to intervene proactively, preventing costly emergency admissions and improving quality of life.

Personalized Medicine and Genomics: Europe is a global leader in advancing personalized treatment. Large-scale national genomics programs, such as those in the UK, Finland, and

DOI: 10.4324/9781003780175-9

Iceland, are creating vast, research-ready biobanks. This is paving the way for treatments tailored to an individual's genetic makeup, particularly in oncology. Doctors can increasingly prescribe therapies targeted to the specific genetic mutations of a patient's tumor, moving away from a one-size-fits-all approach and towards more effective, less invasive treatments.

Robotics and Automation in Surgery and Care: Robotic assistance is enhancing precision in operating theatres across Europe, facilitating minimally invasive surgeries that reduce patient recovery time. Beyond surgery, robotics is addressing critical challenges like staff shortages and an ageing population. We are seeing the deployment of robotic exoskeletons for rehabilitation therapy, helping stroke patients relearn to walk, and assistive robots in care homes to support logistics and combat social isolation among seniors.

Interoperability and the Regulatory Framework: A critical, though less visible, innovation is Europe's focus on interoperability—ensuring devices and systems can communicate with each other. The new European Health Data Space (EHDS) aims to break down data siloes, creating a single market for health data that empowers citizens and fuels innovation. Furthermore, the EU's updated medical device regulation (MDR) ensures that new technologies meet high standards of safety and efficacy before reaching the market.

Wait for it: AI. Fact is we are not calling out AI separately. It is simply part of the everyday experience.

Looking Ahead: A Human-Centric Future

The European approach is not without its challenges, including navigating diverse healthcare systems, ensuring equitable access, and securing sustainable funding. However, the overarching trend is clear: technology is being deployed not to replace human care but to augment it. The focus remains on creating a more sustainable system that empowers clinicians, engages patients as active partners in their health, and ensures that the benefits of innovation are felt by all citizens, not just a privileged few. The future of European healthcare is a seamlessly integrated, data-enabled, and profoundly human experience.

Leadership. We end all of our *Voices of Innovation* books with a similar admonishment. We should not rely on tech, government, or a team of brilliant minds to enable healthcare innovation for the masses. Most of the advances do not happen in a lab, on a bench, or in a classroom. They happen every day to people, like you and me, focused on improving the human experience and taking bold action. Be bold.

Index